IN PURSUIT OF POWER
Heinrich von Kleist's Machiavellian Protoganists

A number of striking parallels link the lives and careers of Machiavelli and Kleist. This study of the influence of one on the work of the other begins with an outline of those parallels, and of the Machiavellian atmosphere in Kleist's first play, *Die Familie Schroffenstein*.

Reeve goes on to focus on the protagonists of Kleist's plays, beginning with Licht in *Der zerbrochene Krug*. He exposes the skill of Licht's behind-the-scenes direction of the course of events to his own advantage and to the detriment of his superior, Adam. Next Reeve offers a detailed analysis of *Die Hermannsschlacht*, in which he demonstrates how Hermann embodies those qualities – the cunning of the fox and the strength of the lion – demanded by Machiavelli in a successful ruler. With these traits Hermann has brought the German princes, his own tribe, his rival Marbod, his wife, and even the Romans to a point where, unwittingly, they have all worked towards the establishment of a united Germany under his leadership.

The chapter on *Prinz Friedrich von Homburg* singles out the underhand manoeuvers of the sadistic Hohenzolern who plots to embarrass publicly both the Elector and the Prince as a subtle manifestation of his personal power over the two leading contenders for political supremacy. The fragment *Robert Guiskard* contains two Machiavellian protagonists, an older, more accomplished practitioner and an up-and-coming young threat, and treats another issue addressed in *Il Principe*: what occurs when an ideal leader at the height of his powers is cut down by a disabling illness?

Indicative of the beginning and the end of Kleist's opus, half of his plays contain the figure of the clandestine schemer who plans the social or political elimination of a rival and, by stealth and skillful manipulation of others, directs the course of events at almost every turn. Reeve concludes with an attempt to explain the presence of the Machiavellian in Kleist's works as the indirect influence of Shakespeare's three villains, the direct example of Napoleon, or the dramatist's own independent insight into the less admirable aspects of the human mind.

WILLIAM C. REEVE is Associate Professor of German at Queen's University.

WILLIAM C. REEVE

In Pursuit of Power:
Heinrich von Kleist's
Machiavellian Protagonists

UNIVERSITY OF TORONTO PRESS
Toronto Buffalo London

© University of Toronto Press 1987
Toronto Buffalo London
Printed in Canada

ISBN 0-8020-5702-0

Canadian Cataloguing in Publication Data

Reeve, William C., 1943–
In pursuit of power
Bibliography: p.
Includes index.
ISBN 0-8020-5702-0
1. Kleist, Heinrich von, 1777–1811 – Criticism and interpretation.
2. Kleist, Heinrich von, 1777–1811 – Characters. I. Title.
PT2379.Z5R44 1986 838'.6 c86-094469-7

To
Professor G.W. Field,
teacher, scholar, and friend

Contents

Acknowledgments

Many people have made contributions, both direct and indirect, to my writing of this Kleist monograph, but I especially owe a debt of heartfelt gratitude to Mrs Margaret Boesch for her patience and counsel, to Professor G.W. Field for his inspiring example, to Professor Ernst Loeb for his generous assistance and constructive criticism, to Professor Martin Swales for his much appreciated encouragement, and to my wife for her continual support.

'An Unsung Villain: The Role of Hohenzollern in *Prinz Friedrich von Homburg*,' *Germanic Review* 56 (1981): 95–110, and 'Ein dunkles Licht: The Court Secretary in *Der zerbrochene Krug*, *Germanic Review* 58 (1983): 58–65. Reprinted with permission of the Helen Dwight Reid Educational Foundation. Published by Heldref Publications, 4000 Albemarle St., NW, Washington, DC 20016 © 1986.

This book has been published with the help of a grant from the Canadian Federation for the Humanities, using funds provided by the Social Sciences and Humanities Research Council of Canada.

Publication of this book was also assisted by a grant provided jointly by the Faculty of Arts and Science and the School of Graduate Studies and Research, Queen's University.

IN PURSUIT OF POWER:
HEINRICH VON KLEIST'S
MACHIAVELLIAN PROTAGONISTS

1

Introduction

At first sight, it might strike the reader as somewhat contradictory to speak of Kleist's Machiavellian protagonists, especially since, as a dramatist, Kleist is usually relegated to the ranks of the romantics. And yet, in *Die Familie Schroffenstein*, his first completed play written under the influence of romanticism, he has Ottokar make the following observation: 'Es zieht des Lebens Forderung den Leser / Zuweilen ab, denn *das Gemeine* will / Ein Opfer auch; doch immer kehrt er wieder / Zu dem vertrauten Geist zurück.'[1] Later in the text, Sylvester, one of the noblest, most sympathetic characters created by Kleist, concedes: 'Ganz rein, seh ich wohl ein, kanns fast nicht abgehn, / Denn wer das Schmutzge anfasst, den besudelts' (1:83). Whereas the young idealist, preferring to dwell in the realm of the 'vertrauten Geist,' only reluctantly acknowledges the demand for coming to terms, however briefly, with life, the older, more experienced man has been taught by 'das Gemeine' the inevitability of losing one's innocence because of the necessity of living in an imperfect human society. Even earlier than *Die Familie Schroffenstein*, Kleist, in a letter to his fiancée from the year 1800, lamented the fact that self-interest was the determining force of politics: 'Ach, Wilhelmine, ich erkenne nur ein höchstes Gesetz an, die *Rechtschaffenheit* [Kleist's emphasis], und die Politik kennt nur ihren Vorteil' (2:504). This same pragmatic assessment of social and political motivation forms the basis of Machiavelli's *Il Principe*: 'There is a wide gulf between life as it is lived and life as it should be lived, and lessons drawn from the latter rather than from the former will teach disaster rather than self-preservation.'[2] The alternatives of disaster and self-preservation could be said to inform Kleist's dramatic world as well.

I should state from the outset that in drawing analogies between *Il Principe* and Kleist's dramas, I do not wish to imply that Kleist read

Machiavelli. In fact, only one critic, Robert Helbling, has alluded to the Italian political theorist in connection with the German playwright, and parenthetically at that: '[Kleist's apparent cynicism] may in equal meaure be due to his candid recognition that a national liberator, not unlike Machiavelli's "ideal" Prince, would have to be cunning, ruthless, and not afraid of dirtying his hands if he were to achieve his goal.'[3] My analysis will demonstrate, however, a remarkable meeting of minds across some three centuries, explicable in terms of what Georg Büchner once decried as 'in der Menschennatur eine entsetzliche Gleichheit'[4] and perhaps in terms of an historical fate with many features in common. Both writers, by their proximity through birth[5] to the ruling class, had first-hand knowledge of the court and its machinations and were thus in a position to observe how power is achieved, exercised, and maintained effectively. Moreover, they both learned from painful personal experience the importance of having a protector or sponsor in high places.[6]

Not only does the titular hero of Kleist's *Hermannsschlacht* match the model of the 'prudent' prince as delineated in *Il Principe*, but also the circumstances surrounding the creation of Kleist's political play conform to those involved in the writing of what Walter Eliot has called 'the handbook for a Resistance, to be completed by a Liberation.'[7] After the Battle of Ravenna in 1512 that resulted in the restoration of the Medici in Florence, Machiavelli sought to return to government service but was refused because of his too prominent association with the fallen Soderini régime. Denied reinstatement in the Florentine civil service, he came to know serious financial difficulty, and being a vain man – a personality trait he shared with Kleist – he felt extremely bitter that the ruling house chose not to make use of his abilities. Out of sheer frustration and abhorrence of idleness (like Kleist he dreamed of 'die grosse Tat' and could be said to have lived it vicariously in his literary activity), he composed his political tract addressed to the Medici. All of this sounds strangely reminiscent of Kleist's unfortunate military and civil-service career, the Battle of Ravenna paralleling the defeat of Prussia at Jena-Auerstedt in 1806 and Machiavelli's attempt at reinstatement corresponding to Kleist's failure to regain the favour of the Prussian court. After his aborted attempt in 1803 to join Napoleon's army, Kleist never fully escaped the stigma of being branded a traitor and as late as 1811 his petition to re-enter the civil service was left unanswered.

Machiavelli remained convinced that Italy, a victim of foreign invasion and subjugation largely through its own fault, had to be brought to a point of total degradation before its inherent excellence would reassert itself.[8] 'In Italy there is no lack of material to be moulded into shape, there is good quality in the mass of people if it be lacking in the leaders' (M 124). For the Renaissance thinker, the central issue was leadership. Italy was both prepared and willing to rise up in revolt if a saviour could be found to put an end to foreign despoiling and partitioning and to heal the rivalries between the various Italian states which, more than any other factor, rendered unification and ultimate victory impossible. This liberator for whom enslaved Italy waited in vain would be characterized above all by *virtù*, which, as Machiavelli uses the word, 'connotes ruthlessness, courage, determination, ability and success in the pursuit of an objective. It has no ethical overtones or undertones whatever.'[9] In *Il Principe*, Machiavelli, consciously avoids idle, idealistic speculation: 'Since, however, I am concerned primarily to give practical guidance to readers, I shall deal directly with the realities of this relationship [between ruler and subjects] and not with imaginary ideals, for there are many who have described utopic republics and despotisms' (M 83), and outlines in a very explicit manner the strategy envisioned and 'the methods proved by the men [he has] set as examples' (M 123). Because he was advocating a resistance movement upon his own native soil against foreign occupational forces with superior means, he knew full well that a successful campaign could only be conducted if a leader from the Italian aristocracy were prepared to resort to deceit, treachery, ruthlessness, or 'the practice of wickedness for use, when necessary' (M 83). If such a man were to come forward and if he were to take to heart the counsel contained in the tract, Italy would undoubtedly welcome him with open arms: 'The present opportunity to provide a saviour for Italy after so long a wait must not be missed. It is important for me to put into words the enthusiasm with which he would be greeted in all the territories which have suffered foreign occupation, the thirst for revenge, the devoted loyalty, the tears of gratitude. What doors would be bolted against him? What population would withhold its obedience? What spite would stand in his way? What Italian would deny him homage? This alien tyranny today stinks in all men's nostrils' (M 125).

If one were to replace Italy-Italian with Germany-German in the preceding quotation, without any further alteration it would read as if it came straight from a résumé of *Die Hermannsschlacht's* political intent. 'Dieses Kleistische Werk,' Kurt May has aptly remarked, 'ist wirklich von der einzigen Absicht bestimmt, in die einmaligen, gegenwärtigen, öffentlichen deutschen Lebensverhältnisse verändernd, nämlich rettend und richtend einzuwirken,'[10] a view substantiated by the most often cited

Kleistian reference to *Die Hermannsschlacht*: 'Sie [Heinrich Joseph von Collin] können leicht denken, wie sehr mir die Aufführung dieses Stücks, *das einzig und allein auf diesen Augenblick berechnet war*, am Herzen liegt. Schreiben Sie mir bald: es wird gegeben; jede Bedingung ist mir gleichgültig, ich *schenke* [Kleist's emphasis] es den Deutschen' (2:824). In full agreement with his Italian predecessor, Kleist also refrained from indulging in vague, idealistic conjecture, for, to use Hermann Korff's formulation, *Die Hermannsschlacht* is 'ein flammender Anschauungsunterricht, wie und wie das *nur* [Korff's emphasis] zu machen ist.'[11] Recognizing that the political exigencies of a resistance movement would inevitably make a shambles of any faith in the universal goodness of man, Kleist, together with Machiavelli, underwent what Sigurd Burckhardt has termed 'the baptism of the gutter.'[12]

Turning to the other plays, one can ascertain what could be called a Machiavellian potential in the atmosphere and motivation underlying *Die Familie Schroffenstein*:

KIRCHENVOGT   Seit alten Zeiten
    Gibts zwischen unsern beiden Grafenhäusern,
    Von Rossitz und von Warwand einen Erbvertrag,
    Kraft dessen nach dem gänzlichen Aussterben
    Des einen Stamms, *der gänzliche Besitztum*
    Desselben an den andern fallen sollte.
JERONIMUS Zur Sache, Alter! das gehört zur Sache nicht.
KIRCHENVOGT Ei, Herr, der Erbvertrag gehört zur Sache.
    Denn das ist just als sagtest du, der Apfel
    Gehöre nicht zum Sündenfall.   (1:57)

Although it is now generally agreed that this revealing exchange can be attributed largely to the influence of Rousseau, the assassination of an opponent's offspring or the general ethos of distrust and hatred symbolized by the prevalence of daggers and poison calls to mind the courtly intrigues of the Borgias. Moreover, according to Machiavelli, 'The urge to acquire possessions [cf 'der gänzliche Besitztum'] and extend dominion is normal and natural' (M 37), a view which runs counter to the Enlightenment's belief in the inherent goodness and perfectibility of man, but a view which Kleist's more pragmatic portrayal of human nature, as exemplified by his Machiavellian protagonists, would seem to support. However, in *Die Familie Schroffenstein*, circumstances tend to govern the individual; hence, there can be no Machiavellian figure since his presence would imply some personal mastery of the dramatic situation. The character most closely approximating the type would be Rupert, but he lacks the requisite cunning and above all the self-discipline under duress. Whereas Hermann almost always has his feelings under strictest control, Rupert comes across as a slave to his emotions: 'Denn niemals hat die blinde Rachsucht, die / Ihn [Rupert] zügellos-wild treibt, mir [Ottokar] wohlgetan' (1:102). One has only to compare Hermann's pursuit of vengeance to see the difference. What Kleist has provided in Rupert is a penetrating study of an essentially weak, cowardly, if not pathetic man in a position of some power who shows a willingness to use others to perform the nefarious deed but, once the deed has been committed, regrets having done it or blames it on others: 'Nicht ein Zehnteil würd / Ein Herr des Bösen tun, müsst er es selbst / Mit eignen Händen tun' (1:117). Furthermore, as Rupert remarks earlier in the tragedy: 'O listig ist die Schlange – 's ist nur gut, / Dass wir das wissen, denn so *ist* [Kleist's emphasis] sies nicht / Für uns' (1:106). The cunning, the deception is almost always presumed to be in the other party and such an attitude, contributing to the ominous ambiance of *Die Familie Schroffenstein*, leaves little space for what Agnes calls 'das Gefühl … der Seelengüte andrer!' (1:99).

The first fully delineated Machiavellian protagonist appears in *Der zerbrochene Krug*, a not surprising development given the less favourable view of human nature and its foibles associated with the comedy. This character type achieves a culmination in *Die Hermannsschlacht*, but reappears in Kleist's masterpiece and final work, *Prinz Friedrich von Homburg*, in his most diabolical form. In addition, *Robert Guiskard*, Kleist's recalcitrant fragment, spanning a majority of his productive years (1801–8), has two Machiavellian protagonists: an older, more accomplished practitioner and an up-and-coming, younger threat. Appearing both at the beginning and the end of Kleist's dramatic career in half of his plays, the figure of the clandestine schemer plots the social or political elimination of a rival and by stealth and skilful manipulation of others determines the direction the action takes at almost every turn. Whereas Goethe had recourse to Mephistopheles to express some reservation about the optimistic eighteenth-century view of man:

Der kleine Gott der Welt bleibt stets von gleichem Schlag
Und ist so wunderlich als wie am ersten Tag.
Ein wenig besser würd' er leben,
Hättst du ihm nicht den Schein des Himmelslichts gegeben;

Er nennt's Vernunft und braucht's allein,
Nur tierischer als jedes Tier zu sein.[13]

Kleist, by consistently making use of the Machiavellian protagonist in both secondary and primary roles, placed a larger question mark after the Enlightenment's faith in the 'Seelengüte andrer.' In the subsequent chapters, I shall endeavour to ascertain the exact nature and function of this question mark and, in the conclusion, explore the degree to which Machiavelli's ideas, conveyed by Shakespeare and demonstrated by Napoleon, may have influenced Kleist.

2

Ein dunkles Licht:
the court secretary in
Der zerbrochene Krug[1]

Although almost every considerable detail of Kleist's *Der zerbrochene Krug*, including its language,[2] the jug itself,[3] even the time and number references,[4] has been scrutinized, a key character, Schreiber Licht, the man most responsible for the final outcome of the comedy, has been accorded only passing reference in the secondary literature. While Richard Samuel concedes a mere functional importance to Licht's role,[5] a view shared by E.L. Stahl,[6] he also alludes to an enigma in what he perceives to be the secretary's motives: 'We never know what he knows and what he does not know, whether he is an arch-intriguer or whether his blandness is genuine.'[7] For both Manfred Schunicht and Hans Schrimpf, however, Licht embodies the unscrupulous, ambitious careerist: 'Der eigentlich negative Charakter des Stücks ist der Gerichtsschreiber, ein blutloser Ehrgeizling aus dem Geschlecht der "Wurm" und "Leonhard", der hinterhältig nur seinen einzigen Zweck im Auge hat, selbst Dorfrichter zu werden.'[8] Despite the astute observations and for the most part correct generalizations made by Schunicht[9] and Schrimpf, no one has undertaken to outline in detail Licht's specific participation in the chain of events leading to Adam's exposure, nor has anyone detected a relationship between Licht's Machiavellian techniques and those of another clandestine villain in *Prinz Friedrich von Homburg*, Graf Hohenzollern.

Several critics[10] have remarked that Kleist's preface to *Der zerbrochene Krug*, written more than four years after completion of the play, furnishes an inaccurate account of the Le Veau engraving alleged to have inspired the comedy. 'Der Richter,' notes Schrimpf, 'thront zwar gravitätisch, donnert aber keineswegs den Burschen an. Und der Gerichtsdiener sieht mehr aus wie ein junger adliger Patron, der dem Gerichtsgang beiwohnt. Es ist durchaus nicht zu erkennen, dass er den Richter misstrauisch anblickt.'[11] The preface may therefore be of greater value as an indication of the dramatist's conscious or unconscious intent. For example, Kleist's observation together with its parenthetical supposition: 'und der Gerichtsschreiber sah (er hatte vielleicht kurz vorher das Mädchen angesehen) jetzt den Richter misstrauisch zur Seite an' (1:176) establishes a link between the girl and the judge through the intermediary of the 'Gerichtsschreiber.' Whereas the use of 'misstrauisch' implies some doubt as to the judge's integrity, 'zur Seite' conveys the impression of a surreptitious functionary who, being less than candid, cannot be fully trusted. In the preface Kleist suggests that the court clerk has an awareness denied the other participants, and since he is the only person to infer the culpability of the judge as well as an inkling of the latter's crime, he clearly performed an important task in the author's perception of the comedy. Hence, Licht appropriately has the first words of the play: 'Ei, was zum Henker, sagt, Gevatter Adam! / Was ist mit Euch geschehn? Wie seht Ihr aus?' (1:177), lines which, by virtue of an expletive and the form of address, allude from the outset to some form of intimacy between judge and secretary.

One of the questions begging an answer is at what stage Licht gains full knowledge of Adam's offence. News travels fast in a small town such as Huisum. The nosy Frau Brigitte has already heard that morning, before the trial begins, 'Was bei Frau Marthe Rull geschehn' (1:235) and Licht, who has learned of Walter's impending surprise visit from a farmer returning from Holla, obviously has his ear to the village grape-vine. A number of seemingly innocuous details point to his having some intimation of his superior's nocturnal escapade. In fact, this first expositional scene has all the earmarks of an interrogation conducted by prosecuter Licht, commencing with the initial line of the play. He also emphasizes the uncomplimentary, compromising parallel between the judge's actual fall and the metaphorical fall of his biblical namesake with its sexual con-notations[12] and singles out almost immediately two crucial issues which will eventually precipitate Adam's social fall: the time that the alleged accident took place – 'Wann trug sich die Begebenheit denn zu?' (1:177) – and the incriminating involvement of the club-foot – 'Und wohl den linken obenein? ... Der ohnhin schwer den Weg der Sünde wandelt?' (1:177). Prepared to exploit the weaknesses or sensitivities of others, Licht is quick to prod a vulnerable spot, despite Adam's protests to the contrary, and refuses to allow his victim an escape: 'Erlaubt! Da tut Ihr Eurem rechten Unrecht. / Der rechte kann sich dieser – Wucht nicht rühmen, / Und wagt sich eh'r aufs Schlüpfrige' (1:178). This assertion not only represents the third reference in less than thirty lines to a potential for evil harped upon by the clerk, two of which relate to sex, but it also provides an excellent example of suggestive ambiguity. The 'Schlüpfrige' chosen by Licht ties in with Adam's explanation in its literal meaning of 'slippery,' while in a figurative sense it designates the lascivious, the indecent, or the obscene. Frequently, Licht's utterances hint at the barely concealed hostility and frustration of the subaltern compelled by circumstances to show respect for a superior whom he feels to be his intellectual inferior. For instance, all of his comments relating to the accident, far from being reassuring to the injured party, blatantly seek to magnify the damage: 'Ein Stück fehlt von der Wange, / Wie gross? Nicht ohne Waage kann ichs schätzen' (1:178).

Equally suspicious are the subsequent comparisons which, although expressed in apparent innocence, come amazingly close to the truth:[13] 'Ein Schaf, das, eingehetzt von Hunden, sich / Durch Dornen drängt, lässt nicht mehr Wolle sitzen, / Als Ihr, Gott weiss wo? Fleisch habt sitzen lassen' (1:178). Whereas Adam has just insisted that the incident occurred in the court house, Licht jumps to the correct conclusion that his associate has left some incriminating flesh-and-blood 'Gott weiss wo.' Later in the scene, Adam characterizes Walter as 'der wackre Mann, der selbst / Sein Schäfchen schiert' (1:179). Licht first proposed a partial but potentially damaging loss of wool, while Adam, open to his subordinate's suggestion, casts himself in the same role but with even more devastating consequences: he now sees himself as one of the sheep shorn by the district judge, a prophetic image.[14] The second comparison made by Licht strikes even closer to home: 'Ei, hier liegt / Querfeld ein Schlag, blutrünstig, straf mich Gott, / Als hätt ein Grossknecht wütend ihn geführt' (1:178). A condition contrary to fact actually states the facts: Ruprecht, a 'Grossknecht' on his father's farm, in a rage delivered this blow with the door knob. The final parallel: 'So gehts im Feuer des Gefechts' (1:178) again sounds strangely out of context if one accepts Adam's explanation, for the image approximates what in reality did transpire – a battle, with elements of sexual and physical violence. Licht's reaction to Adam's further fabrication of having fallen against the stove: 'lacht. Gut, gut ... Der erste Adamsfall, / Den Ihr aus einem Bett hinaus getan' (1:179) signifies both his rejection of the obvious falsehood and his continual insistence upon the relationship between his superior's physical fall and his moral degradation. The tumble from bed is false in an 'unbildlich' (1:177) sense, but quite true in the 'bildlich,' because sex has caused Adam's fall from social grace.

Essentially, the same procedure of obliging the unwilling Adam to face the reality of an unpleasant turn of events continues as Licht warns his colleague of Walter's imminent arrival. Giving further evidence of his ability to read Adam's mind, Licht perceives a danger. Adam, thinking only of the bribable Wachholder, refuses to come to terms with his ostensibly incorruptible successor, but Licht insists that the meeting take place, partly out of fear for his own position, since Walter 'Richter dort [Holla] und *Schreiber* [suspendierte]' (1:180). This menace posed by Walter results in a significant exchange between judge and clerk which more than any other explains the motivation of the latter throughout the rest of the drama. Unable to elude the inspection, Adam tries to intimidate and blackmail his right-hand man in an effort to silence him: 'Jetzt gilts Freundschaft. / Ihr wisst, wie sich zwei Hände waschen können. / Ihr wollt auch gern, ich weiss, Dorfrichter werden, / Und Ihr verdients, bei Gott, so gut wie einer' (1:181). Recognizing Licht as a dangerous rival, Adam asks him to deny his ambition on this particular occasion and endeavours to ingratiate himself by acknowledging Licht's worthiness and by promising to support his future career. Not only does Licht seek to deny the charge: 'Dorfrichter, ich! Was denkt Ihr auch von mir?' (1:181), but he even goes so far as to disavow the relationship: 'Wir zwei Gevatterleute! Geht mir fort!' (1:181) that he himself was anxious to establish in the opening line of the play: 'Ei, was zum Henker, sagt, Gevatter Adam!' (1:177). In the first instance he stressed a bond of friendship in order to encourage Adam to disclose his intimate affairs, a tactic designed to give the subordinate subtle power over his superior. But now, always with an eye to his own advantage, Licht objects to being 'tarred with the same brush.' When Adam persists in his attempt to bribe his secretary, the latter retorts in righteous indignation: 'Geht mir mit Eurem Argwohn, sag ich Euch. / Hab ich jemals – ?' (1:181). On the verge of protesting his innocence, he is unable to complete his sentence as signaled by the dash, an implied confirmation of his guilt. Finally, as his last trump, Adam resorts to a concealed threat:

> Seht, ich, ich, für mein Teil,
> Dem grossen Griechen [Demosthenes] folg ich auch. Es liesse
> Von Depositionen sich und Zinsen
> Zuletzt auch eine Rede ausarbeiten:
> Wer wollte solche Perioden drehn? (1:182)

Licht has involved himself in questionable financial dealings, specifically the misuse of debtors' funds; however, the only person aware of his complicity and thus in a position to inform against him is Adam. The secretary's three subsequent responses: 'Nun, also!,' 'Ich weiss,' and 'Das sag ich auch' (1:182) betoken his reluctant agreement to concur with the cover-up.[15] Being smart enough to know when he has been backed into a corner, he concedes apparent defeat rather than run the risk of being implicated by a potentially dangerous Adam and has no choice but to appear to go along with his superior. Even though he secretly wants to eliminate Adam, out of self-interest he must avoid discrediting him openly. This consideration will determine the remainder of the secretary's calculated behaviour before and during the trial.

Whereas Adam goes to great lengths to avoid the confrontation with Walter, Licht is equally adamant that it come about, partly because such an encounter could well redound to the public embarrassment of Adam. Throughout the confusion created by the messenger's announcement, the secretary displays composure, presence of mind, and the ability to assume complete control if necessary. An implied threat, this time made by Licht: 'Das fehlt noch, dass Ihr [Adam] auf den Weg ihm [Walter] leuchtet' (1:183), represents the deciding argument convincing Adam to agree to the fateful meeting. But even before Walter appears on stage, there are signs that Licht has switched loyalties and is manoeuvring to gain the confidence and favour of the opposing side by a show of feigned solicitude: 'Es ist dem Herrn Gerichtsrat, will ich hoffen, / Nichts Böses auf der Reise zugestossen?' (1:184). Adam recognizes the game that his clerk is playing: 'Ihr [Licht] gebt Euch bloss, Gevatter. / ... Ihr seid verlegen' (1:184), while Licht's reaction: 'Wieso?,' 'Was!,' 'Ich, verlegen!,' and 'Es war ein Miss-verständnis' (1:184–5) suggests the criminal caught in the act as he continues to justify himself despite the fact that it is quite evident that Adam, having forgotten about the incident, is more concerned with putting the registry in order.

The critical issue of the exact time that the alleged accident took place is again raised quite innocently by the two maids whose collaborating statements place the mishap at 'Gestern abend – / Glock eilf – ' (1:185), an assertion which contradicts Adam's earlier declaration and which the ever alert Licht immediately seizes upon: 'Habt Ihr die Wund seit gestern schon?' (1:185). When Adam justifies the absence of his wig by having recourse to the falsehood of the cat and her litter, Licht's response to this makeshift expedient: 'Die Katze? Was? Seid Ihr – ?' (1:186) dem-onstrates that he is not deceived and that only the awareness of his precariously dependent relationship with his superior prevents him from 'letting the cat out of the bag.' However, this awareness does not hinder him from ironically aiding in the fabrication of the story to underscore how preposterous the whole excuse is: 'Drauf nimmt die Katze sie [Perücke] ins Maul – ... / Und trägt sie unters Bett und jungt darin' (1:186). Adam, fearing his subordinate's intervention, endeavours to regain control of his own fiction: 'Ins Maul? Nein – ' (1:186), but this proves to be a fatal mistake: 'Nicht? Wie sonst?' In other words, try to get out of this one! Put on the spot, Adam recognizes that he has been caught: 'Die Katze? Ach, was!' and since his usually agile mind cannot think fast enough to extricate itself from this predicament, he falls even farther into the trap skilfully set for him. Having fun at Adam's expense, Licht playfully proposes a way out of the dilemma: 'Nicht? Oder Ihr vielleicht?' – not a very plausible one, but one which the judge, anxious to save face, eagerly resorts to: 'Ins Maul! Ich glaube – ! / Ich stiess sie [Perücke] mit dem Fusse heut hinunter, / Als ich es sah' (1:186). Licht has achieved his objective. From a position of strength he has toyed with Adam, compelling him to change his story and thus demonstrating that the whole tale is nothing but a lie. As signalled by the complacency of Licht's final comment relating to this episode, 'Gut, gut' (1:186), he has clearly gained the upper hand.[16]

Once Adam has recounted his self-condemning dream, Licht seeks both to minimize its prophetic content and to exploit it as a vehicle to frighten his superior into acquiescence. While in actual fact the secretary does everything to realize indirectly the 'Traum vom ausgehunzten Richter' (1:187), at the same time he manages to preserve a semblance of non-intervention or sympathy towards Adam who could still conceivably thwart Licht's ambitions. Even at this stage he may have some idea of the judge's nocturnal indiscretion, but in any case he remains quite eager that the court be called into session, since there is a good chance, as the pedant Licht well knows, that Adam will disgrace himself in a purely legal, 'vorschriftsmässig' (1:187) sense. After Licht obsequiously states his position and volunteers his years of service, a further attempt to ingratiate himself, he intervenes soon thereafter in a Walter-Adam dialogue, ostensibly to set the record straight. Adam has rather foolishly revealed his knowledge of the inspection tour to Holla. To Walter's enquiry, 'Woher wisst Ihr das?' (1:189), Adam answers with a misrepresentation: 'Woher? Euer Gnaden Diener –.'[17] At this very point, Licht rudely interrupts to contradict his superior and by so doing puts him in an uncomplimentary light: 'Ein Bauer sagt' es, / Der eben jetzt von Holla eingetroffen' (1:189). Throughout this scene, Licht efficiently provides the necessary information, while Adam, unsure of himself, proves unable or is not permitted to complete his sentences:

WALTER Sagt doch, Ihr habt ja wohl Gerichtstag heut?
ADAM – Ob wir –?
WALTER   Was?
LICHT   Ja, den ersten in der Woche.
WALTER. Und jene Schar von Leuten, die ich draussen
    Auf Eurem Flure sah, sind das –?
ADAM   Das werden –
LICHT Die Kläger sinds, die sich bereits versammeln.   (1:189–90)

As the proceedings open and Adam turns to Licht, his only apparent source of support, the court secretary diminishes the importance of the impending case and is sufficiently confident to order his superior to sit down. When Adam makes one last desperate attempt to avoid presiding over the trial by feigning illness, Licht utters what seems to be a conflicting statement: 'Ich glaub, Ihr rast, im Ernst. Soeben kommt Ihr –? / – Meinethalben. Sagts dem Herrn Gerichtsrat dort. / Vielleicht erlaubt ers. – Ich weiss nicht, was Euch fehlt?' (1:195). In the initial reaction (prior to the dash), Licht pursues his primary aim: to have Adam try the case and bring reproach upon himself, but the double dash marks a brief time lapse during which the secretary reconsiders what would ultimately be in his own best interest. Returning to bed could be equally damaging to Adam and would give Licht an opportunity to demonstrate his expertise on the judge's bench. One must also bear in mind that, although there is as yet no conclusive evidence, he may know full well 'was [Adam] fehlt.' Still unable to reach a decision, Adam remarks, 'für sich'. Verflucht! Ich kann mich nicht dazu entschliessen – ! / – Es klirrte etwas [the jug], da ich Abschied nahm –' (1:196). There is no sign that Licht overhears this aside and in an effort to bring the judge back to the demands of the situation at hand, 'ihn [Adam] aufschreckend,' the secretary exclaims, 'Herr Richter! Seid Ihr –?' (1:196) The 'Seid Ihr' means something to the effect, 'Are you in your right mind?' or, as Licht later suggests in explanation, 'Ob Ihr taub seid, fragt ich' (1:197). I feel that Schunicht is only partly correct in his assumption: 'Hier weiss Licht, der die Wahrheit sehr früh ahnt, das "Stichwort" zu geben, das blitzartig alle täuschenden Schichten durchstösst.'[18] Licht, more concerned that Adam proceed with the trial and 'judiziert den Hals ins Eisen [sich]' (1:187), only accidentally hits upon the correct stimulus, specifically an incriminating 'Seid Ihr' (1:196)

response to Adam's previous query, 'Ei, wer zerbrach den Krug?' (1:195).
Assuming that Licht intended to say 'Are you the one who broke the
jug?,' Adam quickly denies it: 'Ich? Auf Ehre nicht!' (1:196) but, then
in his confusion, perhaps engendered by the sound of his colleague's
voice, he makes a further confession completely out of context: 'Ich hatte
sie behutsam drauf gehängt' (1:196), which can only relate to his previous
excuse made in Licht's presence, 'Ich hatte die Perücke aufgehängt, / Auf
einen Stuhl, da ich zu Bette ging' (1.186). Temporarily alienated, as
anticipated by his dream, Adam responds on two levels which consciously
he has endeavoured to separate: the jug, a night crime, and the wig,
an alleged morning accident, but which unconsciously he brings together
in this reflex and indirect admission of guilt fortuitously triggered by
Licht's question.

During the trial, Licht surreptitiously pursues his judicial ambitions
by two means. First, he strives to exhibit his greater legal acumen at
Adam's expense. One particular episode typifies this approach. Because
Adam is keen to stress the fact that the case concerns only the broken
jug, he insists, 'Ein Krug. *Ein blosser Krug.* Setzt einen Krug, / Und schreibt
dabei: dem Amte wohlbekannt' (1:198). Earlier, in a statement meant for
Adam, Licht had maintained: 'Lärm um nichts; Lappalien. / Es ist ein
Krug zerbrochen worden' (1:195), a minimizing description which Adam
now seizes upon. In an effort both to call into question his superior's
forensic ability as well as to underline indirectly the seriousness of the
case, Licht now retracts in Walter's presence his former assertions. 'Auf
meine hingeworfene Vermutung / Wollt Ihr, Herr Richter –?' (1:198). As
Licht's contribution to the cat fabrication proved, he is not really after
the truth unless it serves his purpose, and hence the insistence upon
proper procedure can only be regarded as part of a scheme to discredit Adam in terms of legalistic know-how and thus to succeed him.
It proves effective. Licht's superficially helpful counsel: 'Wollt Ihr nicht
förmlich–?' (1:199), prompted by another of Adam's blatant improprieties,
finally elicits the desired response in Walter: 'Wenn Ihr [Adam] Recht
anders nicht, als so, könnt geben, / So tretet ab: vielleicht kanns Euer
Schreiber' (1:199). In fact, somewhat later in the proceedings, the district
judge offers Adam's office to Licht. The latter, not averse to the idea:
'Ob ich – ei nun, wenn Euer Gnaden–' (1:207), continues to play up to
Walter. Second, Licht seeks to expose Adam's involvement in the case
being heard without actually seeming to point the accusing finger himself.
Although he may have considerable circumstantial evidence from the very
beginning,[19] he achieves complete awareness only with the exchange

occasioned by the door knob. Because Adam could not see what struck
him as he hung helplessly in the trellis, he is curious to learn the nature
of the weapon:

ADAM Wars eine Klinke? ...
RUPRECHT   Ja, die Türklinke.
ADAM Darum.   (1:210)

Licht, instantly detecting the implied acknowledgment contained within
the 'Darum' and setting a trap, asks innocently: 'Ihr glaubtet wohl, es
war ein Degen?' (1:210). The use of the past tense could relate to Ruprecht's
testimony but really alludes to Adam's assumption at the time when
he received the blow. Licht has hit upon Adam's actual train of thought;
the judge, however, professing ignorance, quickly covers his trail: 'Ein
Degen? Ich – wieso?' Licht now knows the culprit. Since he has been
blackmailed into silence and cannot risk denouncing a powerful associate
publicly, he wisely withdraws: 'Je nun! / Man kann sich wohl verhören.
Eine Klinke / Hat sehr viel Ähnlichkeit mit einem Degen' (1:210).[20] None
the less, Licht persists in his interference: 'Bei meiner Treu! Der Stiel,
Herr Richter?' (1:210). If Walter were the least bit observant, he would
notice the irregularity of Licht's participation in the cross-examination
and the fact that the secretary addresses his question not to the witness
but to the judge who supposedly was not present during the crime.

ADAM Das umgekehrte Ende wars der Klinke!
LICHT So! So!
RUPRECHT   Doch auf dem Griffe lag ein Klumpen
    Blei, wie ein Degengriff, das muss ich sagen.
ADAM Ja, wie ein Griff.
LICHT   Gut, wie ein Degengriff.
    Doch irgend eine tücksche Waffe musst es
    Gewesen sein. Das wusst ich wohl.   (1:210–11)

Licht's ironic 'So! So!' reveals that he can now fill in all the details, while
the observation, introduced by the self-satisfied 'Gut,' with its two past
tenses, 'musst' and 'wusst' harps back to the opening scene in which
he described Adam's wound as a battle scar inflicted by a 'Grossknecht.'
    From this point until the eleventh scene, Licht is rarely heard from,
but as Schrimpf has noted, 'Unterdessen waltet er, Fäden spinnend, im
Hintergrund.'[21] Once Adam has ordered Licht to send the bailiffs to fetch

Frau Brigitte, Walter asks the secretary to investigate the affair himself. Since Licht has given ample evidence of his legal erudition to Adam's detriment and has also successfully managed by calculated intervention to sow some seeds of doubt and suspicion, this request should not surprise us. The subsequent scene illustrates just how susceptible Walter is to suggestion: he interrogates Adam to determine the origin of his wounds to which Licht has deviously drawn attention by dwelling upon the door knob as a lethal weapon.

With the entry of Frau Brigitte, Licht, as he had done in the exposition, openly dominates the trial, adroitly staging the public exposé of his 'Gevatter.' Apprised of Frau Brigitte's testimony beforehand and hence aware of its damaging consequences for Adam, far from attempting to conceal it, he promotes its disclosure and confidently assumes control of the interrogation, insisting that she not be interrupted. In keeping with his Machiavellian character, he lets Frau Brigitte perform the unpleasant task of denunciation and even though he rejects her superstitious interpretation, he none the less confirms and gives credence to the salient details of her report. This approach achieves its desired effect, for when Adam suggests that the Synode in Utrecht be consulted as to whether the devil could be considered the culprit, Walter, disparaging Adam, turns to the man who has earned his confidence: 'Ein Antrag, wie ich ihn von Euch [Adam] erwartet. / Was wohl meint *Ihr* [Kleist's emphasis], Herr Schreiber?' (1:236).

From Frau Brigitte's account of how she and Licht followed the perpetrator's tracks in the snow, the latter's duplicity is divulged to the audience, but not to the other protagonists on stage: 'Gut, sagt er [Licht], Frau Brigitte, ein guter Einfall; / Vielleicht gehn wir uns nicht weit um, / Wenn wir zum Herrn Dorfrichter Adam gehn' (1:236). Because the secretary already knows where the trail will lead, he can thus indulge in this cruel innuendo that on the surface presents the law embodied by Adam as one's natural recourse. This situation is ideal for Licht. By exploiting Frau Brigitte's ignorance and naïveté, he successfully manipulates this scene in such a way that it cannot but embarrass his superior, while giving himself the semblance of the innocent, unsuspecting bystander obliged to become involved by circumstances beyond his control. Once the destination of the footprints has been established, Walter asks Frau Brigitte, ' War eine Spur vornaus?' (1:237). Significantly, Licht intrudes at this juncture to declare, 'Vornaus, verzeihn Euer Gnaden, keine Spur' (1:237). If this testimony were allowed to stand without qualification, although not false, it would still constitute a misrepresentation, for, as

Frau Brigitte goes on to state, 'Ja, vornaus war der Weg zertreten' (1:237). In telling the truth but not the whole truth which would concede the possibility that the guilty party might have only passed through the court house and does not necessarily reside within, Licht betrays his hostility.

Since Licht has already put forward the obvious explanation for the clovenfoot imprint: 'Fuss eines Menschen, bitte, / Doch praeter propter wie ein Pferdehuf' (1:236), Walter eventually poses the follow-up question: 'Sagt doch, ihr Herrn, ist jemand hier im Orte, / Der missgeschaffne Füsse hat?' (1:238), to which Licht responds: 'Hm! Allerdings ist jemand hier in Huisum – / ... / Wollen Euer Gnaden den Herrn Richter fragen – ' (1:238). Again, the secretary refrains from drawing the self-evident conclusion as his recommendation allows for a twofold interpretation. It could signify that Walter should ask the judge if the latter knows of anyone with a misshapen foot, the meaning which Adam chooses to infer, but it could also imply that Adam has the incriminating limb. In any case, Licht's ambiguous counsel draws attention to Adam and no doubt serves to jog the others' memories about his physical defect.

The wig that finally convinces several characters of Adam's guilt[22] achieves this pre-eminence in part through Licht's shrewd handling of the incriminating exhibit.

ADAM Glaubt Ihr, ich hätte, ich, der Richter, gestern,
    Im Weinstock die Perücke eingebüsst?
WALTER Behüte Gott! Die Eur' ist ja im Feuer,
    Wie Sodom und Gomorrha aufgegangen.
LICHT Vielmehr – vergebt mir, gnädger Herr! Die Katze
    Hat gestern in die seinige gejungt.   (1:239)

Licht simply repeats Adam's first expedient invention, which the secretary himself helped to embellish, and so doing, he proves that his colleague is a liar by juxtaposing the double fiction and thus singling out the contradiction. Licht lets Adam figuratively hang himself, the literal fate of his associate in Holla. But the public embarrassment does not stop there: 'Hm! Die Perücke passt Euch doch, mein Seel, / Als wär auf Euren Scheiteln sie gewachsen. / Er setzt sie ihm auf' (1:240). Licht's animosity, his determination to destroy Adam, comes to the surface in this assertion and gesture and thus the individual who has set the stage appropriately supplies the decisive visual confirmation. Even in this instance, however, he pretends to be somewhat surprised at the excellent fit, even though he makes this observation *before* placing the damning piece of evidence upon Adam's head.

The only time in the whole drama when Licht attacks his superior *directly* occurs soon after the village judge has been fully exposed and has fled from the courtroom: 'Die Order! Was! Der Sünder, der!' (1:243). In Adam's absence, he can permit himself this show of self-righteous indignation with impunity. As further proof that the secretary has acquired the district judge's trust, Walter does not hesitate to use him to substantiate his own statements: 'Herr Schreiber Licht, sagt selbst, ist das die Order, / Die man aus Utrecht jüngst an euch erliess?' (1:243). This implied dependency reflects adversely upon Walter's power of judgment, one of several signs that cast some doubt upon his wisdom and impartiality,[23] for Licht is a more subtle and hence more dangerous rogue than Adam, who comes across much more sympathetically.[24] Somehow we forgive his human weaknesses and even see him as a victim of his physical ugliness, whereas little can be said in defence of a man who only serves his own ambition and seeks to satisfy a sadistic streak as manifested in his concluding statement: 'Seht, wie der Richter Adam, bitt ich euch, / Berg auf, Berg ab, als flöh er Rad und Galgen, / Das aufgepflügte Winterfeld durchstampft!' (1:243). Fittingly, the protagonist largely responsible for Adam's social fall leaves the audience with its last image of the village judge, while the comparison 'als flöh er Rad und Galgen' suggests what the secretary might well have in mind for his rival if he were in a position of absolute power.[25] This cruelty and callousness are highlighted when seen in relation to Walter's more compassionate attitude: 'Geschwind, Herr Schreiber, fort! Holt ihn zurück! / Dass er nicht Übel rettend ärger mache' (1:244). And ultimately Licht does achieve his objective: 'Von seinem Amt ist er [Adam] suspendiert, / Und Euch [Licht] bestell ich, bis auf *weitere* / Verfügung, hier im Ort es zu verwalten' (1:244). Many critics have pointed to Licht's *temporary* appointment as evidence of the thwarting of his ambition,[26] but up to this point Walter has given no indication that he harbours any suspicion vis-à-vis Licht and there is every reason to believe that he has been completely duped by the secretary's skilfully applied strategy. One thing, however, has become clear: Walter is a stickler for proper legal procedure; even though he is convinced of Adam's guilt, he refrains from suspending him from his post as long as he officially occupies the bench. Furthermore, in what can be interpreted as an attempt to preserve some vestige of dignity and respect for the authority of the court, Walter promises, 'Doch sind die Kassen richtig, wie ich hoffe, /

Zur Desertion ihn zwingen will ich nicht' (1:244). Not only is the audience aware that debtors' funds have been misappropriated, but the district judge himself recognizes that the books will never balance: 'ich [Adam] stehe für nichts [in der Registratur] ein. / WALTER. Ich auch nicht' (1:238). Hence, there is a distinct possibility that 'auf weitere Verfügung' represents a mere formality and if one were to take into consideration Licht's dexterity in turning everything to his own advantage, Walter's less than perfect administration of justice, or Kleist's obsession with 'die unerklärliche Einrichtung der Welt,' there would seem to be some justification for viewing Licht's tenure of office as more than temporary in keeping with the pessimistic undercurrent peculiar to Kleist's comedies.

In summary, it may be said of Licht that, purporting to be a friend, 'Gevatter,' of the main protagonist whenever it suits the secretary's purpose, he occupies a position of considerable influence between two power figures by virtue of a greater awareness denied the other principals and an amazing ability to exploit his knowledge of human motivation. Pursuing at all times his own subtle advantage, he indirectly controls both parties without becoming ostensibly involved himself. As a means to disparage a 'friend' in the presence of others or to influence a superior against an inferior, he supports a contrary opinion at a rival's expense, plants an idea in an associate's mind by which the latter eventually does damage to himself, or requests the elucidation of an incident although he already knows that whatever account is offered will be a fabrication and thus will further jeopardize the individual being questioned and place him even further under the authority of the interrogator. One can also ascertain a well-developed tendency to set the stage so as to manoeuvre a protagonist into an embarrassing predicament which will obviously imperil his public image, or into a mental state under whose influence he draws what appears to be his own conclusion when in actual fact Licht has deviously led him to that very conclusion. If someone has to do the dirty work, Licht cunningly avoids becoming the perpetrator. This clandestine domination can achieve such proportions that the unwitting victim often becomes totally dependent upon his confidant. Even though he supplies the appropriate cues to bring the distracted character back to a painful reality, the advice offered turns out to be more harmful than beneficial to the recipient. But above all, instead of revealing the truth, Licht opts to conceal it until a stage is reached where its disclosure, circuitously engineered, will prejudice a rival and thus promote Licht's own personal aspirations.

All of the foregoing observations illustrate just as accurately the

Machiavellian machinations of another largely ignored evil-doer in Kleist's opus, Count Hohenzollern, whose dubious distinctions will be dealt with in a later chapter. Indeed, the parallels are quite striking.[27] Hohenzollern and Licht, being privy to a dream related by the main protagonist who has just awakened, deviously contribute to its realization to the detriment of the dreamer. Practising duplicity in their apparent loyalty to two men, they change allegiance whenever it suits their purpose and always take care to be on the winning side. In both dramas a nocturnal incident, during which an individual's sensitivities have been exploited in a vulnerable state, receives several interpretations, each coloured by the witnesses' or victims' bias, but it falls to Licht and Hohenzollern con-fidently[28] to provide or confirm the final version, one which shows off a rival in an unflattering light. Lastly, these two villains share an especially reprehensible feature: a propensity to indulge in gratuitous, diabolical cruelty. Hohenzollern is the only character to laugh in *Prinz Friedrich von Homburg*, and in both instances, the laughter, a spontaneous reaction, implies pleasure derived from witnessing the avoidable suffering of a 'friend' (Homburg), or the bloody destruction of an enemy (the Swedish cavalry). Although Marjorie Gelus has documented the nature of 'Laughter and Joking in the Works of Heinrich von Kleist,'[29] she has failed to note the presence of sadistic merriment. Adam only laughs once under conditions which Gelus' study covers in a general sense: 'Among the different types of joking and laughter in Kleist's works, the most common is to be found among characters who *knowingly* [Gelus' emphasis] face a situation that is unacceptable or unpalatable to them. Their jokes attempt to diminish the magnitude of the problem, or to delay the moment in which they must accept and act on it.'[30] Because unwanted attention has been drawn to Adam's wounds, he finds temporary relief in a defensive display of humour: 'ADAM *lacht*. Nein, Gott sei Dank! Fraunnägel sind es nicht' (1:226). The only other person to laugh, in fact the first to do so, is Licht, in response to Adam's tale about having fallen against the stove: 'LICHT *lacht*. Gut, gut' (1:199). The secretary exhibits sadistic amuse-ment at an excuse which he knows to be a lie; he clearly enjoys the discomfort and embarrassment experienced by the judge, and he mocks his superior in circumstances that would normally elicit sympathy and concern. The laughter therefore signals a sly expression of power over Adam, the self-complacency of which is reinforced by the smug, 'Gut, gut.'

3

Die Hermannsschlacht

In my investigation of the role of Licht in *Der zerbrochene Krug*, I have endeavoured to expose the skilfully concealed presence of the Machiavellian protagonist clandestinely controlling the dramatic action. Kleist's court secretary does, however, have a significant successor in Hermann just as the latter anticipates his direct descendent, Hohenzollern. Reminiscent of Licht, Hermann leads a 'friend' into a false sense of security, while secretly undermining his position. Exploiting an alleged ally in their respective bid for power, both the functionary and the prince show no mercy in the pursuit of their enemy's total elimination achieved by the calculated release of damaging information at the crucial moment. By the conclusion of the two plays, all the characters unite against the common foe at the prompting of the schemer. Hence, *Die Hermannsschlacht* does not necessarily represent as radical a departure from Kleist's previous works as has been maintained, for example by H.A. Korff: 'Mit der *Hermannsschlacht* nimmt Kleist als Dichter eine neue Wendung'.[1] The general type exemplified by Hermann is not new, only the relative position he occupies within the drama: whereas Licht may be said to influence *indirectly* the direction the plot takes, with *Die Hermannsschlacht* one man determines the full course of events, both *indirectly* and *directly*.[2] Ernst Stahl's contention, shared by several commentators, that the play consists of 'four separate but closely-knit parallel actions and one almost independent subplot'[3] does not recognize Hermann's manipulation of the German[4] princes, the Romans, Marbod, Thusnelda, and above all her relationship with Ventidius which remains the very key to the success of Hermann's secret strategy. Many critics, too caught up with the political allusions and the morality debate over which there would appear to be no unanimity, have been deceived by Hermann and have failed to perceive and to evaluate his total mastery from the initial scene to his final speech with which *Die Hermannsschlacht* ends. This domination, deplored by some as a regrettable one-sidedness,[5] none the less confers a psychological unity upon the work as a whole.

Written to promote a self-evident political goal and conceived of with typically Kleistian enthusiasm and commitment, *Die Hermannsschlacht* has met with either a warm or a cool reception upon the stage, almost solely on the basis of the current German political climate. When aspirations towards national unity reached a high point in the 1870s after German forces defeated France in the Franco-Prussian war[6] and during the early years of the Hitler period with the Nazi transformation of Hermann into the prophet of the Third Reich,[7] the play achieved considerable socio-political prominence. This predominantly political orientation is equally reflected in the evaluation of the work by the secondary literature where it has been classified rather consistently as a '"patriotic" play,'[8] 'ein aktivistisches Drama,'[9] or 'ein politisches Tendenzstück mit nur wenig verhüllten Anspielungen auf zeitgenössische Personen und Ereignisse.'[10] Such a political bias, justifiable in terms of Kleist's professed intent, has led critics to ignore or to make only passing reference to literary merit, and to date, with the notable exception of Sigurd Burckhardt's informative reappraisal,[11] Ruth Angress's comparative analysis of *Die Hermannsschlacht* and 'Die Verlobung in St. Domingo' under the aspect of total politics,[12] Ilse Graham's contemporary philosophical approach,[13] an important article by Lawrence Ryan,[14] and Hans-Dieter Loose's socio-political study,[15] there has been little attempt to examine the work in any depth. Most commentators appear to be in general agreement with Walter Müller-Seidel's evaluation: 'Nur mit immer erneut auszusprechenden Vorbehalten wird man dieses Stück in das dichterische Werk Kleists einbeziehen dürfen.'[16] This failure to come to terms with the whole text and to ascertain its inherent poetic idiom has resulted in erroneous statements: 'Am Anfang des Stückes verlassen die deutschen Fürsten Hermann,'[17] (significantly, the actual order is reversed!); inappropriate generalizations: '[Thusnelda's] descent into bestiality is a symbolic re-enactment of man's animal nature in war'[18] (the only 'war' in the Thusnelda-Ventidius episodes involves the battle between the sexes); and some remarkable contradictions: Robert Helbling speaks of 'the *pathological* excesses of human emotion,'[19] while Friedrich Gundolf calls the drama 'sein bis dahin verhältnismässig

gesündestes, entdumpftes, enthitztes [Werk].'[20] Fricke, Gundolf, and Korff
see in *Die Hermannsschlacht* an illustration of 'die vernunftlose Verabso-
lutierung eines Gefühls';[21] Rolf Linn and Burckhardt respectively point
to 'Hermann's cool and methodical pursuit of his aim'[22] and 'a coldly
planned and executed ambush.'[23] For Joachim von Kürenberg, 'Herman
[ist] nichts anderes ... als ein idealisierter, von allen Hemmungen befreiter
Kleist,'[24] but in Helbling's view, 'The author obviously intends to create
in the audience the same critical distance from the political machinations
of his hero as he himself as capable of.'[25] Kürenberg's assertion: 'Thusnelda
ist aufrichtig und zuverlässig, hierin auch Alkmene gleich'[26] gainsays
Helbling's contention: '[Thusnelda has] no scruples in exploiting the
attraction she exerts on Ventidius'[27] while a close reading of the play
will invalidate both of these statements as complete misunderstandings
of the 'heroine.' Earlier in this chapter, I spoke of a psychological unity,
a penetrating, objective portrait revealing the motivation and techniques
of a skilled power politician in the tradition of Machiavelli's *Il Principe*
and it is to this singularly one-sided dramatization of what Jeffrey Sammons
calls Hermann's 'adamant concentration on the larger purpose'[28] that I
shall now direct my attention.

HERMANN'S MACHIAVELLIAN MANOEUVRES

No sooner does a group of German hunters appear on stage than one
of them, Wolf, in the first symbolic act of the drama, '[wirft] sich auf
dem [sic] Boden' (1:535). This introductory visual gesture of defeat and
despair, setting the general tone, is reinforced by the images of his
subsequent opening speech, all of which emphasize a downward, inferior,
subservient status. While Rome parallels the Colossus of Rhodes in its
dominant, standing posture, its enemies are being trampled underfoot:
'Rom ... Den Fuss auf Ost und Westen setzet,' cast into the dust: 'Er
wirft auch jetzt uns Deutsche in den Staub' or subjugated by the emperor:
'Gueltar, der Nervier, und Fust, der Fürst der Cimbern, / Erlagen dem
Augustus schon' ('erliegen' also implies a low, prostrate position before
a superior foe). The Germans seem to be caught up in an irresistible
general collapse, '[im] allgemeinen Sturz Germanias,' (1:535) and the only
apparent means of remaining upright is to become an ally of Rome: 'Aristan
hat, der Ubier, / Der ungrossmütigste von allen deutschen Fürsten, / In
Varus' Arme treulos sich geworfen' (1:536). The operative verb remains
'werfen,' but in this instance the traitor is held up by the arms of the
enemy, an unconscionable position dictated by self-centred survival. The

attitude of the princes towards one another emphasizes this 'down-beat' note, creating an overwhelming impression of hopelessness. When Dagobert announces that Augustus has promised him the realm of the Narisker in return for his support, he proceeds to use the possibility of his joining an alliance against the enemy as emotional blackmail to oblige a fellow German prince to make an important concession: 'Und wenn er [Selgar] mir [Dagobert] Gerechtigkeit verweigert, / Selbst jetzt noch, da er meiner Grossmut braucht, / So werd ich mich in *euren* Krieg nicht mischen' (1:536). His blind egotism surfaces in his formulation 'euren Krieg': the war is their war, not his. Selgar's emotional response: 'Eh ich, Unedelmütgem, dir / Den Strich am Lippgestade überlasse, / Eh will an Augusts Heere ich / Mein ganzes Reich, mit Haus und Hof verlieren!' (1:536-7), divulges the pernicious influence of traditional rivalries: rather than lose face and relinquish the contested strip of land, he is prepared to sacrifice his whole realm! Concerned only with property, the princes cannot raise their eyes above their own narrow, self-oriented perspective, a shortcoming which the Romans have been using to their advantage by setting one tribe off against the other. Cognizant of this central function of possessions in human motivation, Machiavelli warns that 'in no circumstances must [the ruler] touch [his people's] property' (M 89).

Critics have consistently overlooked the fact that right from the very first scene of *Die Hermannsschlacht*, Kleist has gone to considerable lengths to stress the duplicity and untrustworthiness of the Romans. If it is a question of foreign conquest, the only principle that they recognize and that determines their behaviour is to win by whatever means are required. Thuiskomar expresses outrage at Varus' failure to keep his word: 'Ein förmlicher Vertrag ward jüngst, / Geschlossen zwischen mir und ihm [Varus]' (1:535), but this did not protect the German prince when, on the pretext of attacking the Friesen, Varus invaded his ally's own country. '[It] should be noted,' cautions Machiavelli, 'that a prudent prince must beware of taking sides with a more powerful neighbour in a quarrel with a third, unless he cannot possibly avoid it. As what I have just stated shows, he must lose the independence which rulers must at all costs preserve' (M 109). Since, however, in drawing attention to the Roman's 'Gaunerstreich' (1:536) Thuiskomar unintentionally discloses his own willingness to sell out a neighbour in order to save his own skin, the audience gains insight into a general lack of ethical standards on *both* sides. Kleist constructed this introductory scene essentially to perform three tasks, all of which relate directly or indirectly to the titular protagonist: to stress the total unreliability of the Romans, Hermann's hunting guests; to reflect the narrow-minded, materialistic mentality of the German princes, the main obstacle that Hermann must overcome; and to acquaint the audience with Hermann's reputation as the 'letzten Pfeiler' capable of keeping the Germans upright in the 'allgemeinen Sturz' (1:535).

The next scene has to be one of the most carefully devised in the whole play, beginning with its underlying message contained in the stage directions: '*Thusnelda, den Ventidius aufführend. Ihr folgt Hermann, Scäpio, ein Gefolge von Jägern und ein leerer römischer Wagen mit vier breitgespannten weissen Rossen*' (1:537). Ventidius is permitted to occupy centre stage, to be the ostensible focal point; Hermann, in his first appearance, does not choose to take the leading position. His entry suggests visually both his alleged subservience and the existence of a stronger physical bond between Thusnelda and the Roman than between husband and wife. In retrospect the empty Roman chariot raises some doubt as to Hermann's subordination since he opts not to ride in it. The Roman gift is simply dragged along, symbolic of Hermann's true intent: to be perceived as fraternizing with the Romans but to elude any iron-clad commitment to their cause.

From the initial lines of this scene: '*Heil dem Ventidius Carbo! Römer-ritter! / Dem kühnen Sieger des gehörnten Urs!*' (1:537), the Roman is being 'set up' as the hero of the hour, a process aided and abetted by Thusnelda. There remains some question as to the degree of her candour throughout the incident; however, one particular comment together with its stage direction: '*mutwillig. Was sollt ich fürchten, Scäpio, / So lang Ventidius mir zur Seite stand*' (1:538) would seem to portray Thusnelda as a coquette of questionable sincerity, eager to gratify the male ego. Alternatively, she could also be secretly flattered and unconsciously attracted by his courtesy and attention which stand in marked contrast to the blunter German approach.

At first Ventidius magnanimously gives the honour of the kill to Thusnelda:

Ihr deutschen Herrn, der Ruhm gehört nicht mir!
Er kommt Thusnelden, Hermanns Gattin,
Kommt der erhabenen Cheruskerfürstin zu!
Ihr Pfeil, auf mehr denn hundert Schritte,
Warf mit der Macht des Donnerkeils ihn nieder ...   (1:537)

Consistent with the downward thrust of scene one, the wild beast has been thrown down, a particularly appropriate symbolic act since, as becomes apparent later, the 'Ur' is associated with the Germans. Although Ventidius soon reverses himself, claiming credit for having dispatched the aurochs: 'Du [Thusnelda] warst des Todes gleichwohl, wenn ich fehlte' (1:538), the play intimates that Thusnelda performed the deed herself with unnecessary help from Ventidius, a reflection of the political situation: the fatal stroke of bringing down the German beast was administered not by the Roman but by the German princess. The fact that Ventidius contradicts himself by maintaining that Thusnelda owes him her life discloses his eager acceptance of the gallant role ('Römer*ritter*') being offered to him and his susceptibility to flattery. The audience later learns that he is a product of the corrupt Roman court and as Machiavelli warns, 'Courts are nurseries of adulation. Men tend to be engrossed in their own affairs and are seldom objective about them, so that they are easy preys to this plague' (M 113). This scene provides a case in point.

Of particular relevance in this episode is Hermann's behind-the-scene contribution as a stage manager. He first exclaims in support of the heroic image: 'Hier, seht, ihr Freunde! / Man schleppt ihn [Ur] bei den Hörnern schon herbei!' (1:537) and then remains silent, observing the debate as to whether or not Thusnelda faced any real danger. However, when the experienced hunters, Wolf and Thuiskomar, attempt to prove that the aurochs would never have charged into the woods where the archers were standing but would have kept to the trail ('Wildbahn'), Hermann immediately intervenes to suspend all further discussion of the incident: 'HERMANN *abbrechend*. Kurz, Heil ruf ich Ventidius noch einmal, / Des Urs, des hornbewehrten, Sieger, / Und der Thusnelda Retter obenein!' (1:538). He wants to appeal to the Roman's already manifested vanity by celebrating his unearned fame, a technique ultimately rendering him more pliable to Hermann's secret plans. If Ventidius is made to believe the Germans owe him a debt of gratitude for having rescued Thusnelda, he will be encouraged to harbour excessive confidence and a feeling of security that will put any suspicions to rest.

As the hunting party prepares to return to Teutoburg, Ventidius and Thusnelda '*sprechen heimlich zusammen*' (1:539), an interlude which the audience must interpret as an illicit dialogue on the basis of the former's preceding amorous aside 'Wie, Göttliche, du willst –?' (1:539). While this flirtation takes place, the remaining characters seem to be engaged in admiring the quadriga, but a telling stage direction: 'HERMANN *zerstreut*' indicates that the German leader is not watching the main attraction, Augustus's gift, but rather the side attraction, the conversation between his wife and the Roman legate. This same pattern repeats itself at the end of act three, the scene most crucial to the final outcome of the drama: Hermann, again described as '*zerstreut*' (1:576), is supposed to be observing the entry of the Roman army into Teutoburg, but, as the stage directions reveal, '*Er beobachtet Varus und Ventidius, welche heimlich mit einander sprechen*' (1:576). In both instances the dramatist furnishes indirect evidence that Hermann always concentrates on the central issue: what is going on in the mind of his enemy. Hermann's query: 'Ventidius Carbo! Willst du sie [Thusnelda] begleiten?' (1:539) ties in neatly with the conclusion of the Ventidius-Thusnelda exchange and adds credence to the view that not only is he aware of the improper relationship but he even abets it to suit his own, at this stage, unspecified purpose. 'VENTIDIUS. Mein Fürst! Du machst zum Sel'gen mich – / *Er gibt Pfeil und Bogen gleichfalls weg*' (1:539). Promoting the flirtation by providing the opportunity and by pretending to be ignorant of its very existence, Hermann renders his foe defenceless: of his own accord he surrenders his weapons and, in his overconfidence, makes himself fully vulnerable. Then, when Ventidius requests an audience to deliver a message from the emperor, Hermann, playing the Roman toady, replies in total deference to his guest: 'Wenn du begehrst, Ventidius!' (1:539). The stage departure also contains a related visual message: '[*Hermann*] *hebt, mit Ventidius, Thusnelda in den Wagen; Ventidius folgt ihr*' (1:539). In cleverly orchestrating this finale, Hermann is employing sex to manipulate the enemy, a practice not unlike those of modern espionage. Whereas the Roman assumes and is subtly urged to assume that he has the two Germans, husband and wife, 'eating out of his hand,' the scene actually anticipates how Ventidius, and with him the Romans, will eventually go to their deaths as staged by Hermann.

This episode contains five imperatives, all of which originate with the true master of ceremonies, Hermann, who, with a minimum of words, indirectly dominates the action. The sharpness of 'Wolf! Selgar! Redet!' (1:539) distinguishes a man accustomed to being unquestionably obeyed. It almost seems as if the princes need his permission before they may speak, a sign of Hermann's autocratic supremacy. Moreover, he has the final say in the scene, again a direct command implying his management of the event: 'Wohlauf, ihr Jäger! Lasst das Horn dann schmettern, / Und bringt sie [Thusnelda and Ventidius] in Triumph nach Teutoburg!' (1:539). This exploitation of both friend and foe prefigures the general thrust of the opening dream sequence from *Prinz Friedrich von Homburg*: neither Hermann nor Hohenzollern is ostensibly the main source of dramatic interest in either of these scenes, although both characters, being extremely knowledgeable about human nature, pull the proper strings, and by so doing, attempt to focus attention on another individual (Ventidius and Homburg, respectively) whom they hope to destroy. In his list of those qualities ensuring the political success of his model, Caesar Borgia, Machiavelli includes 'his astonishing shrewdness in the handling of friends and enemies' (M 53). *Die Hermannsschlacht* will continue to provide ample testimony to Hermann's expertise in this same area.

The detailed examination of act two, scene two, has disclosed a leader who, by his cunning, surreptitiously maintains control of the situation. The manner by which he has overseen the conclusion to the hunt precludes fortuity and suggests a degree of conscious intent, notwithstanding the fact that the observer still has no inkling of the aim to which it is directed. In any assessment of the third and final scene of act one, by far the most difficult, at times most contradictory sequence of the whole work, one must bear in mind the inferred message of the preceding scene as well as an important parenthetical remark made by Hermann towards the end of the act: 'wie ich schon einmal euch [the princes] sagte' (1:546). On a previous occasion, Hermann had made his drastic proposal of total commitment, the condition for his acceptance of supreme command, to the German princes, but had met with refusal. Hence, he is aware of their self-centredness before the third scene begins, and the extreme measures to which he resorts have been dictated in large measure by the known deplorable attitude of his fellow rulers.

Once a convivial atmosphere has been engendered with the aid of wine, and the conversation turns to the Romans, 'diesen Kindern des Betruges' (1:541), Thuiskomar again deplores Roman treachery and his own betrayal of the Friesen prince. Hermann's remark: "Ich hab davon gehört, Thuiskar. / Ich sprach den Boten, der die Nachricht / Dir eben aus Sicambrien gebracht' (1:541), indicative of his being informed of all developments, supplies a sign for the alert spectator that his apparent neutrality or indifference conceals a very real concern since he himself went out of his way to speak to the messenger. Thuiskomar's subsequent speech makes Hermann's dilemma more obvious to the audience: 'Was nun – was wird für *dich* [Hermann] davon die Folge sein?' (1:541). Caught up in his own egocentricity, he is only capable of imputing his own self-serving motives to Hermann and thus dwells solely on the consequences for the individual, Hermann, and not for the nation, Germania. In this same vein Thuiskomar mentions another danger: 'Marbod, der herrschensgierge Suevenfürst, / Der ... seinem Szepter (so erklärt er) / Ganz Deutschland siegreich unterwerfen will' (1:541). As the aurochs incident has already symbolically suggested, the enemy within represents a much greater threat than the enemy without. Clearly a major power struggle is in progress and the issue at the back of the minds of many is: who will ultimately rule all the German tribes, Augustus, Marbod, or Hermann? Thuiskomar's political evaluation also includes the first direct acknowledgment of Hermann's main strength, his cunning, by means of which he has managed to exclude the Romans from his territory: 'Den *schlausten* Wendungen der Staatskunst nur / Gelang es, bis auf diesen Tag, / Dir [Hermann] den bösartgen Gast entfernt zu halten' (1:541). With Marbod threatening to invade from the east and the Romans perched on his western frontier, Hermann's position does not seem enviable as he himself concedes: 'Gewiss. Da siehst du richtig. Meine Lage / Ist in der Tat bedrängter als jemals' (1:541), but what the princes fail to realize is that Hermann has already foreseen this scenario and has planned accordingly.

HERMANN Nach allem, was geschehn, find ich
    Läuft nun *mein* Vorteil ziemlich mit dem Varus,
    Und wenn er noch darauf besteht,
    So nehm ich ihn in meinen Grenzen auf.
    . . .
DAGOBERT   Zu welchem Zweck?
HERMANN – *Mich* gegen Marbod zu beschützen,
    Der den Tribut mir trotzig abgefordert.   (1:542)

Die Hermannsschlacht proves quite conclusively that Hermann has no such intent: he only wishes to create the illusion of such an intent. Sounding like a carbon copy of the princes by professing to be acting according to his own best interests, Hermann now plays the *ingénu* in an effort to shock his listeners into an awareness of their only means of defence. When Thuiskomar informs Hermann of Rome's double-dealings with Marbod, we may safely take for granted that Hermann is fully apprised of the Roman strategy of playing one side against the other, leaving the choice of ally until the last minute. Since Hermann has successfully donned the mask of the Roman toady, he has prepared the way for the enemy to throw in their lot with him against Marbod. The Romans will opt for the Cheruskian prince who appears to be more willing to acquiesce to their wishes. (The fourth act will illustrate that Marbod is too independent and lacks Hermann's ability to dissemble.)

HERMANN Ihr Freund', ich bitt euch, kümmert euch
  Um meine Wohlfahrt nicht! Bei Wodan, meinem hohen Herrn!
  So weit im Kreise mir der Welt
  Das Heer der munteren Gedanken reichet,
  Erstreb ich und bezweck ich nichts,
  Als jenem Römerkaiser zu erliegen.   (1:542)

This particular declaration bears the major responsibility for most of the confusion surrounding *Die Hermannsschlacht*, largely because many critics have made the mistake of taking this Machiavellian protagonist at his word.[29] As Machiavelli pointed out some three hundred years before Kleist, 'a ruler who intends to keep his office must learn the practice of wickedness for use, when necessary' (M 83), and telling lies – Hermann has already told one: his plan to form an alliance with Rome against Marbod – is but a small part of 'the practice of wickedness.' This speech, dripping with irony, should clearly not be taken too literally or seriously. The very salutation: 'Ihr Freund'', in view of Thuiskomar's betrayal of his friend, the Friesen prince, for personal gain, contains a measure of sarcasm underlined by the subsequent statement: 'Ich bitt euch, kümmert euch / Um meine Wohlfahrt nicht!' Their last thought is Hermann's welfare and he well knows it.[30] If then Hermann has no intention of succumbing to the Romans as the second scene of act one implies and the remainder of the drama obviously demonstrates (he only concedes the possibility of defeat through chance or the will of the gods [II/10]), then we must assume that Hermann is employing reverse psychology. In a different context, Burckhardt makes a revealing comment quite applicable to this situation: '[Hermann] does not try to praise the Germans into patriotism; he tries to shame and whip them into the resolution of despair.'[31]

  Das aber möcht ich gern mit *Ruhm*, ihr Brüder,
  Wies einem deutschen Fürsten ziemt:
  Und *dass* [Kleist's emphasis] ich das vermög, im ganzen vollen Masse,
  Wie sichs die *freie Seele glorreich* denkt –
  Will ich allein stehn, und mit euch mich –
  – Die manch ein andrer Wunsch zur Seite lockend zieht, –
  In dieser wichtgen Sache nicht verbinden.   (1:542)

The second half of this speech begins with an implied insult, critical of the princes' former behaviour which has been dictated by their preoccupation with property and individual power. This whole utterance, although, in fact, only partially truthful, dwells on a non-materialistic level emphasizing such concepts as 'Gedanken,' 'Ruhm,' 'freie Seele,' and 'glorreich' and thus obliging his 'brothers' to consider a more ideal attitude. He purports to want to die in a final blaze of glory, by implication something that would not be possible were he to join forces with his German allies. Hermann's concept of the 'freie Seele' together with 'Ruhm' looks forward to Homburg's final resolve: 'Ich will das heilige Gesetz des Kriegs, / ... / Durch einen freien Tod verherrlichen!' (1:704). As will be shown later, in both Homburg and Hermann the patriotic motivation is at best questionable and at heart not as altruistic as it may first appear. Whereas Homburg in the last act does in fact desire to die gloriously in isolation to achieve an immortality of sorts, a *Nachruhm*, Hermann, having no such ambition, prevaricates when he speaks of his standing and dying alone: he really hopes to bring his listeners around to his way of thinking.[32] By describing his imaginary defeat in a fashion so unpalatable that the princes will have to feel some compunction, Hermann could also be playing the pedagogue, reminding them of how they have all acted independently in the past and how this leads inevitably to disaster: 'jenem Römerkaiser zu erliegen' (1:542). My contention that Hermann's public statements in this scene are all part of a carefully and cunningly devised scheme gains some support from his interjection: 'Die manch ein andrer Wunsch zur Seite lockend zieht'; he dangles the carrot of an alternative before their noses, but does so incidentally, thus cleverly concealing his true design.

'SELGAR. – Man kann nicht sagen, / Dass hoch Arminius das Ziel sich stecket!' (1:543). Hermann does achieve his objective of outraging his interlocutors at the prospect of independent action without any hope of success. His reaction to their criticism betrays in part his pride of intellect and his strong sense of superiority, not the sort of answer one would expect from someone planning to go down to defeat:

> So! –
> Ihr würdet beide euren Witz vergebens
> Zusammenlegen, dieses Ziel,
> Das vor der Stirn euch dünket, zu erreichen.
> Denn setzt einmal, ihr Herrn, ihr stündet
> (Wohin ihr es im Lauf der Ewigkeit nicht bringt)
> Dem Varus kampfverbunden gegenüber;
> Im Grund morastger Täler er,
> Auf Gipfeln waldbekränzter Felsen ihr: ,   (1:543)

Hermann is obviously taunting them. His interpolation aims to accomplish precisely that which it maintains is impossible: by telling someone that he cannot do something, you appeal to his vanity and pride to prove you wrong in your appraisal. Hermann puts the princes down, hoping that they will rise to the occasion and live up to their better selves.

This speech also suggests that Hermann has already devised a very forward-looking plan that determines his every move. His vision of the confrontation – the Romans in swampy lowlands and the Germans on higher forested areas, hence in a strategically superior position – matches the final configuration in the Teutoburg Forest. Aristan announces to Varus in the last act: 'Den Teutoburger Wald umringen sie [Marbod and Hermann], / Mit deinem ganzen Heere dich / In der *Moräste Tiefen* zu ersticken!' (1:607), while during the actual hostilities, there are references to the Germans' higher vantage point: '*Marbod, von Feldherren umringt, steht auf einem Hügel*' (1:621). Is this mere coincidence or a sign that Hermann already has the ambush in mind? 'A commander,' Machiavelli maintains, 'lacking knowledge of the use of ground lacks the first of the qualities of a soldier. It is essential for reconnaissance, siting of camps, selection of route and choice of positions for battle, in short for successful campaigning' (M 81). The fifth act will demonstrate Hermann's turning to account *all* these aspects related to 'knowledge of the use of ground.'

> So dürft er [Varus] dir nur, Dagobert,
> Selgar, dein Lippgestad verbindlich schenken:
> Bei den fuchshaarigen Alraunen, seht,
> Den Römer lasst ihr beid im Stich,
> Und fallt euch, wie zwei Spinnen, selber an. (1:543)

Although Hermann was not present during the first scene, this statement proves conclusively that he has a thorough grasp of the whole problem: the real obstacle to vanquishing the enemy is the lack of unanimity among the Germans themselves, their petty rivalries and disputes which the Romans have already exploited. Victory will only be gained if they can achieve a common front against the common foe and sacrifice their private interests for the general welfare. Since he has almost 'tipped his hand' as a comment made by Wolf, the most perceptive and likeable of the princes, connotes: 'Du hältst nicht eben hoch im Wert uns, Vetter! / Es scheint, das Bündnis nicht sowohl, / Als die Verbündeten missfallen dir' (1:543), Hermann, changing his approach, resorts to praise and flattery to placate his friends and disguises his true aim: 'Wollt ich auf Erden irgend was *erringen* [Kleist's emphasis], / Ich würde glücklich sein, könnt ich mit Männern mich, / Wie hier um mich versammelt sind, verbinden' (1:543). This assertion amounts to yet another untruth determined by a manipulative tactic outlined in *Die Familie Schroffenstein* by the bastard Johann: 'Weil ich mich edel nicht erweise, nicht / Erweisen will, machst du mir weis, ich seis, / Damit die unverdiente Ehre mich / Bewegen soll, in ihrem Sinn zu handeln?' (1:80). Hermann is likewise trying to compel his listeners to ignore their differences and adopt a more noble frame of mind. When Thuiskomar proposes the possibility of victory through alliance, Hermann, again displaying his knowledge of Rome's ultimate plans for Germania, paints a hopelessly black picture in order to frighten the individual rulers into a united, desperate last stand:

> Nein, nein! Das eben ists! Der Wahn, Thuiskar,
> Der stürzt just rettungslos euch ins Verderben hin!
> Ganz Deutschland ist verloren schon,
> Dir der Sicambern Thron, der Thron der Katten dir,
> Der Marsen dem, mir der Cherusker,
> Und auch der Erb, bei Hertha! schon benannt. (1:544)

It is worth noting in passing that Machiavelli, conscious of human materialism, advocated a similar scare tactic: 'It might be objected that the citizens who have farms and lands in the countryside and see them burnt and wrecked will lose patience and begin to consider their own interests rather than the ruler's. To this I shall retort that a well-established and dogged prince can usually overcome this difficulty by persuading his subjects that their troubles will soon be over, frightening them with the ferocity of the enemy' (M 66).

By inviting contradiction, Hermann incites the princes to meet the challenge. This circuitous approach may be said to prefigure Hohenzollern's strategy with Homburg subsequent to the initial garden scene. The Count baits a defenceless victim to establish how much he knows, and, by negative example, as in the instance under investigation, proposes a means to extricate the Prince from his predicament (who was the 'süss[e] Traumgestalt?' [1:639]). Intentionally using the wrong name, Hohenzollern narrows down the field of candidates, in our case, the alternatives still left open to the princes, and points to the obvious and only solution as well as the means to realize the desired end. This would seem to be what Hermann is attempting to accomplish: to manoeuvre his allies towards his own point of view and thus to gain greater control over them.

When Wolf contends that Hermann considers the Romans 'ein Geschlecht von höhrer Art' in comparison with 'uns roh're Kauze' (1:544), the latter rejoins by praising his people's potential in words smacking of racism: 'Ich glaub, der Deutsch' erfreut sich einer grössern / Anlage, der Italier doch hat seine mindre / In diesem Augenblicke mehr entwickelt' (1:544). One must, however, take into account the remainder of Hermann's speech where he also acknowledges:

> Wenn sich der Barden Lied erfüllt,
> Und, unter *einem* [Kleist's emphasis] Königsszepter,
> Jemals die ganze Menschheit sich vereint,
> So lässt, dass es ein Deutscher führt, sich denken,
> ein Britt', ein Gallier, oder wer ihr wollt.   (1:544)

Anyone from any nation, including significantly even the French ('Gallier') whose emperor and his pernicious ways this *drame à clef* impugnes,[33] could assume the reins of world leadership, 'Doch nimmer jener Latier, beim Himmel! / Der keine andre Volksnatur / Verstehen kann und ehren, als nur seine' (1:544). Hermann claims not to despise the Romans per se, but rather their deplorable attitude vis-à-vis other national characters and traditions, their arrogance in imposing by force of arms their own customs and their refusal to respect the natural right of national self-determination. Hence critical comments such as 'Der Mangel an deutschem Nationalbewusstsein provoziert als Gegentendenz einen masslosen Nationalismus, der mehr durch den Hass gegen andre Völker als durch die Liebe zum eignen genährt wurde';[34] or '[This speech] has no less puzzled some of Kleist's interpreters who find it incompatible with the seemingly fierce national thrust of the play'[35] neglect to take into consideration Hermann's anachronistically enlightened view as substantiated by the rest of the drama. 'Dieser Hass trägt einen Verteidigungscharakter,' declares Siegfried Streller. 'Es ist kein blinder Nationalhass.'[36] In act four, when Thusnelda protests the total annihilation of the enemy, her husband retorts: 'Solang sie [Dämonenbrut] in Germanien trotzt, / Ist Hass mein Amt und meine Tugend Rache!' (1:594). On the basis of the proviso introduced by 'Solang,' we must conclude that this is not the blind hatred of a foreign people, but an understandable, if not forgivable, hatred of a foreign aggressor.

To describe the inherent capacity of the world's peoples to become a major political force, Hermann has recourse to an image of the ocean. Roman domination will continue largely unchallenged, 'bis die Völker sich, die diese Erd umwogen, / Noch jetzt vom Sturm der Zeit gepeitscht, / Gleich einer See, ins Gleichgewicht gestellt,' (1:545). The 'Völker,' in their present disarray, are compared to a sea blown in several directions and thus producing mere squalls; they fail to direct their consolidated strength, a tremendous source of power, against the foe. Later in the fifth act, a variation of this maritime image confirms this potential while contributing to the overall poetic unity of the drama: 'Zerschellt ward nun das ganze Römerheer, / Gleich einem Schiff, gewiegt in Klippen, / Und nur die Scheitern hülflos irren / Noch, auf dem Ozean des Siegs, umher!' (1:622). The German tribes are still equated with the sea but a sea united in its fury against a foreign object, a ship and its crew, which it easily destroys.[37]

Up to this point in the dialogue, the princes, and to a lesser degree the audience, must be truly puzzled by Hermann's performance. On the one hand he remarks that if the Germans were to form an alliance to defeat the Romans, they would undoubtedly end up fighting against each other; on the other hand, despite this serious reservation, he maintains, 'Wollt ich auf Erden irgend was *erringen* [Kleist's emphasis] / Ich würde glücklich sein, könnt ich mit Männern mich, / Wie hier um mich versammelt sind, verbinden' (1:543), a clear contradiction. Wolf, obviously perplexed by Hermann's statements, assumes capitulation without resistance to be Hermann's aim, a misunderstanding which elicits the following fiery outburst with its six exclamation marks:

Behüte Wodan mich! Ergeben! Seid ihr toll?
Mein Alles, Haus und Hof, die gänzliche
Gesamtheit des, was mein sonst war,
Als ein verlornes Gut in meiner Hand noch ist,
Das, Freunde, setz ich dran, im Tod nur,
Wie König Porus, *glorreich* es zu lassen!
Ergeben! – Einen Krieg, bei Mana! will ich
Entflammen, der in Deutschland rasselnd,
Gleich einem dürren Walde, um sich greifen,
Und auf zum Himmel lodernd schlagen soll!   (1:545)

Wolf's criticism must have touched a sensitive spot to bring forth Hermann's least controlled utterance of the scene. A man of strong feelings, Hermann is quite capable of losing his equanimity, of boiling over and exposing his real purpose under the influence of emotion. But even this anger could well be fabricated, for he never loses sight of his goal, his endeavour to win his allies to his point of view. Overemphasizing all of his personal possessions by a double repetition, the second containing a redundant adjective: 'die *gänzliche* / Gesamtheit,' he asserts his resolve to renounce them in a noble death, a position contrary to that espoused by his listeners. At the same time, in the second half of the speech, he again, perhaps unwittingly, perhaps intentionally, betrays his true plan to involve the whole of Germany in his war, although he still persists in presenting the final battle as a hopeless individual act for the sake of personal glory.

Hermann returns to the inevitability of defeat in order to force his interlocutors to convince him of the opposite. Whereas he declares that he is obliging his own troops 'In dem gefährlichen Momente der Entscheidung, / Die ungeheure Wahrheit anzuschaun' (1:545), he more likely intends the warning for the German princes. By a roundabout route, cunningly conveyed as a directive to his own men, he indicates how the princes have deluded themselves, have ignored an unpleasant truth and, caught up in their own private sphere, have never considered the total picture. Expanding their horizons, he wants to compel them to come to grips with the hopelessness of their plight and hence the need for drastic, concerted action. The speech concludes with the alleged intent to die '[d]en schönen Tod des Helden' (1:546), marking the third time that Hermann has mentioned or implied the concept of glory or fame in this scene. Although conceivably part of his strategy to shame his 'brothers' into a more ideal stance, this repetition none the less intimates a personal preoccupation or an unconscious motivation that will attain greater prominence in his final confrontation with Varus.

Told by Selgar that he will not go far with such a defeatist attitude, Hermann, his vanity obviously piqued, retorts: 'Nicht weit? Hm! – Seht, das möcht ich just nicht sagen. / Nach Rom – ihr Herren, Dagobert und Selgar! Wenn mir das Glück ein wenig günstig ist' (1:546). Again he contradicts himself, for these are not the words of a leader whose only intention is 'alles zu *verlieren* [Kleist's emphasis]' (1:543) if he seriously contemplates the feasibility of bringing the war to the very gates of Rome. 'Und wenn nicht ich, wie ich *fast* zweifeln muss, / Der Enkel einer doch, wag ich zu hoffen, / Die hier in diesem Paar der Lenden ruhn!' (1:546). Now he qualifies the pride and confidence of the first half of his utterance; however, the 'fast' still allows for the possibility of a victory, not just over Varus, but over the whole of Rome. This appeal achieves its objective in Wolf at least who is prepared to accept Hermann's leadership and proposes a toast to 'Hermann ... der Befreier Deutschlands' (1:546). After

Wolf's embrace and pledge, Hermann submits his proposal of total commitment to the war effort for the second time as signalled by his parenthetical subordinate clause: 'wie ich schon einmal euch sagte' (1:546). When the princes insist upon pursuing their own narrow interests and prove incapable of total surrender to the ideal of freedom, the universal perspective they have lost sight of, Hermann, realizing that he can expect no assistance from them, takes his leave: 'Ihr Herrn, ihr hörts; so kann ich euch nicht helfen' (1:547).

This puzzling, only superficially contradictory scene depicts an unsuccessful second attempt on the part of Hermann through shock tactics to bring potential allies around to his committed point of view with its repudiation of self-oriented materialism. Hermann is in fact willing to assume the supreme command, but only on his own terms since he astutely recognizes the necessary conditions to assure some potentiality of success against a better-equipped, better-trained, more-sophisticated hostile force. Because the princes and the audience have no clear indication of Hermann's ultimate purpose and because he gains our attention by making some preposterous claims such as his wanting to be defeated by the Romans, Kleist confronts us with an intriguing dramatic enigma in his portrayal of the isolated German ruler who plays cat and mouse with his 'brothers.'[38] As Sammons has astutely observed, 'With his allies he plays the sardonic fool for a time in order to draw them into their appropriate roles.'[39]

The second act opens with 'Hermann auf dem Thron' (1:547), while Ventidius 'steht vor ihm,' a dramatic reminder of Hermann's superior position before this Roman who, as the subsequent dialogue will intimate, is a mere pawn in the German's overall scheme. This meeting underscores again Roman double-dealing: Augustus has offered Hermann help against Marbod 'zum Drittenmal,' but Hermann also knows that the same proposal has been made to Marbod; Ventidius maintains that Hermann should regard the three proffered legions as his own, but Hermann realizes that they will ultimately be used against him. After pointing out the suffering inflicted upon a territory by 'einem Heereszug,' he inquires, seemingly out of innocence: 'Meinst du nicht, alles wohl erwogen, / Dass ich im Stande wär, allein / Cheruska vor dem Marbod zu beschützen?' (1:548). Hermann is toying with the legate by putting him in a difficult position to see how he will extricate himself without insulting his host. The permission for free passage, as Hermann fully comprehends, is but a pretext to occupy his country. Ventidius' response: 'Nein, nein, mein Fürst! Den Wahn, ich bitte dich, entferne!' (1:548) indicates that his German ally has hit a very sensitive nerve, indeed. Eager to impress upon Hermann how desperate his situation will be without Roman assistance, Ventidius stresses Marbod's military might: 'Wo ist der Wall um solchem Sturz zu wehren?' and inadvertantly tips his own hand: 'Die Römer werden Mühe haben, / Die weltbesiegenden, wie mehr, o Herr, denn du, / Dein Reich vor der Verschüttung zu beschirmen' (1:548). Machiavelli notes in *Il Principe* how the Romans always sided with the weaker party against the stronger both of which they eventually destroyed (M 35). Hermann has skilfully managed to extract from his enemy an indirect confession of the same intent: to unite Roman forces with what they believe or have been led to believe to be the lesser threat, Hermann, against the greater danger, Marbod.

In an obvious attempt to create a misleading image of himself as a stay-at-home family man, Hermann pursues his tactic of lulling the Roman into a false sense of security:

> Freilich! Freilich! Du hast zu sehr nur recht.
> Das Schicksal, das im Reich der Sterne waltet,
> Ihn [Marbod] hat es, in der Luft des Kriegs,
> Zu einem *Helden* rüstig gross gezogen,
> Dagegen mir, du weisst, das sanftre Ziel sich steckte:
> Dem Weib, das mir vermählt, der Gatte,
> Ein Vater meinen süssen Kindern,
> Und meinem Volk ein guter Fürst zu sein.   (1:548)

To the alert spectator, this is a total misrepresentation. In the previous scene he had insisted upon his aim of dying '[d]en schönen Tod der Helden' (1:546), while here he attributes the heroic stance exclusively to Marbod. He then pretends that, having been intimidated by the military strength of the Romans, he will accommodate their demands. At all times deferential to Ventidius, he is merely living up to an image of the pusillanimous, ineffectual leader which he has expressly created for foreign consumption. His guest, completely taken in by this subservient, sycophantic attitude, hears only what he wants to hear and hence suspends all critical judgment and caution: 'Gewiss! Die Weisheit, die du mir [Ventidius] entfaltest, / Füllt mit Bewundrung mich' (1:549)

Ventidius now insists that Hermann must decide 'zwischen Marbod und Augustus' (1:549), a case of retrospective irony when we learn at the end of the act that Hermann has already opted for Marbod as part of the general strategy intimated in the first act. By playing the weak sovereign, Hermann encourages his guest to have no fear of him and hence unwittingly to disclose his true intent, specifically 'dass Augustus / Die Oberherrschaft keinem gönnen kann, / Der, auf ein Heer, wie Marbod, trotzend, / Sich selbst sie nur verdanken will' (1:549). Since the Romans will not tolerate an independent power, it follows that they intend to make all the German tribes subservient to their rule. In an effort to bribe Hermann into compliance, Ventidius continues:

> ... ja, wenn
> Er [Augustus] je ein Oberhaupt der Deutschen anerkennt,
> Ein Fürst es sein muss, das begreifst du,
> Den er, durch einen Schritt, verhängnisvoll wie diesen,
> Auf immer seinem Thron verbinden kann.   (1:549)

Again, Hermann's attitude may be said to cause the naïve Roman unwittingly to expose his true intent. At the beginning of the scene, Ventidius sought to flatter his host by portraying him as his superior: 'Die drei Legionen, ... Betrachte sie wie dein!' (1:547–8), but by specifying that the nominal head must be subject to Rome and hence derive his authority from the emperor, he contradicts his earlier statement.

HERMANN *nach einer kurzen Pause.*
> *Wenn* [Kleist's emphasis] du die Aussicht mir eröffnen könntest,
> Ventidius, dass *mir* [Kleist's emphasis]
> Die höchste Herrschgewalt in Deutschland zugedacht:
> So würd Augustus, das versichr' ich dich,
> Den wärmsten Freund würd er an mir erhalten. –
> Denn dieses Ziel, das darf ich dir gestehn,
> Reizt meinen Ehrgeiz, und mit Neid
> Seh ich den Marbod ihm entgegeneilen.   (1:549)

This speech quoted in its entirety strikes me as being a masterpiece of cunning, disclosing an uncanny knowledge of human psychology. Even the introductory pause implies Hermann's scheming for effect. Having convinced his listener of his total intimidation, he now enlarges his theatrical role to include the envious, resentful puppet ruler, the typical Roman ally, eager to form an alliance at all cost before his rival can do likewise. Because this compliant posture has encouraged Ventidius not to perceive his host as a threat, the Roman feels sufficiently secure to tell him to lay no store in the rumour that Augustus intends to establish a nephew as prefect in Germany 'sobald es nur erobert' (1:549), even though this practice has been followed in 'Nariska, Markoland und Nervien.' Still appealing to Hermann's vanity, he maintains, 'Ein Deutscher kann das Ganze nur beherrschen! / Der Grundsatz, das versichr' ich dich, / Steht, wie ein Felsen, bei Senat und Volk!' (1:549–50). When considering the issue of morality in *Die Hermannsschlacht*, one should recall this declaration, a conscious fabrication as will be disclosed to the audience by a dialogue between Varus and Ventidius in the third act:

VARUS Wieso? Meinst du vielleicht, die Absicht sei, Cheruska
    Also ein erobertes Gebiet – ?
VENTIDIUS   Quintilius,
    Die Absicht, dünkt mich, lässt sich fast erraten.   (1:577)

The willing slave now speaks those words that the Roman has wanted to hear: 'Nun denn, Legat der römischen Cäsaren, / So werf ich, was auch säum ich länger, / Mit Thron und Reich, in deine Arme mich!' (1:550). However, two considerations call his sincerity into question: his attitude in the preceding scene – 'einen Krieg, bei Mana! will ich / Entflammen' (1:545) – and his dismounting from his throne as he makes this major concession. He only utters this speech of rank servitude once he has vacated the symbol of his authority.

The concluding line of this scene: 'Vergönne, dass ich die Minute nütze' (1:550) leads the audience into the next sequence in the Ventidius-Thusnelda affair. The intervening short episode in which Hermann contradicts Eginhardt's assumption of the direction taken by the exiting Ventidius and proves correct: 'Rechts! Der Vorhang rauschte. / Er bog sich in Thusneldens Zimmer hin' (1:550) provides a subtle indication of the extent to which Hermann knows what is going on not only in the general but in the personal realm as well. He has a remarkable grasp of the situation as becomes even more obvious in the next scene when he orders his wife into the presence of the enemy, the modern equivalent of using sexual favour to compromise or gain influence with a foreign agent: 'Geschwind! Ventidius sucht dich. / ... / Zurück, mein Herzchen! *liebst du mich*! Zurücke! / In deine Zimmer wieder! Rasch! Zurücke!' (1:551). He sees in Ventidius the key to the success of his plan based on deception since the Roman official will finally determine both his country's attitude to the Cheruskian prince and the choice between the two rival German factions. It is therefore crucial that Ventidius not sense any danger. Having recourse to emotional blackmail: 'liebst du mich!' Hermann exploits his spouse as bait ('Er [Ventidius] riecht die Fährt ihr ab' [1:551]) and obliges her to deceive her alleged admirer against her will. If Ventidius believes that he has some control over the ruler's wife, he will have an inordinate amount of confidence in his ability to manipulate this tribe of harmless, naïve barbarians. Thusnelda's reluctance to go along with her husband's request can be traced to a feeling of some sympathy for the young Roman and an element of vanity. She does not like to be used: 'Lass mich mit diesem Römer aus dem Spiele' (1:551). Hermann's reply: 'Dich aus dem Spiel? Wie! Was! Bist du bei Sinnen? / Warum? Weshalb?' (1:551) by its very tone, denotes the dominant male accustomed to getting his own way and, by his reiteration of her 'Spiel' formulation, suggests that he views the scenario himself in this manner. But it is also a deadly serious political game which should not be isolated from the personal sphere.[40] This is only the second time in the drama that the observer can detect a strong emotional outburst in Hermann, the first being his response to the allegation that he will surrender without a fight: 'Behüte Wodan mich! Ergeben? Seid ihr toll?' (1:545). Since both then and now he accuses his interlocutors of madness, this reaction would seem to stress the central importance of Thusnelda's part in Hermann's overall plan of luring Ventidius into a trusting state of mind so that he neglects to see the trap that is being set for him and the Romans generally. The Thusnelda plot does indeed have a significant 'causal connection with the main action' and hence I take issue with Burckhardt's contention: 'What Thusnelda says and does has no effect on Hermann's schemes; it neither furthers nor impedes them.'[41]

'By way of an epilogue to act I, scene 2,' remarks Linn, 'the hunting incident is reviewed in act II, scene 3.'[42] Thusnelda, aware of the deception perpetrated at Ventidius' expense, expresses reluctance to comply with it because of his supposed affection for her: 'Er *wähnte* [Kleist's emphasis] doch, mich durch den Schuss zu retten, / Und wir verhöhnen ihn!' (1:551). She realizes that in fact her husband scorns the Roman for his vanity and naïveté. Hermann's rejoinder discloses an amazing awareness of the subtlety of which the human mind is capable, a psychological acuteness to which the early Kleistian essay 'Über die allmähliche Verfertigung der Gedanken beim Reden' also bears witness. 'Er wähnt ja auch, du Törin, du, / Dass wir den Wahn der Tat ihm danken!' (1:551). Ventidius knows that he cannot claim responsibility for the death of the aurochs; yet he believes the Germans none the less attribute this feat to him. They stand so much in awe of this representative of the master race that they are not able to distinguish between illusion – 'Wahn' – and reality. Therefore, he interprets this incident as a clear manifestation of how easily these ingenuous people can be duped. Since this is precisely what Hermann wants Ventidius to think, we have yet another example of quite sophisticated intrigue. This telling confrontation between husband and wife, closing with a command and an implied threat: '– Du sei mir klug, ich rat es dir!' (1:551), again underscores the decisive leader who will not tolerate any objection; she must become a tool in his overall scheme to conquer the enemy.

Before Ventidius meets with Thusnelda, he announces to Scäpio that the messenger should wait until he (Ventidius) has completed a still unknown 'Geschäft / Für Livia ... , die Kaiserin' (1:552). Kleist includes this as yet puzzling piece of information to alert the audience that the Roman is not all that he seems and to minimize any sympathy we may feel later when he reaps the rewards for his guile.

The relating of a dream which invariably has a prophetic function in Kleist's works also occurs in Die Hermannsschlacht but with a noteworthy variation. Thusnelda purports to have dreamed about the aurochs episode and yet she realizes, as does the audience, that Ventidius did not really save her. The nightmare and her alleged reaction to it: 'Ich hätte durch die ganze Nacht, / Ventidius! Ventidius! gerufen' (1:552) most likely represent a fiction motivated by the obedience to her husband's order and by her own conceit: she secretly enjoys the young man's attention. However, on a different level, bearing in mind the later explicit association of the 'Ur' with the Germans generally, one could see in the wild beast of her fantasy her barbaric roots, an indirect manifestation of an unconscious threat to herself from a deep-seated aggressiveness that she chooses not to acknowledge. (The dream episode in Prinz Friedrich von Homburg fully documents Kleist's familiarity with the psychic phenomenon now called repression.) Her lines: 'Ein fürchterlicher Tod, Ventidius, / Solch einem Ungeheu'r erliegen!' (1:552) prove especially ironic in retrospect since both Ventidius and Thusnelda may be said to succumb to the beast, the former physically, the latter mentally.

During this confrontation, the first time we observe them alone on stage, each participant gives some evidence of being genuinely attracted to the other sexually, but the overall impression is one of role-playing. As Ventidius' stylized, artificial language intimates, he is performing the part of an eighteenth-century gallant blinded by his passion, seeking a token from the 'Vergötterte' (1:553), while Thusnelda, in keeping with Hermann's demand, assumes the character of the neglected wife who perhaps would not be averse to a little affair on the side, although she constantly protests her innocence and insists upon propriety. When Ventidius fails to gain the lock of hair through emotional pressure: 'Die kannst du mir, geliebtes Weib, nicht weigern, / Wenn du nicht grausam mich verhöhnen willst' (1:553), he casts himself at her feet and grasps her hand in an effort to compromise her indirectly, confident that she will not inform on him. Thusnelda obviously finds this unexpected behaviour embarrassing; he has gone farther in this conventional love scene than she anticipated. She does not particularly mind a flirtation over which she has some influence, but as the stage directions indicate, she soon extricates herself from this potentially damaging situation: '*Thusnelda steht auf und sieht ihn an. Ventidius lässt sie betreten los und erhebt sich. Thusnelda geht und klingelt*' (1:554). This is not the conduct of a defenceless, easily manipulated female; she has full mastery of herself and the capacity to put the Roman in his place. Ventidius, surprised at this display of composure, finds her reaction unnerving (at one point, she even stands above him in a physically dominant position), for he is accustomed or has been made accustomed by Hermann to being ostensibly in control. Since she does not accede to his wishes, this little pantomime amounts to a defeat of sorts and a caution, one which he unwisely does not take to heart.

The subsequent scene commences immediately with Thusnelda's indirect warning to Ventidius couched in verse and song, an admonition to respect the innocent beauty of their relationship. The key note of the song is possession, the attempt to gain power over something by owning it. Since she wishes to be worshipped from afar – there are unmistakable signs that she enjoys his adulation – he should avoid physical contact as it will only destroy the lovely image. As soon as the boy (Ventidius) tries to seize the moonlight, he loses it. The poem is especially appropriate, for at the very moment of its performance, Ventidius manages to steal one of Thusnelda's golden locks, the equivalent of the song's 'Mondenschein.' This gesture becomes an act symbolic of his desire to possess and use her.[43] In hindsight, several parallels also come to mind. Ventidius' later simile of the stag in heat desirous of plunging himself into the stream (1:618) looks back to the boy's putting his hand into the water. The drama continually connects Ventidius as the rococo lover with moonlight. In the third act, Hermann asks his wife, 'Was macht Ventidius, dein Mond?' (1:567) and the final fatal tryst between Thusnelda and Ventidius is conducted under the double auspices of moonlight and water: 'Hier, meint' er [Ventidius], sei es still, wie an dem Lethe, / Und keines lästgen Zeugen

Blick zu fürchten, / Als nur der Mond, der ihm zur Seite buhlt' (1:615). The reference to Lethe, one of the rivers from the realm of the dead whose waters had the power of oblivion, underscores the seductive nature of water, the female element, while alluding to the ultimate loss of consciousness, death. Not only does Thusnelda tell Ventidius to appear 'beim Untergang des Mondes' (1:615), but the latter, as a prelude to the assignation, exclaims ecstatically, 'Wie mild der Mondschein durch die Stämme fällt! / Und wie der Waldbach fern, mit üppigem Geplätscher, / Vom Rand des hohen Felsens niederrinnt!' (1:617), the third time in the play that water and moonlight have been juxtaposed in the sexual context of a *Liebestod*.

Ventidius presses the purloined lock 'leidenschaftlich an seine Lippe' (1:554), a performance for Thusnelda's benefit. She is meant to see it and in fact does as the next scene indicates: 'Drückt' er sie, glühend vor Entzücken, an die Lippen' (1:556). The hyperbolic language of the gallant lacks the ring of sincerity and further suggests histrionics. Although the theft is designed in part to flatter the female ego, it also compromises a married woman: something illicit now exists between them. However, her reaction to his deception and to his demeaning attitude in this battle of the sexes: 'Und ging, mit Schritten des *Triumphes* / ... mit seiner *Beut* hinweg' (1:556) shows her outrage at his taking advantage of her and reinforces the idea that she is not a woman to be toyed with: 'THUSNELDA *steht auf*. Ventidius Carbo, du beleidigst mich!' (1:555). In the subsequent conversation with her husband, she does disclose exactly what has happened, something which Ventidius in his confidence could not conceive of and which further testifies to Hermann's command of the overall situation. Very little escapes his notice.

HERMANN   Du gabst sie [die Locke] ihm – ?
THUSNELDA Ich – ? ihm die Locke geben!
HERMANN   Was! Nicht? Nicht?   (1:555)

By taking for granted that his wife freely gave the requested token, Hermann fails to recognize her partial emotional involvement. He assumes that she will play along and do whatever is required to entice the Roman into his carefully devised trap and, to prepare her, he hints at the enemy's real intention: 'Käm er daher, mit seinen Leuten, / Die Scheitel ratzenkahl dir abzuscheren: / Ein Schelm, mein Herzchen, will ich sein, / Wenn ich die Macht besitz, es ihm zu wehren' (1:556). This oblique warning also outlines his own impotence as he has no choice in his present political dilemma other than to appear to throw his lot in with Augustus. Thusnelda's perplexity: 'Ich weiss nicht, was ich von dir denken soll' (1:556) probably approximates that of the audience at this stage in *Die Hermanns-schlacht*. Hermann, the enigma, does not behave or speak in the straightforward, heroic manner one would normally expect of a titular protagonist. We know that he is up to something but what precisely is still not clear.

Thusnelda's longest speech in this important dialogue seems to have been overlooked by most commentators. Helbling, for example, comments, 'In fact, both [Thusnelda] and Arminius have no scruples in exploiting the attraction she exerts on Ventidius for the purpose of lulling the Roman official into a false sense of security.'[44]

THUSNELDA *streng.*
> Armin, du hörst, ich wiederhol es dir,
> Wenn irgend dir dein Weib was wert ist,
> So nötigst du mich nicht, das Herz des *Jünglings* ferner
> Mit falschen Zärtlichkeiten, zu entflammen. (1:556)

If Thusnelda is bait, she is clearly unwilling bait. She does in fact have reservations about using feigned emotions to deceive her suitor; however, it is not really a question of ethics but rather of vanity. At heart she is annoyed that her husband does not take offence at this younger rival's behaviour and intent. Her pride is hurt by Hermann's seeming indifference, his tendency to treat the matter, as the stage direction indicates, '*mit Humor.*' Although the age issue is never directly mentioned, it does add a significant dimension to the triangle. At the beginning of the scene, and throughout the drama for that matter, Hermann persists in treating his mate and in referring to her as his 'Kind' (1:555), while Thusnelda just as consistently categorizes the Roman as a 'Jüngling' (1:551, 556, 557, 595), one who obviously pays more attention to the neglected, younger wife than the older, politically dedicated husband for whom his spouse exists primarily as a sex object to render an enemy unsuspecting, more compliant, and hence vulnerable.

> Bekämpf ihn, wenn du willst, mit Waffen des Betrugs,
> Da, wo er mit Betrug dich angreift;
> Doch hier, wo, gänzlich unbesonnen,
> Sein junges Herz sich dir entfaltet,

Hier wünsch ich lebhaft, muss ich dir gestehn,
Dass du auf offne Weise ihm begegnest.

(1:556)

'Thusnelda's flaw,' observes Burckhardt, 'is that she shows self-respect and generosity.'[45] This comment also misses the point. The emphasis in almost everything Thusnelda does or says is upon the self, and ultimately the 'generosity' of which Burckhardt speaks is extended not to Ventidius, but mainly to the self as in this particular instance. By implication, Ventidius may well deceive Hermann, but in Thusnelda's case, when he flatters her, when he cannot but fall in love with her, he may be indiscreet but certainly not insincere. Her conceit, as pronounced as that of her admirer, blinds her to Ventidius' rather obvious theatrics to the point that she is taken in just as much as the Roman legate who thinks that she agreed to see him privately of her own accord, whereas the meeting actually took place at Hermann's behest.[46] Thusnelda's speech concludes with the imperative: 'Sag ihm, mit einem Wort, bestimmt doch ungehässig, / Dass seine kaiserliche Sendung / An dich, und nicht an deine Gattin sei gerichtet' (1:556). Her insistence that her husband reprimand Ventidius in a non-objectionable manner further highlights her interest in the young Roman, an ironic request in retrospect since part of his imperial mission (Livia) does indeed involve her.

Being an objective observer and a much better judge of character,[47] Hermann is not deceived by the game Ventidius is playing, but his attempts to disabuse his wife at this stage prove unsuccessful. When he calls into question the sincerity of the Roman's feeling, she retorts 'Gewiss, glaub mir, ich fühls, und fühls mit Schmerz, / Dass ich den Irrtum leider selbst, / Der dieses Jünglings Herz ergriff, verschuldet' (1:557). Once more this amounts to indirect self-praise; she blames herself (because how could the young man be expected to resist her charms) and her husband who encouraged her to assume her deceptive role: 'Er hätte, ohne die betrügerischen Schritte, / Zu welchen du mich aufgemuntert, / Sich nie in diese Leidenschaft verstrickt' (1:557). Since she has been touched by what her egotism interprets as Ventidius' genuine passion and since there are hints of her being attracted to him, she now wants honesty to exist between them. Hermann's blunt appraisal, comparing her to less than his dog or a sucked-out orange in the Roman's eyes, may be a close approximation, but is not designed to enhance her self-esteem; hence his attempted rude awakening, falling on deaf ears, only elicits the following defensive response:

THUSNELDA *empfindlich*.
> Dich macht, ich seh, dein Römerhass ganz blind.
> Weil als dämonenartig dir
> Das Ganz' erscheint, so kannst du dir
> Als sittlich nicht den Einzelnen gedenken.   (1:557)

These lines have often been quoted as if they represented the dramatist's opinion or were uttered by 'the spokeswoman for humanitarianism.'[48] Because a naïve, self-centred, spoiled young woman who is deluded by her own excessive vanity makes this pronouncement, we are not encouraged to set any store by what she says and this consideration alone should call into question the validity of her statement under the given circumstances. The drama will prove that Hermann's 'Römerhass,' far from being blind, renders him more perceptive than his spouse, because it remains under the rigid control of a cunning, pragmatic mind. Moreover, in singling out Ventidius, Thusnelda has in fact chosen the worst possible example to justify any moral discrimination.

> Meinst du? Wohlan! Wer recht hat, wird sich zeigen.
> Wie er die Lock, auf welche Weise,
> Gebrauchen will, das weiss ich nicht;
> Doch sie im Stillen an den Mund zu drücken,
> Das kannst du sicher glauben, ist es nicht.   (1:557)

The lock of hair and the use it is put to will prove decisive as Hermann prophetically sets up a contrast between Ventidius' ostentatious display designed for Thusnelda's eyes and an as yet unknown employment once the Roman removes his mask. The play will verify Hermann's cynical estimation of human motivation rather than his mate's ostensibly more enlightened view. The dialogue between husband and wife then comes to an end with the former's promise: 'In drei Tagen, / Soll sein [Ventidius'] Besuch dir nicht zur Last mehr fallen!' (1:557), the first definite sign that Hermann is following a plan with even a specific schedule.

What has been merely implicit in many of Hermann's utterances and actions up to this point becomes explicit in the last two scenes of the second act as Hermann outlines to Eginhardt and Luitgar both his knowledge of the Roman intent to divide and rule and his resolve to forge an alliance with Marbod, his greatest rival for the overall leadership of Germania:

> Doch, um dich [Luitgar] in den Stand zu setzen,
> Sogleich jedwedem Irrtum zu begegnen,
> *Der etwa nicht von mir berechnet wäre,*
> Will ich umständlich, von dem Schritt,
> Zu dem ich mich entschloss, dir Kenntnis geben. (1:558)

This preamble furnishes the first piece of conclusive evidence that Hermann is working with a particular aim in mind. Although he has tried to foresee all contingencies, he still recognizes the key role of chance, the importance of timing, to achieve his goal. Machiavelli, outlining the careers of great men such as Moses, Cyrus, Romulus, and Theseus, records that they were able to rally their peoples behind them in a seemingly hopeless situation: 'Opportunity was what these leaders required, their abilities enabled them to seize it' (M 45). By his own admission, Hermann has calculated what he believes to be the opportune moment and even though he acknowledges that if fate is against him, he will never prevail, he none the less leaves very little to chance. As proof of his good faith, he sends with the letter to Marbod his two sons and a dagger, another symptom of the general atmosphere of distrust among the German tribes as well as a mark of his total commitment. Not only is he prepared to sacrifice (or use) his own children, but he is also willing to renounce his ambition to become supreme ruler. Humble submission to a rival does not come easy to Hermann. On the surface it would seem that love of country or hatred of the enemy is the prime motive; however, the first act has proven that this step represents the only possible means of survival. Either he submits to Marbod, his traditional opponent, or they will both be eliminated by the Romans:

> Das Schicksal Deutschlands lehrt nur allzudeutlich mich,
> Dass Augusts letzte Absicht sei,
> Uns beide, mich wie ihn, zugrund zu richten,
> Und wenn er, Marbod, wird vernichtet sein,
> Der Suevenfürst, so fühl ich lebhaft,
> Wird an Arminius die Reihe kommen. (1:559-60)

'The experience of many rulers,' observes Machiavelli, 'has shown that they have met with more useful and reliable support from men who were initially their opponents than from their original backers [cf. the German princes or the Romans]' (M 105). Although Hermann accepts in name the status of being Marbod's vassal, there are several intimations that the titular protagonist still retains the real authority. His play on 'mir' versus 'ihm' underlined in the text itself (1:559) and conveying an almost pedagogical tone, suggests his ascendancy; *his* plan will be responsible for vanquishing the Romans. 'An dem Alraunentag rück ich nunmehr so fehllos, / *Als wär es sein Gebot*, aus meinem Lager aus, / Und steh, am Nornentag, vorm Teutoburger Wald' (1:561). While he is still anxious to flatter Marbod into concurrence: 'Nach seiner [Marbod's] höhren Weisheit' (1:561) and to give the appearance of obedience, in effect the 'Suevenfürst' will be the supreme commander in name only because Hermann is agreeing to obey an order which he himself issued but which he now attributes to his rival. Also his submission to Marbod is conditional to the defeat of the Romans: 'Sobald wir über Varus' Leiche uns / Begegnet - beug ich ein Knie vor ihm, / Und harre seines weiteren Befehls' (1:561-2). Can Marbod be realistically expected to assent to this magnanimous offer? Is not Hermann shaming him into compliance by a subtle form of emotional blackmail as already employed in his unsuccessful campaign to elicit total commitment from the princes? If the proposed plan leads to victory, one due almost entirely to Hermann, can Marbod be expected to reap the rewards rightfully earned by his rival? He would reign knowing full well that he owed his crown to the foresight and magnanimity of another. But, in Hermann's defence, we must acknowledge that he clearly faces a real dilemma: he is fully convinced of the correctness of his solution to their common problem, but success hinges upon enlisting the support of a life-long opponent. He must both humble himself and at the same time assure absolute adherence - 'die Kraft nun des Gesetzes' (1:561) - to his strategy, a diplomatic *tour de force*.

The second act concludes with the *Realpolitiker*'s concession to an authority, not human but divine and hence greater than himself: 'Wer wollte die gewaltgen Götter / Also versuchen?! Meinst du, es liesse / Das grosse Werk sich ohne sie vollziehn?' (1:562). One might be tempted to see this as a devious manipulation of religious sentiment in order to give the German cause the aura of a religious mission,[49] a gifted performance for the benefit of his listeners; however, he does appear to have a fatalistic belief in fate or the gods as the final arbiter of human destiny, a view also shared by Machiavelli: 'since there is surely a certain liberty of choice left to us, I think that it may well be true that fate determines part of our actions but allows our freedom of will to control the other' (M 117). The authenticity of Hermann's religious feeling will be further substantiated in the last act when Hermann must temporarily relinquish command under the strong sentimental influence of the 'Chor der Barden'

(1:613–4), one of the rare occasions on which his calculating mind succumbs to debilitating emotion.

The teichoscopic introduction to the third act confronts the audience both with a visual representation of Hermann's ascendancy – his tent upon a hill, the oak tree emblematic of indigenous strength, and the historically inaccurate tiger skins suggestive of primitive vigour – and with a further demonstration of his full grasp of the situation:

HERMANN Das ist Thuiskon, was jetzt Feuer griff?
ERSTER ÄLTESTER Vergib mir, Herthakon.
HERMANN   Ja, dort zur Linken.
   Der Ort, der brannte längst. Zur Rechten, mein ich.
ERSTER ÄLTESTER Zur Rechten, meinst du. Das ist Helakon.
   Thuiskon kann man hier vom Platz nicht sehn.
HERMANN Was! Helakon! Das liegt in Asche schon.
   Ich meine, was jetzt eben Feuer griff?
ERSTER ÄLTESTER Ganz Recht! Das ist Thuiskon, mein Gebieter!
   Die Flamme schlägt jetzt übern Wald empor. –
Pause
HERMANN Auf diesem Weg rückt, dünkt mich, Varus an?   (1:563)

Reminiscent of a dialogue in act two, scene two, in which Hermann divulged his awareness of Ventidius' intent to make a secret visit to Thusnelda's tent, this exchange also provides more evidence of the mental shrewdness of which the German prince is capable. He asks a question to which he already knows the answer in order to single out surreptitiously to a representative of his people the perpetrator(s) of the destruction entailed by what amounts to an occupation. That pillaging is inevitable, Hermann has already noted in the first scene of the second act: 'Freund [Ventidius], dir ist selbst bekannt, wie manchem bittern Drangsal / Ein Land ist heillos preis gestellt, / Das einen Heereszug erdulden muss' (1:548), and yet he has wittingly called this fate upon his country. To cite Machiavelli: 'The result [of an invasion] is the hostility of the occupied people' (M 31), precisely what Hermann is counting on. Now with the audience in the picture, he continues to practise his deceptive role as the Roman toady, insisting that full hospitality to be extended to his alleged allies while at the same time he secretly goes to great lengths to poison his people against the Romans, a process already initiated by their entry into Cheruska.[50]

What has only been insinuated in the initial speeches becomes painfully obvious to the spectator in the following scene as Hermann elaborates upon actual atrocities as a means to compound their adverse impact upon public opinion. 'Drei [seiner] blühndsten Plätze,' plundered by the Romans, are transformed into 'sieben' (1:564); to a slaughtered mother and child, a father is added; and an unintentional sacrilege is presented as a forced conversion. Particularly noteworthy is Hermann's reaction to these reports: 'heimlich und freudig' (1:564). In a manner calling to mind the sadistic laughter of Licht or Hohenzollern at the misfortune of others, he joyfully welcomes the heinous crimes committed against his own people. Here, as elsewhere in the drama, the end, the annihilation of the Romans, justifies any means. He is more than willing to delude the masses by increasing the magnitude of the incident in order to depict the foe as a merciless, inhuman monster and thus, to use the Florentine's formulation, to 'fright[en] [his subjects] with the ferocity of the enemy' (M 66). All that matters is the successful execution of the plan; the fact that this entails the death of many innocent people does not concern him in the least. This deplorable attitude culminates in his order to Eginhardt to have a group of Germans disguised as Romans 'auf allen Strassen, / Die sie durchwandern, sengen, brennen, plündern' (1:566). 'Seitdem die Hitlerfaschisten in gleicher Weise verfahren sind, um ihrem Eroberungskrieg einen Vorwand zu schaffen,' remarks Streller, 'seit dem Fall Gleiwitz und der Bombardierung von Freiburg im Breisgau durch deutsche Flugzeuge sind derartige Handlungen selbst als poetische Möglichkeiten unerträglich geworden.'[51] Speaking from a Marxist point of view, Streller sees some justification for Hermann's use of these deceitful tactics in that the 'Volksmassen,' at that time, are still 'blind and unmündig.' Because they lack the necessary insight, Hermann, to preserve the principle of national self-determination, has no other alternative but to resort to such extreme measures. One might be persuaded to go along with this line of reasoning on the purely pragmatic grounds outlined by Machiavelli: 'There are circumstances in which righteousness spells ruin, while evil is essential to security and self-preservation' (M 84), provided that Hermann exhibited some regret rather than pleasure at the destruction wrought upon his own subjects. Moreover, if one takes account of Hermann's apparently sincere reluctance to shed German blood, his forgive-and-forget attitude of the final act, the drama seems to contain a contradiction, but a closer examination discloses an underlying consistency. In his command to Eginhardt he shows no compunction to sacrifice some 'incidental' people whose death will advance the greater political goal of German unity just as before the decisive battle he will advocate a policy of sparing German traitors, again in the interest of a consolidated German nation.[52]

The first two scenes of the third act have conveyed to the audience the extent to which Hermann has foreseen both the actions of the Romans and the reactions of his own people. He does not, however, limit his manipulation of others to the enemy and his own subjects but includes as well the person who should be closest to him, his wife. The spectator's censure of Hermann for his sexual exploitation of Thusnelda is somewhat mitigated, however, by her second function in the drama: she reflects the decadence imported from Rome, the main concern of the first segment of their third-act confrontation.

THUSNELDA *den Sitz betrachtend.*
> Der Sybarit! Sieh da! Mit seinen Polstern!
> Schämst du dich nicht? – Wer traf die Anstalt hier?
Sie setzt sich nieder.
HERMANN Ja, Kind! Die Zeiten, weisst du, sind entartet – . (1:566–7)

Thusnelda accuses her husband of over-refinement but then immediately succumbs to it herself, a visual display of her acquiesence. In addition, by her own admission, she is 'Geschmückt ... beim hohen Himmel, / Dass [sie] die Strassen Roms durchschreiten könnte!' (1:567), a statement which harks back to Hermann's recognition of the general corruption of the age. Even in the way she dresses, Thusnelda betrays her secret desire to be a part of this new world, whereas Hermann, hiding behind a mask of conscious self-irony: 'Holla, schafft Wein mir her, ihr Knaben, / Damit der Perserschach vollkommen sei!' (1:567), is merely going along in an effort to appease for the moment a potentially dangerous adversary.

HERMANN Potz! Bei der grossen Hertha! Schau! – Hör, du!
> Wenn ihr den Adler seht, so ruft ihr mich.
Der Knabe, der ihn bedient, nickt mit dem Kopf.
THUSNELDA Was?
HERMANN   Und Ventidius war bei dir? (1:567)

Concerned only with his political intrigue, Hermann has no time to compliment her toilette nor to play up to her conceit. Although he makes a somewhat overstated attempt to compensate for his inattentiveness, much as one would to a child, in the same line he breaks off, as signalled by the dash, to issue an order in keeping with his overriding preoccupation. Thusnelda's 'Was?' registers her lack of regard for anything other than herself, as she is too caught up in the effect she hopes to have upon the Roman guests to appreciate the importance of the events surrounding her. In this non-dialogue between husband and wife, Hermann's query about Ventidius further underscores the diverse interests separating this couple: *she* can only see Ventidius from her personal point of view, on this occasion, as the man from whom she has received instructions in the Roman hair and dress styles, her superficial female concerns, while *he* views the legate as an exploitable political pawn.

The mention of hair provides Hermann with the opportunity to continue his devious campaign to turn his wife against Ventidius by appealing to her weakness, her vanity: 'Aber, Thuschen! Thuschen! / Wie wirst du aussehn, liebste Frau, / Wenn du mit einem kahlen Kopf wirst gehn?' (1:568). There are definite signs that Hermann has succeeded in shaking some of her confidence: 'THUSNELDA *lacht.* Das muss ich sagen! Der [Varus] wird doch / Um meiner Haare nicht gekommen sein?' (1:568). The laughter signals a growing sense of unease or insecurity. Then Hermann asks her if she remembers the fate of the 'Ubierin':

HERMANN   Das weisst du nicht mehr?
THUSNELDA Nein, Lieber! – Dass drei Römer sie, meinst du,
  In Staub gelegt urplötzlich und gebunden – ?   (1:569)

At first, she denies all knowledge, as if she had completely forgotten the incident, but with time to reconsider, (indicated by the dash) the details come back to her in their entirety. What Kleist is suggesting here is that she has been unable to repress fully this story which has in fact haunted her. Hermann now advances further particulars, including the victim's loss of hair and teeth:

THUSNELDA Ach, geh! Lass mich zufrieden.
HERMANN   Das glaubst du nicht?
THUSNELDA Ach, was! Ventidius hat mir gesagt,
  Das wär ein Märchen.   (1:569)

Her protestations emphasize her vulnerability to this line of attack, for she would prefer to ignore an unpalatable truth. Also, the fact that she sought a disclaimer from Ventidius signifies her deep-seated fear: she needed reassurance from the man to whom she feels secretly attracted. Since in Kleist's very unstable world lovers are continually in need of such reassurances, especially in the case of self-gratifying passion, love can very quickly turn into hate if any external indication appears to call the loved one's fidelity into question.

Intimations continue to accumulate that Hermann has seriously threatened his wife's equanimity by his revelation of the use to which the plundered teeth and hair will be put, a disclosure designed to outrage her sense of dignity: 'THUSNELDA *glühend*. Bei allen Rachegöttern! Allen Furien! / Bei allem, was die Hölle finster macht! / Mit welchem Recht, wenn dem so ist, / Vom Kopf uns aber nehmen sie sie weg?' (1:570). While preparing the audience for her own bloody vengeance, this strong emotional outpouring, the first real manifestation of her volatile nature as she invokes the gods of revenge, contrasts effectively with her husband's controlled and calculated anger. 'HERMANN *lacht*. Nun wird *ihr bang*, um ihre Zähn und Haare' (1:570). This laughter, quite different from the defensive variety emitted by a worried Thusnelda, denotes the sadistic pleasure derived from the obvious discomfort and dismay of his interlocutor. Condescension may also be detected in the choice of 'ihr,' the third person rather than the more intimate 'dir.' Relishing his superior position, Hermann is guilty of the very crime of which he accuses the Romans: specifically of taking advantage of other people as instruments to promote the glorification of the state and its power. One could argue in his defence that, as the pedagogical tone of his utterances implies, he is merely seeking to educate a child to the danger she faces. To disabuse someone who can rarely see beyond her own self-interest requires harsh measures, but the regrettable fact still remains that he really does enjoy the distressful reaction he has occasioned in his wife: 'HERMANN *ebenso* [i.e. *lacht*]. Wie sie nur aussehn wird! Wie'n Totenkopf!' (1:570).

Once Hermann's scare tactics convince Thusnelda, her thoughts turn to self-preservation: 'Und diese Römer nimmst du bei dir auf?' (1:570). Hermann's answer: 'Soll ich, um deiner gelben Haare, / Mit Land und Leut in Kriegsgefahr mich stürzen?' (1:571) presents his politically desperate plight in a manner to which she in her self-centredness can relate directly. Her subsequent response verifies the correctness of this approach: 'Um meiner Haare! Was? Gilt es sonst nichts? / Meinst du, wenn Varus so gestimmt, er werde / Das Fell dir um die nackten Schultern lassen?' (1:571). She persists in viewing the national crisis exclusively from her subjective point of view; making no mention whatsoever of the well-being of her country, she is only aroused at the prospect of losing her husband. 'Sehr wahr, beim Himmel!' exclaims Hermann, 'Das bedacht ich nicht. / Es sei! Ich will die Sach mir überlegen' (1:571). This seemingly good-natured admission adheres to his skilfully contrived procedure for dealing with a childish mentality. Playing the naïve *ingénu*, a role already familiar to the audience from its performance at the expense of Ventidius, the vain male, Hermann has her reach a self-evident conclusion which he knew from the beginning and then gives her the credit in order to flatter her ego.

Even if Hermann already possessed the letter proving Ventidius' betrayal, he could not risk a Thusnelda inimical to the Roman legate since she still has an important social function to perform as hostess at the reception being prepared in Varus' honour. Hence he offers the child the reassurance she requires by telling her a further untruth: 'Gestehs mir [Thusnelda] nur: du scherztest bloss? / HERMANN *küsst sie.* Ja' (1:571); none the less, his psychological manipulation has prepared the ground for the 'Bärin' episode:

> THUSNELDA Nun, meine goldnen Locken kriegt er nicht!
> Die Hand, die in den Mund mir käme,
> Wie jener Frau, um meiner Zähne:
> Ich weiss nicht, Hermann, was ich mit ihr machte.
> HERMANN *lacht.* Ja, liebste Frau, da hast du recht! Beiss zu! (1:571)

A final confirmation of her egocentric attitude to the general calamity, this preoccupation with her physical appearance causes her to dwell upon the 'Ubierin' incident out of fear of the possible consequences for herself. Hermann's laugh substantiates for a third time his sadistic streak, while his advice, 'Beiss zu!,' forebodes Ventidius' fate.[53]

Once Varus arrives, Hermann reverts to the tone of abject servility always adopted in the presence of the Romans; however, he also endeavours to undermine their position by downplaying or making excuses for the atrocities committed by the Roman army since reparation or atonement would only serve to improve the invader's popular image. To ingratiate himself with Varus and to put his fears to rest, he minimizes the public-relations problem: the Roman commander has only to protect the sacred oaks to earn the full confidence and loyalty of the German people.

When Varus introduces his host to his three German supporters, Hermann actually takes the initiative in approaching Fust. He once fought at Hermann's side against the Romans and he will lead the revolt of Rome's German allies against their master (1:607). Now Hermann addresses him directly: 'Wir kennen uns' (1:575). Gueltar who, through no fault of his own, arrived too late for the battle, Hermann asks, 'Dich, Gueltar, auch sah ich an diesem Tag?' (1:575), but to Aristan, the traitor, he poses the telling question: 'Wo war Aristan an dem Tag der Schlacht?' The almost imperceptible movement is from the most intimate first-person plural by which Hermann directly associates himself with Fust to the personal 'dich' which establishes a link with Gueltar to the most remote third person 'Aristan' from whom Hermann wishes consciously but subtly to distance himself: 'Arminius bewundert seine Weisheit' (1:575). Hermann even goes as far as to employ the third person to characterize himself! Aristan who always seeks his own advantage with the least risk incarnates the worst aspects of the German princes with which Hermann must contend: 'Aristan hat das Schwert niemals / Den Cäsarn Roms gezückt, und er darf kühnlich sagen: / Er war ihr Freund, sobald sie sich / Nur an der Schwelle von Germania zeigten' (1:575). Il Principe also describes the self-centred attitudes of local princes whose opportunism renders the conqueror's task all the easier: '[States governed by hereditary rulers] are not difficult to overrun with the support of a disgruntled or ambitious noble or two. Such men, by reason of their position, ... can open the gates to an invader and make the conquest possible' (M 40).

'The Romans,' according to Machiavelli, 'were remarkable in their anticipation of trouble and always ready to face it' (M 35). This ability to foresee problems before they threatened their superiority enabled them to found their vast empire. In Die Hermannsschlacht Kleist has reversed the roles, for it is not the Romans but rather Hermann who is 'remarkable in [his] anticipation of trouble and always ready to face it.' On several occasions he has managed to mask his true intent by projecting an image of himself as an ineffectual puppet ruler. The key to the false impression, as Hermann fully realizes, has been Ventidius, sent by Rome to pave the way for Varus' campaign. Ventidius' dealings with his host, combined with his flirtation with Thusnelda as stage-managed by Hermann, have enhanced the Roman official's high opinion of himself, convinced him of Hermann's dependence on and loyalty to his Roman allies, and thus blinded him to the real danger. A dialogue between Varus and Ventidius discloses the complete success of Hermann's stratagem:

VARUS zu Ventidius. Was also, sag mir an, was hab ich
   Von jenem Hermann dort mir zu versehn?
VENTIDIUS Quintilius! Das fass ich in zwei Worten!
   Er ist ein Deutscher.

In einem Hämmling ist, der an der Tiber graset,
Mehr Lug and Trug, muss ich dir sagen,
Als in dem ganzen Volk, dem er gehört. –
VARUS So kann ich, meinst du, dreist der Sueven Fürsten
Entgegenrücken? Habe nichts von diesem,
Bleibt er in meinem Rücken, zu befürchten?
VENTIDIUS So wenig, wiederhol ich dir,
Als hier von diesem Dolch in meinem Gurt – .   (1:576)

The Romans' general low opinion of the barbarians causes them to underestimate their foe, but, in addition, Hermann has clearly lived up to their expectations of the simple-minded, noble savage. Although Varus does anticipate possible trouble, he listens to the legate's counsel, fails as a result to take the necessary precautionary measures, and exposes his most vulnerable flank to his most bitter enemy.

One of the 'moral' dilemmas posed by *Die Hermannsschlacht* and singled out for special consideration by the secondary literature is the alleged contradiction that the exemplary actions of the drama belong exclusively to the villains, whereas the so-called heroes display a total disregard for any ethical standards. 'Varus and Septimius,' in Burckhardt's opinion, 'are noblemen next to these German princes, the 'best' of whom, in his resolute reserve, is the unregenerate and unforgiven Aristan.' Burckhardt goes on to contend that the *manner* of presentation does make a difference in our moral perception of the play and consequently, 'Roman posturing, however noble' comes across more sympathetically than 'Teutonic feeling, however revolting.'[54] But this argument does not take cognizance of the third act's conclusion where Kleist obviously goes to some lengths to expose the deception, the total lack of good faith in this noble posturing. To state the case bluntly, Hermann beats the Romans at their own game, or as Korff puts it, '[Hermann] zeigt sich ... als ein so gerissener Fuchs, ein so gelehriger, ja perfekter Schüler der römischen Politik.'[55] Machiavelli delineates approvingly the basic principles of this 'römischen Politik' in *Il Principe*: 'The extinction of the native dynasty in such [conquered] territories is a factor of security for the new ruler ... [The Romans] made settlements, protected minorities, without granting them authority, destroyed local leadership and combated penetration by alien powers' (M 32, 34). The text makes it quite apparent that Rome has a similar fate in mind for Cheruska and its ruler:

VARUS ... Meinst du vielleicht, die Absicht sei, Cheruska
Als ein erobertes Gebiet – ?

VENTIDIUS   Quintilius,
  Die Absicht, dünkt mich, lässt sich fast erraten.
VARUS – Ward dir etwa bestimmte Kund hierüber?
VENTIDIUS Nicht, nicht! Misshör mich nicht! Ich teile bloss,
  Was sich in dieser Brust prophetisch regt, dir mit,
  Und Freunde mir aus Rom bestätigen.   (1:577)

At first one may be inclined to regard Varus in a positive light as an
unconscious tool in the hands of a power-hungry, treacherous Rome. This
more favourable assessment is due in part to the implied contrast with
Ventidius, the palace intriguer who thrives on the secret machinations
of the court and deals in rumour, a type to whom Kleist appears to have
harboured a particular aversion.[56]

VARUS Seis! Was bekümmerts mich? Es ist nicht meines Amtes
  Den Willen meines Kaisers zu erspähn.
  Er sagt ihn, wenn er ihn vollführt will wissen. –
  Wahr ists, Rom wird auf seinen sieben Hügeln,
  Vor diesen Horden nimmer sicher sein,
  Bis ihrer kecken Fürsten *Hand*
  Auf immerdar der Szepterstab entwunden.
VENTIDIUS So denkt August, so denket der Senat.   (1:577)

Varus' rationalization, an unfortunate characteristic of the military mind
(it is not his to question but to obey), calls into serious doubt his designation
as 'die rundeste und nobelste Figur des Dramas'[57] because it reveals his
willingness to become the *conscious* tool of an immoral Rome. Even though
he may speak in a seemingly noble fashion, his conduct is essentially
a lie: it lacks a moral will to make it personally meaningful. He treats
Hermann as his colleague, will call him his friend: 'Weisst du noch sonst
was anzumerken, Freund?' (1:578) and '*nimmt ihn vertraulich bei der Hand*'
(1:577), the very hand from which he has just approved the forceful removal
of the 'Szepterstab.' This patent duplicity stressed by Kleist's juxtaposing
of the Varus-Ventidius and the Varus-Hermann dialogues invalidates the
noble posture as the deceptive veneer of an alleged superior civilization.
In his undisguised brutality, his unsophisticated revenge and cruelty,
Hermann comes across as somehow more authentic although no less
reprehensible.[58] Both sides of the conflict would seem to have taken to
heart Machiavelli's observation: 'No one will contest that it is praiseworthy

for a ruler to keep his promises and be frank and open in his dealings rather than tortuous. Nevertheless, in our times we have seen men who took their pledges very lightly, and confounded people by trickery, go a long way, and in the end get the better of others who were guided by the principle of integrity' (M 91). 'But', as Machiavelli also is quick to point out, 'it is important in practices of this sort to be careful about appearances' (M 92). Hence the act is brought to a close with the continued semblance of total obedience, of total self-effacement on the part of Hermann:

VARUS – Weisst du noch sonst was anzumerken, Freund?
HERMANN Nichts, Feldherr Roms! Dir übergab ich alles,
  So sei die Sorge auch, es zu beschützen, dein.   (1:578)

The issue of trust, a central underlying concern of the third act and a major preoccupation of Kleist, continues to elicit the audience's attention with the first speech of the fourth act spoken by Marbod:

  Was soll ich davon denken, Attarin?
  – Arminius, der Cheruskerfürst,
  Lässt mir durch jenen wackern Freund dort melden:
  Varus sei ihm, auf Schutz und Trutz, verbunden,
  Und werd, in dreien Tagen schon,
  Mich am Gestad der Weser überfallen! –   (1:579)

The general atmosphere of distrust is so severe that Hermann has to surrender his own flesh and blood as proof and guarantee of his good faith. Clearly, without the presence of his children, the alliance would not have taken place and thus we have yet another indication of his mind's capacity to encompass the full political spectrum. In the ensuing interrogation of the two boys, the spectator gains some insight into the past relationship between the two principal contenders for the position of supreme ruler over the German tribes: 'In Teutoburg, vor sieben Monden, / Als *ich* den Staatenbund verhandeln wollte, / Hab ich die Jungen, die dort stehn, / Wie oft an diese alte Brust gedrückt!' (1:580). There have been attempts to effect a common front and Marbod evidently regards himself as *the* key figure in these prior unsuccessful talks. Although he offers no specific cause for the failure of the negotiations, a power struggle between the two most prominent leaders does come to mind, especially since they both believe in the desirability of a confederation. Now that a crisis has been reached, the question of mere survival takes precedence over such internal matters. They are unequivocally united in their hatred of the Romans, and if one takes heed of the marks of affection shown by Marbod to Hermann's children, some form of personal attachment must exist between them.

This initial episode is also designed to alienate further any sympathy one might feel for the enemy. Attarin, Marbod's sceptical confidant, finds it inconceivable that after all the displays of commitment to his master's cause, the Romans could be contemplating betrayal of the Sueven: 'Hat er [Roms Cäsar] mit Waffen dich, dich nicht mit Geld versehn, / In ihre Staaten [i.e., the Cherusker] feindlich einzufallen?' (1:582). Hermann has been fully apprised of this treachery from the beginning and has played his cards in such a way as to assure his being chosen as Rome's ally. Hence the Roman double-dealing confirmed by the letter should come as no surprise to the audience.

MARBOD *liest.*

Du hast für Rom dich nicht entscheiden können,
Aus voller Brust, wie du gesollt:
Rom, der Bewerbung müde, gibt dich auf.
Versuche jetzt (es war dein Wunsch) ob du
Allein den Herrschthron dir in Deutschland kannst errichten.
August jedoch, dass du es wissest,
Hat den Armin auf seinem Sitz erhöht,
Und dir – die Stufen jetzo weist er an! (1:583)

Marbod is much too self-reliant, proud, and powerful to be a serious candidate for an alliance with Rome. Ventidius has been led to believe that the Romans have completely intimidated Hermann by the latter's cunning show of abject servility, and by comparison Marbod appears to be the stronger and more independent of mind of the two. Therefore, Rome, in keeping with its traditional approach to foreign conquest, throws in its lot with what it incorrectly presumes to be the weaker party, a tactical mistake engineered by Hermann the fox. Having played into Hermann's hands, the Romans, by divulging their intent to Marbod, inadvertently clear the way for the next stage of the master plan: 'Und welchen Tag, unfehlbar und bestimmt, / Hat er [Hermann] zum Fall der Würfel festgesetzt?' (1:583). Hermann is now in charge. All of Marbod's subsequent military actions will conform to 'des Arminius Kriegsentwurf' while the contentious issues of ultimate authority is left in abeyance:

'Den Teil [of Hermann's letter], der mir von seiner Huldgung spricht, / Als einem Oberherrn, den lös ich ab – ' (1:584).

One of the few emotional outbursts on the part of Hermann introduces the third scene of the fourth act: 'Tod und Verderben, sag ich, Eginhardt! / Woher die Ruh, woher die Stille, / In diesem Standplatz römscher Kriegerhaufen?' (1:584). Generally, Hermann displays a very cold, disciplined disposition. Only if the plan is being realized beyond his expectations, or if the chain of events does not follow the pattern he has foreseen, is he capable of a quick, unguarded response whether it be joy at a calamity which suits his purpose, or anger, as in this instance, when the Romans' good conduct frustrates his intent.

> Ich aber rechnete, bei allen Rachegöttern,
> Auf Feuer, Raub, Gewalt und Mord,
> Und alle Greul des fessellosen Krieges!
> Was brauch ich Latier, die mir Gutes tun?
> Kann ich den *Römerhass*, eh ich den Platz verlasse,
> In der Cherusker Herzen nicht
> Dass er durch ganz Germanien schlägt, entflammen:
> So scheitert meine ganze Unternehmung!   (1:585)

What Hermann has described here is a propaganda technique quite familiar to our century, which consists in portraying the adversary in as negative a light as possible. The accuracy of this representation matters little since one must bring the masses to the point of hating the anonymous enemy. 'Hate and fear both drive men to hostility' (M 55), a political fact of life at the basis of several intrigues documented in *Il Principe*. This speech also implies Hermann's low opinion of his own people: given the opportunity, he is confident that he can direct and dominate their attitudes and feelings.

Hermann's knowledge of human character is again brought to the attention of the audience when Eginhardt proposes informing Wolf, Thuiskomar, and the other native leaders of the master plan. Hermann's analysis proves correct: the princes waste their time indulging in conspiracies, while refusing to act out of fear of risking their own security: 'Die schreiben, Deutschland zu befreien' (1:585). The reference to writing recalls Thuiskomar's priorities in the first act – it was he who insisted: 'Er [Hermann] *muss* [Kleist's emphasis] hier diese Briefe lesen!' (1:535) – and in response to Hermann's scorched-earth policy, it was again Thuiskomar who exclaimed: 'Das eben, Rasender, das ist es ja, / Was wir in diesem Krieg verteidigen wollen!' (1:547). The drama also confirms Hermann's more positive assessment of Wolf: 'Wolf ist der einzge, der es redlich meint' (1:585). He makes the perceptive summation at the end of the first scene: 'Es bricht der Wolf, o Deutschland, / In deine Hürde ein, und deine Hirten streiten / Um eine Handvoll Wolle sich' (1:537), the desperate cry concluding the first act: 'O Deutschland! Vaterland! Wer rettet dich, / Wenn es ein Held, wie Siegmars Sohn nicht tut!' (1:547) and the first triumphant salutation of Hermann after his victory over the Romans: 'Heil, Hermann! Heil dir, Sieger der Kohorten! / Germaniens Retter, Schirmer und Befreier!' (1:625). In all three of these key utterances, Wolf addresses himself to the welfare of the German nation as a whole ('Deutschland,' 'Vaterland,' or 'Germanien'), best realized in his view under Cheruskian leadership. Hermann knows whom he can count on.

'Now, the maintenance of autocratic rule in dynastic monarchies,' Machiavelli argues, 'is a far easier business than it is in the newly established. All that is needed is the avoidance of a breach with tradition in institutions, and opportunism in the face of events' (M 30). Hermann is undeniably an autocratic, dynastic ruler, one whose authority over his own tribe is never questioned. He does seem to respect traditions, especially the religious customs of his people, but above all he knows how to exploit a situation, or if need be, to create one to exploit. So desperate is he for an excuse, for some provocation derived from Roman excesses, that he even contemplates manufacturing an incident himself: 'Ich stecke, wenn sich niemand rührt, / Die ganze Teutoburg an allen Ecken an!' (1:586), a further irrational reaction to circumstances which imperil his scheme.

EGINHARDT Nun, nun! Es wird sich wohl ein Frevel finden.
HERMANN Komm, lass uns heimlich durch die Gassen schleichen,
    Und sehn ob uns der Zufall etwas beut. (1:586)

The opportunity soon presents itself: the Hally episode, Kleist's adaptation of an Old Testament story from the book of Judges.[59]

The success of Hermann's secret campaign depends upon his ability to provoke in his people a 'Römerhass.' Because '[h]atred is aroused most readily by interference with the property and the women of subordinates' (M 94), the violation of a young woman by the enemy together with her violent death at the hands of her infuriated relatives who view her as a piece of property over which they have life-and-death authority furnishes the German ruler with the 'perfect' atrocity at the most opportune moment. Interestingly enough, Kleist does not leave the assailants unpunished:

'Drei'n dieser geilen apenninschen Hunden, / Als man die Tat ihm [a young Roman captain] meldete, / Hat er das Herz gleich mit dem Schwert durchbohrt!' (1:586). This has to be regarded as a positive act, in part an indemnification for the rape, and yet, except for the old man's exclamation: 'Vergib mir, Gott! ich kann es ihm [the Roman captain] nicht danken!' (1:587), it is completely ignored from this point on. Why did Kleist include this information since it mitigates against an exclusively negative appraisal of the enemy? Obviously, one is encouraged to make a distinction between the dramatist and the titular protagonist. The former does not engage in the practice of presenting the foe solely as a voracious monster as he goes to some length to demonstrate that not all Romans are bad, while the latter strives to create a consciously distorted, pejorative image of his adversary as a means to alienate public sympathy. This is but one of several instances where Kleist remains fairly objective despite his unmistakable bias in favour of the German cause.

HERMANN Was gibts?
DER ERSTE CHERUSKER Was! Fragst du noch? Du weisst von nichts?
HERMANN Nichts, meine Freund! Ich komm aus meinem Zelte. (1:589)

It should come as no surprise to the alert observer that Hermann will turn this situation to his advantage. In fact, his first statement of the episode is a lie. By his own admission at the end of the third scene of the act, he was sneaking ('schleichen,' 1:586) about the streets (and not in his tent), searching specifically for such an incident.

DER ZWEITE CHERUSKER *halblaut.* Eine ganze Meute
Von geilen Römern, die den Platz durchschweifte,
Hat bei der Dämmrung schamlos eben jetzt –
HERMANN *indem er ihn vorführt.*
Still, Selmar, still! Die Luft, du weisst, hat Ohren.
– Ein Römerhaufen?
EGINHARDT Ha! Was wird das werden? (1:589)

Not the victim, but those responsible for this 'Greuel' attract his immediate attention. He does not even allow the speaker to finish his report, so eager is he to confirm the identity of the transgressors who have aroused the people to such a pitch. Although at the back of his mind he has already evaluated the feasibility of using this crime against the enemy, he still does not know if it will meet his needs and he must avoid revealing his intent too prematurely to the Romans who may have spies present. As indicated by Eginhardt's rhetorical question, Hermann's confidant also foresees the potential.

> *Sie sprechen heimlich zusammen. Pause.*
> HERMANN *mit Wehmut, halblaut.*
>   Hally? Was sagst du mir! Die junge Hally?   (1:589)

The pause supplies the time necessary to devise the best method to exploit this outrage as a means to put his people in the desired hostile frame of mind. Then, for their benefit, he focuses on the victim with a suitable show of public grief and concern.

The play frequently furnishes evidence of Hermann's consummate histrionic ability in his dealings with both the Romans and his own tribe,[60] for with Machiavelli, he knows that the 'mass is taken in by appearances' (M 93). He begins and ends his seemingly incredulous response with the victim's name, thereby establishing a personal, intimate link with his audience and further plays on emotion by alluding to her youth. Once the details have been confirmed, Hermann confidently turns to the crowd:

> HERMANN *zum Volke.*
>   Kommt, ihr Cherusker! Kommt, ihr Wodankinder!
>   Kommt, sammelt euch um mich und hört mich an!
> *Das Volk umringt ihn; er tritt vor Teuthold.*   (1:590)

The situation is strongly reminiscent of Mark Antony's speech over Caesar's body: both orators skilfully utilize a corpse to stir up the gullible masses against the perpetrators of a violent crime. Whereas Mark Antony ingratiates himself with his audience by addressing the citizens as 'Good friends, sweet friends,'[61] Hermann flatters his listeners by calling them the children of the most powerful god, thus reminding them of their heritage or potential strength and implying an almost sacred obligation to appease Wodan for such a heinous offence. The visual image of the people gathered about Hermann dramatizes precisely what the schemer hoped to achieve.

> DER ZWEITE CHERUSKER.
>   Hermann, dein Rächer ists, der vor dir [Teuthold] steht.
> *Sie heben ihn empor.*

TEUTHOLD Hermann, mein Rächer, sagt ihr? – Kann er Rom,
   Das Drachennest, vom Erdenrund vertilgen?
HERMANN Ich kanns und wills! Hör an, was ich dir sage.   (1:590)

Hermann has so masterfully staged this incident that the call to avenge the rape comes to him from the people. In other words, the people ask him to do what all along he has been planning to do. This enables him to appear as the chosen instrument of his subjects' will and to have the populace firmly behind him. At the propitious moment and with a full voice, not the 'halblaut' at the beginning of the scene, he now announces openly his actual aim and as Teuthold's response proves: 'Gebeut! Sprich! Red, o Herr! / Was muss geschehn? Wo muss die Keule fallen?' (1:590), he has his audience 'eating out of his hand.' The people unite behind the concrete symbol of Germania's desecration, Hally's body: 'Empörung! Rache! Freiheit!' (1:591), while the implacable nature of the desire for revenge, the firm commitment to the cause, becomes explicit in Teuthold's final commands: 'Auf! Greift an! / Bringt sie ins Haus, zerlegt in Stücken sie!' (1:591). Without any apparent qualm, Teuthold orders his own daughter's body to be torn into pieces.

HERMANN Komm, Eginhardt! Jetzt hab ich nichts mehr
   An diesem Ort zu tun! Germanien lodert:
   Lass uns den Varus jetzt, den Stifter dieser Greuel,
   Im Teutoburger Walde suchen!   (1:591)

Implicit within this utterance is a lack of sincere concern at Hally's death. (Indeed Hermann was willing to put the torch to his own village if it would inflame the masses.) He has managed to turn to account the perfect opportunity which he set out with Eginhardt to find and which advances him one step farther along the way to the attainment of his ultimate goal. When it is a question of his subjects in a narrower context, Hermann consistently reveals himself to be the ruthless totalitarian prince described at length in *Il Principe*.[62]

The short dialogue between Hermann and Septimius in the next scene is intended to give an additional example of the former's cunning management of the enemy. The Romans wanted to divide the Cheruskian army into smaller, more manageable 'Manipeln' '[n]ach Römerart,' but Hermann had insisted that he be present during this operation and then intentionally stayed away. Playing the innocent: 'Was! So ist alles noch im Heer, wie sonst?' (1:591), he maintains that he had assumed Septimius would '[a]uch ohne [ihn] hierin verfügen können' (1:592), while consciously frustrating the enemy's strategy. By an apparent oversight, presented as regrettable but, in actual fact, deliberate, Hermann succeeds in retaining full control of his men as a single force without arousing the least suspicion in Septimius and thus thwarts the Romans' attempt to impose more direct authority over their German 'allies': 'Nun – wird es wohl beim alten bleiben müssen' (1:592).

Hermann's only soliloquy of the play anticipates Homburg's second monologue in *Prinz Friedrich von Homburg*. The two speeches occur at the turning point in the career of the speaker who faces the prospect of a trip into the unknown: 'DER PRINZ VON HOMBURG. Das Leben nennt der Derwisch eine Reise' (1:686); 'HERMANN. Nun wär ich fertig, wie ein Reisender' (1:592). Even though the speculations of the titular protagonists deal with death, at first glance, there would seem to be a major distinction: Hermann appears to be more altruistically concerned with the welfare of his country; Homburg is preoccupied with his own individual fate. However, the first person singular occurs only twice in Homburg's eleven lines, while Hermann employs it five times in ten lines. Not only does Hermann affirm the unpredictable nature of his country's destiny; he also stresses the fact that he alone holds that destiny in *his* hands. Cheruska becomes so much baggage that he chooses to take along on his journey: 'Cheruska, wie es steht und liegt, / Kommt *mir*, wie eingepackt in eine Kiste, vor: / Um einen Wechsel könnt *ich* es verkaufen' (1:592). He dwells upon the consequences of failure for his nation, but significantly he presents this potential destruction as if it were done to him or because of him personally: 'Roms Feldherr steckte gleich *mir* alle Plätze an' (1:592). This soliloquy creates the strong impression that Hermann enjoys exercising his power and affirming it even in the present desperate situation which he views primarily in terms of his own personal dimension.[63]

The most crucial exchange between Hermann and Thusnelda takes place '*nachdem er Schild und Spiess weggelegt*' (1:592). Like Achilles in *Penthesilea* and Ventidius, he approaches the woman he loves 'unarmed' and hence vulnerable, and only later, once he has taken official leave of her and is brought back to the reality of war, does he pick up his weapons again. I am reminded of Nietzsche's dictum: 'Zweierlei will der ächte Mann: Gefahr und Spiel. Deshalb will er das Weib, als das gefährlichste Spielzeug.'[64] In Kleist's world, if men let down their guard, it can be fatal, and as we shall ascertain, Thusnelda is Hermann's 'Achilles' heel.'

Thusnelda confronts her husband, allegedly concerned over the rumoured fate in store for the three cohorts. After Hermann confirms her worst fears, she incredulously inquires, 'Die Guten mit den Schlechten, rücksichtslos?' (1:593). He then answers with the seemingly contradictory assertion: 'Was! Die Guten! / Das sind die Schlechtesten! Der Rache Keil / Soll sie zuerst, vor allen andern, treffen!' (1:593). This dialogue has given rise to several misconceptions. For example, Burkhardt sees a commendable side to Thusnelda's character in that 'she does protest against Hermann's refusal to make any distinction between the individual and the social group to which he happens to belong.'[65] What Burckhardt has overlooked is that all of Thusnelda's arguments, no matter how compelling, are motivated by one selfish concern: her desire to save the young Roman to whom she feels unconsciously attracted. In interpreting Hermann's reply to his wife, Burckhardt explains: 'For if [the good Romans] were truly good, they would have to feel a deep and personal shame at having a part in reducing other human beings to such meanness. Their moral superiority – displayed with such style, such pithy and devastating wit – who is furnishing them with the moral means for it if not the cringing creature at their feet?'[66] The conversation between Varus and Ventidius at the end of the third act surely goes a long way to dispel any illusion of 'moral superiority.' The noble posturing, albeit 'displayed with such style, such pithy and devastating wit,' amounts to a mask to disguise the corruption of Roman civilization as epitomized by Ventidius. Kurt May's analysis of the same lines stands up better to close scrutiny, but is none the less somewhat misleading: 'Denn immer bleibt [ein Römer von vornehmer Gesinnung oder gutem Herzen] doch einer von denen, die eingedrungen sind ins fremde Reich und das Recht des fremden Volkes verletzt haben. Der Anschein von Güte der Gesinnung und des Handelns auf römischer Seite bedeutet erhöhte Gefahr, weil ein solcher Römer den Gegner irre machen könnte in seinem Wissen von Gut und Böse.'[67] As Machiavelli warns in his pragmatic approach to morality, there are times when to be good could well spell ruin. For Hermann, all that counts in such a struggle against an essentially immoral enemy is survival, a goal presented as being, so to speak, beyond good and evil and necessitating the vilification of the invaders without exception. It follows that the 'good' Roman is the worst since he may weaken the people's resolve to resist foreign subjugation. Also, as Hermann's superficially innocent question implies: 'Nenn einen Namen mir?' (1:594), he fully realizes what prompts Thusnelda's defence of the enemy. This scene functions primarily as the culminating exhibition of his devious exploitation of his spouse: her part is the final detail of the master plan, which must be set in motion before he leaves for battle.

When Thusnelda stubbornly persists in her campaign to obtain mercy for a few Romans, she really has an interest in sparing only one and thus by referring to a centurion who saved a German child she attempts to clothe her personal motive in a more general guise. If '[d]er junge Held' is in fact a surrogate for Ventidius, then Thusnelda's question to her husband: 'Er hätte kein Gefühl der Liebe dir entlockt?' (1:594) takes on a special meaning as an oblique admission of love for the young Roman legate. Hermann's retaliatory response warrants special consideration:

HERMANN *glühend.*
Er sei verflucht, wenn er *mir* das getan!
Er hat, auf einen Augenblick,
Mein Herz veruntreut, zum Verräter
An Deutschlands grosser Sache mich gemacht!
Warum setzt' er Thuiskon *mir* in Brand? (1:594)

The stage direction *'glühend,'* the introductory curse, and the two exclamations underscore an emotional eruption with the usual egocentric basis: the reported incident interferes with his scheme. Although his heart is not unmoved by the centurion's compassionate act, Hermann must refrain from envisioning the enemy as human beings and must not lose sight of the overall goal – 'Deutschlands grosser Sache' – because of one isolated case. Furthermore, as the two dative pronouns 'mir' imply, he interprets both the rescue of the child and the burning of the village, the positive and the counterbalancing negative, as personal affronts to himself. From the first act where Hermann announced his wish to die gloriously alone, there are indications that he views the whole conflict from the subjective perspective of 'I' versus the Romans (cf. 'Roms Feldherr steckte gleich *mir* alle Plätze an' [1:592]). *Die Hermannsschlacht* offers a perceptive psychological study of hate, but what is more remarkable is that the subject, Hermann, remains aware of the mental discipline he must exercise to induce this desired and politically necessary attitude. Once he has made up his mind to despise the Romans, he consciously looks for or even manufactures excuses to justify and reinforce his hatred: 'Ich *will* [Kleist's emphasis] die höhnische Dämonenbrut nicht lieben! / So lang sie in Germanien trotzt, / Ist Hass mein Amt und meine Tugend Rache!' (1:594). By an act of will, he refuses to allow any positive feelings vis-à-vis the foe to weaken his determination, for to do so would be tantamount to paralysing his will to act. This position begins to sound like that of the single-minded fanatic who, having committed himself to a specific cause, will entertain only those emotions (hate and revenge) conducive to the cause. Hermann is much too calculating, much too aware of his own mental manoeuvres, however, to be classified as a 'blind' fanatic.

Hermann's blunt statement of intent finally compels Thusnelda to betray her true reason for pursuing a course of generosity towards the enemy:

THUSNELDA *weinend.*
    Mein liebster, bester Herzens-Hermann,
    Ich bitte dich um des Ventidius Leben!
    Das eine Haupt nimmst du von deiner Rache aus!
    Lass, ich beschwöre dich, lass mich ihm heimlich melden,
    Was über Varus du verhängt:
    Mag er ins Land der Väter rasch sich retten!
HERMANN Ventidius? Nun gut. – Ventidius Carbo?
    Nun denn, es sei! – Weil es mein Thuschen ist,
    Die für ihn bittet, mag er fliehn:
    Sein Haupt soll meinem Schwert, so wahr ich lebe,
    Um dieser schönen Regung heilig sein!
THUSNELDA *sie küsst seine Hand.*
    O Hermann! Ist es wirklich wahr? O Hermann!
    Du schenkst sein Leben mir?   (1:594–5)

The conclusion of this scene will prove that Hermann is ironically toying with his immature wife, playing up to her vanity: 'Weil es mein Thuschen ist, / Die für ihn bittet,' to which he will soon deal a fatal blow. Having no intention of sparing Ventidius, he follows a sly stratagem to render her submissive to his will. Once, he promoted the flirtation because it served his political objective; now he no longer needs it. Since Ventidius has served his purpose by convincing Varus of Hermann's docility and trustworthiness, he can be eliminated. What Hermann prefers to regard as a harmless dalliance, a view shared by several commentators, is obviously much more than that. For instance, when Hermann proposes that Thusnelda write a warning letter to Ventidius, she concurs but adds a significant variation: 'Und dass der Jüngling auch nicht etwa, / Der törichte, um dieses Briefs, / Mit einem falschen Wahn sich schmeichele, / Will ich den Brief in deinem Namen schreiben' (1:595). Thusnelda does not wish the young man to flatter himself that his life is of any concern to her whereas this is clearly the case: 'Du schenkst sein Leben mir?' Exemplifying the peculiar vulnerability of lovers in the initial stage, she avoids giving Ventidius any control over her which he would conceivably gain if he had a definite confirmation of her intervention on his behalf. In addition, the impassioned nature of her plea: 'weinend' (1:594), 'sie küsst seine Hand' (1:595), 'O Liebster mein! Wie rührst du mich! O Liebster!,'(1:595) and 'indem sie sich die Tränen trocknet' (1:595) does betoken a strong emotional commitment. Now that Hermann guarantees Ventidius' survival, she no longer displays any particular moral scruple at the fact that all the Romans, 'Die Guten mit den Schlechten' (1:593) must die:

HERMANN Denn alle andern müssen unerbittlich,
  Die schändlichen Tyrannenknechte, sterben:
  Der Anschlag darf nicht etwa durch ihn [Ventidius] scheitern!
THUSNELDA indem sie sich die Tränen trocknet.
  Nein, nein, ich schwörs dir zu! Kurz vor der Sonn erst!
  Kurz vor der Sonn erst soll er es erfahren! (1:595)

Hermann's speeches up to this point in the scene have been preparing for the sudden reverse precipitated by his reintroduction of Thusnelda's lock of hair:

HERMANN heiter.
  Das tu. Das ist sehr klug. – Sieh da, mein schönes Thuschen!
  Ich muss dich küssen. –
  Doch, was ich sagen wollte – –
  Hier ist die Locke wieder, schau,
  Die er dir jüngst vom Scheitel abgelöst ... (1:595)

Hermann could, of course, have made this revelation towards the beginning of their conversation, but quite intentionally he has managed the dialogue in such a fashion as to elicit from his wife what amounts to an indirect confession of affection for Ventidius. Now, when she has made herself most assailable, has jeopardized her own pride to plead for the life of an enemy, Hermann presents her with a visual confirmation, set aside for the occasion, of that very man's perfidy. Although the double and the two single dashes create a semblance of nonchalance to accompany the exposure, they actually highlight the conscious manipulation of which Hermann is such a master.

Thusnelda immediately tries to give the most positive slant possible to the presence of her lock of hair, positive in terms of her own self-image. First, Hermann must have demanded it from Ventidius: 'Du hast sie dem Arkadier abgefordert?' (1:596). When her husband rejects this alternative, she advances a second innocuous suggestion: 'Ward sie gefunden?,' but Hermann insists upon confronting her with visible reality: 'Gefunden, ja, in einem Brief, *du siehst*, / Den er nach Rom hin, gestern früh, / An Livia, seine Kaiserin, abgefertigt' (1:596). He refuses to spare her feelings or to offer her an honourable retreat because she must continue to act as a pawn in his political game. There is also the possibility of a subtle form of revenge on both his wife and her suitor as Hermann, with his knowledge of human personality, must be dimly aware of his wife's more than superficial emotional involvement with his younger rival. The extent to which she prefers to ignore a truth injurious to her female ego becomes especially evident, however, when in response to the unavoidable fact of the letter addressed '"An Livia, Roms grosse Kaiserin"' (1:596), she comments, '– Freund, ich versteh kein Wort! / – Wie kamst du zu dem Brief? Wer gab ihn dir?' (1:596) Hermann has already explained the origin of the lock and letter twice and must now do so the third time. Then the emphasis shifts from the lock to the content of the letter:[68]

THUSNELDA Das ist ja seltsam, so wahr ich lebe! –
  Was sagt Ventidius denn darin?
HERMANN   Er sagt – :
  Lass sehn! Ich überflog ihn nur. Was sagt er?
  Er guckt mit hinein.   (1:596)

Since Hermann chooses this precise moment to produce the incriminating piece of evidence, the audience realizes that he is lying when he denies full knowledge of the letter's content. He adopts the guise of the naïf in order not to appear to be poisoning her against Ventidius. The latter's own words will oblige her to draw the painful conclusion herself. Thusnelda's reaction: ' – Ei der Verfluchte! / *Sie sieht Hermann an, und wieder in den Brief hinein.* / Nein, ich las wohl falsch?' (1:597) explains why Hermann wanted to be present during the reading of the letter. He knows of her propensity to delude herself and thus constrains her to face the ugly fact of Ventidius' betrayal: '– Stehts anders in dem Briefe da? / Er sagt – :' or 'Nun ja; er will – ! Verstehst dus nicht?' (1:597).

Once Hermann's persistence brings home to Thusnelda the full extent of the treachery practised by the man for whose life only minutes before she had debased herself to plead so ardently, her initial response is purely passive: she is unable to speak: 'Die Sprache geht ihr aus' and when she does, she expresses the desire to run away from this world: 'Nun mag ich diese Sonne nicht mehr sehn' (1:597), a wish symbolically reinforced by her gesture: 'Sie verbirgt ihr Haupt.' Now that she has reached the lowest point of self-esteem, has had both her judgment of others and of herself called into serious question, Hermann can pursue the next objective of this consciously structured meeting: specifically, to determine the precise nature of her retaliation:

HERMANN *leise, flüsternd.*
   Thuschen! Thuschen! Er ist ja noch nicht fort.
Er folgt ihr und ergreift ihre Hand.
THUSNELDA Geh, lass mich sein.
HERMANN *beugt sich ganz über sie.*
                         Heut, wenn die Nacht sinkt, Thuschen,
  Schlägt dir der Rache süsse Stunde ja!   (1:597)

In a conspiratorial, almost diabolical manner, he whispers into her ear; he pursues and seizes her by the hand, not allowing her to escape from his influence and demonstrating his resolve to direct her as he sees fit; and finally he completely dominates her with his physical presence, a dramatization of his absolute authority over her. Another important consideration which this quotation substantiates but which the critics have ignored[69] is the fact that the revenge theme, including its actual setting and even the attitude of the avenger, is initially outlined not by Thusnelda but by Hermann. He first presents the possibility of obtaining satisfaction in a surreptitious, primitively malicious tone: 'Er ist ja noch nicht fort,' the underlying message being: you can still get him! When this approach fails to produce the desired response, he resorts to the more direct method of suggesting a possible scenario for the act of revenge, a staging to which Thusnelda will in fact adhere. '[Wenn] die Nacht sinkt' is the time lovers normally agree upon for a tryst, but in this particular case, it will provide the suitable ambiance for the 'süsse Stunde' of hate. The choice of 'sweet' already foreshadows the sadism of the drama's most repulsive episode, while the inferred love-hate relationship points to an erotically based conflict of emotions corroborated by the fifth act. It may strike one as odd that the proposal should come from the husband, the injured party, so to speak; however, he could well be unconsciously jealous of the younger man's attractiveness, his power over Hermann's possession.

As noted, her impassioned entreaty on Ventidius' behalf would seem to intimate more than a mere infatuation. Therefore, by inciting her to seek revenge on her admirer, the husband achieves a double satisfaction: he destroys a potentially dangerous rival and he forces his wife to do the destroying as a reconfirmation of her loyalty to him.

The full exposure of Ventidius' duplicity causes Thusnelda to turn on everything and everyone, including herself: 'Geh, geh, ich bitte dich! Verhasst ist alles, / Die Welt mir, du mir, ich: lass mich allein!' (1:598). A very immature, irrational outburst, it may none the less expose her true sentiments under the duress of strong emotions.[70] The self-hatred has in all likelihood the same source as that felt by Penthesilea once she believes that she has failed as a woman to captivate the man she loves: 'Staub lieber, als ein Weib sein, das nicht reizt' (1:363). In *Penthesilea* there is a major misunderstanding occasioned largely by cultural differences, whereas in *Die Hermannsschlacht* the wronged woman must confront the distressing realization verified by tangible proof that a more civilized rival, Livia, has gained her suitor's fidelity and that her person has been and will be used to provide a token of that very fidelity:[71]

Nun bin ich [Ventidius] jenes Wortes eingedenk,
Das deinem schönen Mund, du weisst,
Als ich zuletzt dich sah, im Scherz entfiel.
Hier schick ich von dem Haar, das ich dir zugedacht,
Und das sogleich, wenn Hermann sinkt,
Die Schere für dich ernten wird,
Dir eine Probe zu, mir klug verschafft.   (1:597)

Kleist conveys the tremendous impact this disclosure has upon Thusnelda by having her single out and requote the section referring specifically to the fate of her hair, the symbol of her vanity, and by having her immediately thereafter become speechless. The hostility towards her husband could also contain a fair measure of unconscious truth. Thusnelda is portrayed as the neglected younger wife whose husband is too preoccupied with affairs of state to pay court to her conceit and who moreover exploits her as a tool to further his political aspirations.

Throughout this dialogue one gains the unavoidable impression that Hermann, the manipulator, always knows the correct string to pull in order to obtain the desired reflex from his puppet wife. And yet the scene terminates with an unexpected gesture and supporting statement: 'HER-MANN *er fällt vor ihr nieder.* / Thuschen! Mein schönes Weib! Wie rührst du mich!' (1:598). One's first impulse, based on experience, is to interpret this as a further example of good acting since he quite intentionally brought on this crisis in his wife, and the seeds of revenge, surreptitiously planted, do in fact take root. On the other hand, the act of prostrating himself before his wife constitutes a visual image of worship and servitude. After all she has just rejected him, and this proud man, who in the next scene will equate his personal fate with that of the whole country, does not kneel lightly before anyone. From the manner of address: '*Mein schönes Weib!*,' two considerations come to mind: he obviously views her as *his* possession but more importantly in his eyes, she is a physically attractive woman. Although Kleist does not pursue the issue directly, he none the less provides signs of a sexual dependency of the male upon the female, what Brecht was to lampoon as 'sexuelle Hörigkeit,'[72] a submissiveness which proves disruptive in *Amphitryon*, *Der zerbrochene Krug*, *Das Käthchen von Heilbronn*, and *Prinz Friedrich von Homburg*, and destructive in *Penthesilea* and *Die Hermannsschlacht*. As I remarked earlier, Hermann puts away his weapons before he confronts his wife, a concrete affirmation of his vulnerability, and the opening of the next scene demonstrates that concern for his spouse is capable of distracting him from the serious campaign at hand:

EGINHARDT Mein Fürst, die Hörner rufen dich! Brich auf!
Du darfst, willst du das Schlachtfeld noch erreichen,
Nicht, wahrlich! einen Augenblick mehr säumen.
HERMANN *steht auf.*
Gertrud!
EGINHARDT Was fehlt der Königin?
HERMANN   Nichts, nichts!
Die Frauen der Thusnelda treten auf.
Hier! Sorgt für eure Frau! Ihr seht, sie weint.
Er nimmt Schild und Spiess.
Astolf ist von dem Kriegsplan unterrichtet?   (1:598)

Love can be the male's most dangerous delusion. Not until after Hermann has attended to the needs of his wife, does he take up his arms and turn to pressing military matters.

When Hermann takes leave of his spouse, he informs her, 'Thusnelda, mein geliebtes Weib! / Astolf hat deine Rache übernommen' (1:599), the second time that he raises the issue of vengeance or the third if one includes his insinuation: 'Er ist ja noch nicht fort' (1:597). Also, in each of the two specific instances, he deliberately maintains that the avenging act belongs rightly to her: 'Astolf hat *deine* Rache übernommen' and 'Schlägt *dir* der Rache süsse Stunde ja!' (1:597). He therefore continues to follow a practice adopted earlier to handle his mate: he defines a matter of national importance (Ventidius does incarnate the most deplorable aspects of Roman civilization) in terms which Thusnelda with her limited personal scope can readily comprehend. Once again this approach bears fruit:

THUSNELDA *steht auf.* An dem Ventidius?
Sie drückt einen heissen Kuss auf seine Lippen.
                                                                                      Überlass ihn mir!
   Ich habe mich gefasst, ich will mich rächen!
HERMANN Dir?
THUSNELDA   *Mir!* [Kleist's emphasis] Du sollst mit mir zufrieden sein.
HERMANN Nun denn, so ist der erste Sieg erfochten!   (1:599)

What does this passionate kiss represent? Is it only an attempt to convince herself and is it really meant for her husband or merely dictated by the circumstances? Its positioning between the two references to Ventidius suggests an ulterior motive reinforced by the imperative: 'Überlass ihn mir!' Because she cannot have Ventidius, she will destroy him. The pleasure of avenging herself she shall share with no one; he belongs to *her*. On the conscious level she justifies her stance as a means of living up to Hermann's expectations, a rather ironic rationalization if one takes into consideration that she is simply responding predictably to her husband's prompting. None the less, Hermann interprets her new resolve as a good omen, as a sign of having won a collaborator to the cause. On this occasion, however, he is either deceived or deluding himself, for her determination to seek revenge amounts to a totally self-centred response to damaged pride and thwarted passion. Kleist designed this crucial husband-and-wife confrontation both to demonstrate Hermann's exceptional talent for manipulating others, for putting them into a situation where they have to react as programmed, and to denote an undercurrent of tension inherent within this marital relationship. The drama generally confirms Hermann's perceptions and assessments except for those involving the person who should be closest to him, his spouse.[73]

   The fifth act traces the more or less successful realization of Hermann's plan on both the domestic and national levels. Only too late does Varus come to realize that his opponent is not the noble savage but the blond barbarian: 'So kann man blondes Haar und blaue Augen haben, / Und doch so falsch sein, wie ein Punier?' (1:608). Hermann exhibits his usual guile in his secret instructions to the guides to ignore Varus' command on linguistic grounds and in his tactical position enabling him to attack the enemy from the rear:

> Marbod und Hermann
> Verständen heimlich sich, in dieser Fehde,
> Und so wie der im Antlitz mir [Varus],
> So stände der mir schon im Rücken,
> Mich hier mit Dolchen in den Staub zu werfen. (1:605)

The conspirator wields the dagger to stab his unsuspecting victim in the back. This disparaging, if not cowardly image of Hermann stands in quite noticeable opposition to the more heroic dimensions attributed to the Roman leader. Once again Kleist confronts the audience with a moral dilemma. When Varus learns from Aristan of his German allies' desertion, he retorts, 'scharf. Und du, Verräter, folgst dem Aufruf nicht?' (1:608). Varus, assuming that any decent German would in fact heed Hermann's call to arms, repudiates his only loyal ally as a traitor and then, in complete honesty with himself, acknowledges, 'Dass mir der Schlechtste just, / Von allen deutschen Fürsten, bleiben muss! - / Doch, kann es anders sein?' (1:608). Also, once he decides to do battle with the foe, he reluctantly orders the slaughter of his unfaithful German allies only because 'Es fehlt [ihm] hier an Stricken, sie zu binden!' (1:608). Why did Kleist opt to include this further justification for an unavoidable act of self-defence, justifiable from a military point of view? Although Varus' more ethically tenable stance contrasts sharply with Hermann's gratuitous cruelty, the real villain is Rome, best exemplified in Ventidius' duplicity. But, as Hermann asserts, Varus has become 'Germaniens Henkersknecht' (1:610), the willing 'Knecht' of a despicable 'Henker,' and hence must be eliminated.

Whereas the mutiny of Rome's allies adds yet another ominous detail to the accumulation of the conqueror's misfortunes, an apparent revolt within the ranks of Hermann's own forces has the paradoxical effect of strengthening the national cause. Kleist's deft juxtaposition of the two insurrections demonstrates Hermann's mastery of the situation not only on the home but on the enemy front. As if on cue, Egbert, the leader of the German discontents, announces to his leader, 'Dein Heer verweigert mutig dir den Dienst; / Es folgt zum Sturm nach Rom dir wenn du willst, / Doch in des wackern Marbod Lager nicht' (1:609–10). Now, of their own accord, Hermann's people express their determination to unite against the common foe and a categorical refusal to fight against a fellow German, the prerequisite frame of mind proposed by Hermann in act one and now skilfully engendered by him within his own tribe. The conclusion of this scene designed for the propagation of patriotic sentiment continues to underscore Hermann's absolute position. Having faced a potential uprising, he demands a sign of obedience and loyalty from the ringleader: 'Noch eh die Sonn entwich, das merk dir wohl, / Legst du [Egbert] ihn [a Roman eagle] hier zu Füssen *mir* darnieder!' (1:610) and emphasizes by repetition that Marbod's strategically superior position can be attributed to his adherence to his, Hermann's, summons: 'Auf *meinen* Ruf, ihr Brüder, müsst ihr wissen, / Steht er auf jenen Höhn durch eine Botschaft / *Mir*, vor vier Tagen, heimlich schon verbunden!' (1:610).[74] He insists upon exclusive credit for the present turn of events, signalled by the prominent first position of the 'Mir' and 'Auf meinen Ruf.'[75]

The secondary literature most frequently raises the morality issue, which we have already dealt with at considerable length, in connection with the series of scenes climaxing in the summary execution of the noble Roman Septimius. Even before the victim appears before his judge, Hermann and Winfried make sport of a generous enemy who tried to make restitution for his men's excesses:

HERMANN Das gute Herz!
WINFRIED   Wo stahl er doch die Säckel?
HERMANN Dein Nachbar auf der Rechten oder Linken?
WINFRIED Er presst mir Tränen aus.   (1:611)

According to Linn, this 'deliberate drollery fulfills its purpose: it prevents sympathy for an enemy who, like his ilk, must die,'[76] but surely the underlying sadism leaves the spectator uncomfortable, for Hermann is a man who, in Burckhardt's apt formulation, 'enjoys his work.'[77]

HERMANN *kalt.*
    Dein Schwert, Septimius Nerva, du musst sterben.
SEPTIMIUS – Mit wem sprech ich?
HERMANN   Mit Hermann, dem Cherusker,
    Germaniens Retter und Befreier
    Von Roms Tyrannenjoch!
SEPTIMIUS   Mit dem Armin? –
    Seit wann führt der so stolze Titel?

HERMANN Seit August sich so niedre zugelegt.
SEPTIMIUS So ist es wahr? Arminius spielte falsch?
  Verriet die Freunde, die ihn schützen wollten? (1:611–12)

The stage direction '*kalt*' and the abruptness of Hermann's first statement
to the unsuspecting Septimius suggest the matter-of-fact composure of
a butcher about to slaughter an animal, a glaring lack of compassion.
The dramatic structure encourages the spectator to compare this situation
to the one faced by the Roman commander a few scenes before. Whereas
Varus reluctantly and justifiably issues the order to destroy his rebellious
allies because to do otherwise would be suicidal for his own forces,
Hermann, under no immediate pressure, derives pleasure from his harsh
treatment of a noble enemy whom the circumstances of an undeclared
war have delivered into his hands. Moreover, Hermann's unequivocal
declaration of his supreme position contrasts noticeably with his earlier
designation of Marbod as 'Deutschlands Oberherrscher' with 'die Ver-
pflichtung / Das Vaterland von dem Tyrannenvolk zu säubern' and of himself as Marbod's 'Knecht' (1:560). Again the play provides a warning that
this is not the type of man who would lightly renounce his absolute power.
  The moral issue is not clear cut. Perhaps Septimius really does believe
in the sincerity of Roman friendship, but since Hermann and with him
the audience know full well that Rome really intends to put an end to
the German nation, then Septimius, the unconscious instrument, must
be removed along with the conscious instrument, Varus.
  After Septimius surrenders his sword, expecting to be treated as a
captive according to the 'Siegerpflicht' of the military code, Hermann's
sarcastic response: 'An Pflicht und Recht! Sieh da, so wahr ich lebe! /
Er hat das Buch von Cicero gelesen. / Was müss tich tun, sag an, nach
diesem Werk?' (1:612) implies his familiarity with Rome's accommodating
surface morality made possible by Roman political domination, his determination to have his fun at his victim's expense, and his aim of setting
an example for the rest of his men. In a war of self-preservation, the
enemy must be eradicated without exception. Hence, when Septimius
appeals to 'das Gefühl des Rechts, / In [Hermann's] Busens Blättern
aufgeschrieben' (1:612), Hermann, flying in the face of the traditional code
of honour, has recourse to the most basic right of national self-
determination:

HERMANN *indem er auf ihn einschreitet.*
  Du weisst was Recht ist, du verfluchter Bube,

> Und kamst nach Deutschland, unbeleidigt,
> Um uns zu unterdrücken?
> Nehmt eine Keule doppelten Gewichts,
> Und schlagt ihn tot! (1:612)[78]

There exists a very real danger that Septimius will win the audience's sympathy. In Hermann's derogatory epithet and his choice of the means of execution, one senses a primitive, vindictive approach to justice, a might-is-right stance of the 'Barbar' alluded to by the Roman. Kleist's attitude is at best ambiguous, for he allows Septimius to have the final say:[79]

> Führt mich hinweg! – hier unterlieg ich,
> Weil ich mit Helden würdig nicht zu tun!
> Der das Geschlecht der königlichen Menschen
> Besiegt, in Ost und West, der ward
> Von Hunden in Germanien zerrissen:
> Das wird die Inschrift meines Grabmals sein! (1:612–13)

Despite *Die Hermannsschlacht*'s failure to conform to usual moral expectations, the critics have reached a reluctant general consensus that circumstances excuse Hermann's stance as dictated by considerations of self-defence beyond good and evil. Koch, Gundolf, and Fricke see in the drama the glorification of the state whereby the end justifies the means, while Federn, Samuel, Kürenberg, and Streller have singled out parallels with the political manoeuvres advocated or practised by Stein and Gneisenau, Arndt or Engels. Others have sought to defend the preservation of the nation by total war (Hohoff, Linn), by the subjugation of the individual to the whole (May, Koch) and by doing onto the enemy what he would otherwise do unto you (Samuel, Kürenberg). A few commentators, however, have raised a voice of qualified dissent. 'Dieses Drama zeigt,' in Koch's view, 'mit welcher Ausschliesslichkeit und Absolutheit Kleist sich dem Vaterland zugewandt hat, wie daneben alles andere verschwindet, das Ich, die Gerechtigkeit und jeder andere sittliche Wert, wie die Natur für ihn höher steht als die Menschheit.'[80] Such a statement ignores, on the one hand, Hermann's speech of act one, scene two, in which he endorses a greater unity of nations to which Germania will belong and, on the other, the dominant function of Hermann's own ego. Streller speaks of 'die Anwendung der List gegenüber den eigenen Landsleuten, ja gegenüber der eigenen Frau,' as being 'äusserst fragwürdig, weil sie das Vertrauen untergraben muss,'[81] while Stahl deplores the extolling of nationalism leading to 'that confusion of values and that disregard for true standards of ethical conduct which is so deplorable a feature of *Die Hermannsschlacht*.'[82] But, then again, in what is clearly a struggle for survival, does Hermann have any real choice given the weakened, disunited political status of the German tribes and the double standards of the foe? If we return to Septimius' departing speech, the heroic exit with its elevated rhetoric, we must also weigh the Roman's pride as conqueror and thus his convenient blindness in not recognizing how this role implies betrayal of the Germans. As Hermann has just indicated, the enemy had no justification for the invasion of Germania other than to appease Rome's insatiable appetite for conquest. It is thus certainly by design that the more primitive, down-to-earth approach to values proves triumphant over a more complex, sophisticated, but at heart hypocritical, decadent civilization whose representative feels justified in designating a foreign people as subhuman ('Hunde in Germanien'), while voicing a high-sounding standard of behaviour.

To date, only Burckhardt, in pointing out Kleist's insistence upon 'the baptism of the gutter,'[83] has made a case for *Die Hermannsschlacht*'s more pragmatic approach to ethics in the political arena.[84] Kleist had learned from experience that the adoption of an absolute moral stance in a very imperfect world would lead inevitably to disaster. In a poem 'An den König von Preussen,' he demonstrates the deleterious effect of 'die schönste Tugend,' truth: 'Du [the king of Prussia] brauchtest Wahrheit weniger zu lieben, / Und Sieger wärst du auf dem Schlachtfeld blieben' (1:33) and a comment entitled 'Notwehr,' appearing in the *Berliner Abendblätter* on 31 October 1810 maintains that there is no moral obligation to be truthful to an adversary: 'Wahrheit gegen den Feind? Vergib mir! Ich lege zuweilen / Seine Bind um den Hals, um in sein Lager zu gehn' (1:37). One must be prepared to adopt the enemy's outlook and tactics to be able to understand him and to decide on an appropriate defence against him. This same sober insight informs several dialogues from the 'Katechismus der Deutschen.' For example, the father declares, 'Das Geschäft der Unterjochung der Erde soll er [Napoleon] mit List, Gewandtheit und Kühnheit vollziehn, und besonders, an dem Tage der Schlacht, ein grosser Feldherr sein.' (Paradoxically, Napoleon's leadership qualities correspond to those exhibited by Kleist's anti-Napoleon *Wunschbild* Hermann.) To the father's question: 'Meinst du nicht, dass er, um dieser Eigenschaften willen, Bewunderung und Verehrung verdiene?' the son retorts: 'Das wäre ebenso feig, als ob ich die Geschicklichkeit, die einem Menschen im Ringen beiwohnt, in dem Augenblick bewundern wollte, da er mich in den Kot wirft und mein Antlitz mit Füssen tritt' (2:355). Cunning, skill, and boldness are only bad in the eyes of the unfortunate receiver; however, by implication, they can be good and profitable in the eyes of their successful practitioner.

Die Hermannsschlacht may be regarded as a dramatization of many of the practical political recommendations outlined in *Il Principe*. Hermann displays that quality of *virtù* signifying in Machiavelli's usage courage, determination, ruthlessness, perseverance in the pursuit of an objective, and above all an amoral stance. Machiavelli even goes as far as to counsel a leader to 'risk the stigma of ruthlessness for the gain of unity and loyalty from his people,' (M 88). 'Caesar Borgia was known for his cruelty, yet by giving rein to it he made the Romagna a viable state, gave it an organic unity, and established peace and respect for law and order' (M 88). Of course, precisely the same may be said of Hermann whose pitiless cruelty, vis-à-vis not only the enemy but his own people, enables him to attain his goal: the unification of the German tribes under his leadership. Hermann also possesses the single-mindedness of the fanatic and hence lives up to Machiavelli's standard: 'the ruler must be deliberate in sentence and execution and certainly assured' (M 88). Hermann amply demonstrates these features in his treatment of Septimius. Even the ambush which Hermann has prepared for the Romans has a direct parallel with Machiavelli's model: 'The Duke [Caesar Borgia] was forthcoming enough and took every kind of step to convince [the Orsini, his rivals for power] of his friendship by personal gifts, horses, apparel and cash, so that they were induced to walk into his trap at Sinigaglia. Then, when they had been strangled and their subordinates reduced to obedience, he felt his authority in the Romagna reasonably firmly established' (M 51). Kleist has fabricated an even more tangled web of deceit: while the Romans believe that they have duped a gullible, naïve Hermann into becoming their unwitting tool by offering him their friendship and gifts (for instance, the quadriga of the first act), they are at the same time being outwitted and outmanoeuvred by the barbarian 'so that they [are] induced to walk into his trap [in the Teutoburg Forest].' Kleist together with Machiavelli would seem to be arguing in favour of moral relativity in the political arena where the only thing that really counts is success.

The inhuman, sadistic episode concluding with the dispatch of Septimius is succeeded by a warm, sentimental moment disclosing in Hermann a very human weakness triggered by the 'Chor der Barden' '[mit] ihrem herzerhebenden Gesang' (1:613). According to Friedrich Dahlmann's testimony of 1859, Kleist recited these verses 'mit einem so unwiderstehlichen

Herzensklange der Stimme, dass sie [ihm] noch immer in den Ohren tönen.'[85] Both the stage directions and the dialogues directly following the chorus register the equally overwhelming effect of these lines upon the otherwise self-possessed Hermann:

Hermann hat sich, mit vorgestützter Hand, an den Stamm einer Eiche gelehnt. - Feierliche Pause. - Die Feldherren sprechen heimlich mit einander.
WINFRIED *nähert sich ihm.* Mein Fürst, vergib! Die Stunde drängt,
    Du wolltest uns den Plan der Schlacht -
HERMANN *wendet sich.*   Gleich, gleich! -
    - Du, Bruder, sprich für mich, ich bitte dich.
Er sinkt, heftig bewegt, wieder an die Eiche zurück.
EIN HAUPTMANN Was sagt er?
EIN ANDERER   Was?
WINFRIED   Lass ihn. - Er wird sich fassen.
    Kommt her, dass ich den Schlachtplan euch entdecke!   (1:613-14)

Patriotic feeling as accentuated by the oak, symbolic of native strength, occasions a strong, emotional upheaval, but Kleist may also be presenting to his audience a disguised homage to art and its ability to influence even the most calculating of man. Poetry and music, united in the service of a political aim, render one of the most aggressive of Kleist's protagonists momentarily incapacitated. It is thus no accident that the 'Chor der Barden,' positioned 'auf dem Hügel, wo die Fackeln schimmern' (1:613), assumes the same function and achieves the same effect that Kleist envisioned for *Germania*. His introduction to this political periodical reads in imitation of *Die Hermannsschlacht*: 'Hoch, auf dem Gipfel der Felsen, soll sie [*Germania*] sich stellen und den Schlachtgesang herab donnern ins Tal! Dich, o Vaterland, will sie singen; und deine Heiligkeit und Herrlichkeit; und welch ein Verderben seine Wogen auf dich heranwälzt! Sie will herab-steigen, wenn die Schlacht braust, und sich, mit hochrot glühenden Wangen, unter die Streitenden mischen, und ihren Mut beleben, und ihnen Unerschrockenheit und Ausdauer und des Todes Verachtung ins Herz giessen' (2:376). Kleist appreciated and attempted to turn to account the propaganda potential of art. The sacred nature of the oak, Hermann's veneration for his fatherland and the semi-holy status occupied by the 'Barden' in German society also imply a religious moment reminiscent of that experienced by the iconoclasts in 'Die heilige Cäcilie oder die Gewalt der Musik.' This unaccustomed weakness and lack of resolve in

Hermann catch the others present fully unprepared and Winfried is obliged to assume temporary command.

The second verse of the 'Chor der Barden' merits close scrutiny since it adds to the humanizing effect of this scene. Ironically, the chorus first tells Hermann, 'Du wirst nicht wanken und nicht weichen, / Vom Amt, das du dir kühn erhöht' (1:614) at the very moment he proves incapable of occupying the office which, as the song notes, he created for himself. The next two lines: 'Die Regung wird dich nicht beschleichen, / Die dein getreues Volk verrät' caution against compassionate concerns that could weaken his determination to defend his people, a further justification for his brutal treatment of Septimius, and point to his present state of vulnerability brought about by a poetic-musical expression of his country's fate. (Although his concern for the fatherland may be a personal weakness, he associates its destiny with his own: he is Cheruska; he decides what his people think and do [1:599].) The chorus then concludes: 'Du bist so mild, o Sohn der Götter, / Der Frühling kann nicht milder sein: / Sei schrecklich heut, ein Schlossenwetter, / Und Blitze lass dein Antlitz spein!' (1:614). At first, the 'mild' would hardly seem an appropriate characterization for a man who derives such conspicuous pleasure from destroying his enemy, but only an act of will made possible his unqualified hatred of the enemy (he shares with the Romans many of their positive as well as negative features) and he is capable of feeling some pity, what the chorus calls a 'Regung,' for a good Roman; however, a desperate political situation will not allow him to indulge in such human emotions. Also, we may assume that the chorus, voicing the fabricated will of the people, is taken in by Hermann's deceptive social persona of the family man dedicated to 'das sanftre Ziel' (1:548). Significantly, as soon as the song ends, Hermann reverts back to his customary role – the leader of decisive words and actions:

Die Musik schweigt. – Kurze Pause. – Ein Hörnertusch in der Ferne.
EGBERT Ha! Was war das?
HERMANN *in ihre Mitte tretend.* Antwortet! Das war Marbod!
Ein Hörnertusch in der Nähe.
  Auf! – Mana und die Helden von Walhalla!
Er bricht auf. (1:614)

The last section of this scene raises the problem of how to treat those Germans who have gone over to the Roman side. With the object of

German unity in mind, Hermann wants all hostility to be directed solely at the foe: 'Es soll kein deutsches Blut, / An diesem Tag, von deutschen Händen fliessen!' (1:614). In a formulation sounding like a Christian admonition but excluding the command to love one's enemy, he tries to channel the desire for revenge away from members of his own race to the foreign invader: 'Vergebt! Vergesst! Versöhnt, umarmt und liebt euch! / Das sind die Wackersten und Besten, / Wenn es nunmehr die Römerrache gilt!' (1:615). But, once again, Kleist provides a veiled suggestion that this position was neither easily won nor is it easily maintained: 'Hinweg! – Verwirre das Gefühl mir nicht! / Varus und die Kohorten, sag ich dir; / Das ist der Feind, dem dieser Busen schwillt!' (1:615). Hermann must exercise self-discipline in order to stir up in himself the necessary enmity towards the Romans, while suppressing his desire to retaliate against their German allies. For the typical Kleistian protagonist, all is well, provided his/her feeling, the intuitive being, remains in union with his/her environment. In this case, with the imperative proceeded by an emphatic 'Hinweg!,' there is every indication that he has achieved an apparent harmony only at considerable personal expense. An individual with a pronounced vindictive streak, he would like nothing better than to avenge himself on the German renegades and thus his much discussed 'Römerhass' may represent in part a sublimation of his animosity towards his own kind who have turned traitor. Whereas the underlying motivation is clearly irrational (revenge), the calculating mind regulates and conducts the emotive energy into one path: the annihilation of the external foe. In speaking of 'Kleists Angst vor der Vernunft, die in dem Worte "Verwirre das Gefühl mir nicht!" zum Ausdruck kommt,'[86] Korff fails to take into account that the imperative occurs in the context of dealing with Rome's German allies. If anything, the mind, by practising extreme self-control, triumphs over mixed feelings produced not by good Romans, but by bad Germans.[87] Since Hermann gains his position by a Pyrrhic victory of patriotic sentiment over a desire for vengeance, his stance can scarcely be designated 'die Verherrlichung des absoluten Nationalhasses.'[88]

In the case of Hermann, we are made to sense a strong emotional undercurrent held in check; in contrast, the following Thusnelda-Ventidius sequence delineates the consequences of an unbridled irrational eruption as it breaks upon its unsuspecting victim. Thusnelda's revenge has elicited comments ranging from 'grandios'[89] to 'das Abscheulichste, was je die grausame Phantasie Kleists ersann.'[90] As I have already demonstrated, there has been a basic misunderstanding shared by most critics[91] as to the exact nature of the relationship between the German princess and her Roman suitor. Streller, Fischer, and Federn, however, do recognize and pay tribute to the 'geniale Psychologie'[92] with which this scene is constructed, while Fischer alludes to Hermann's use of psychology[93] on his wife who, like most of the other protagonists, becomes one of his unwitting instruments in the greater scheme of things.

Burckhardt's designation of the incident as a 'purifying rite which is to make her "worthy again of Arminius"' I find questionable, but I do concur with his overall verdict that Kleist 'saw, and meant us to see, the purification as a descent, unredeemed and unrevoked, into bestiality.'[94] Throughout this episode, Kleist employs Thusnelda's servant Gertrud to reflect the audience's attitude and reactions to this bestiality:

> Doch, meine grosse Herrscherin,
> Hier werf ich [Gertrud] mich zu Füssen dir:
> Die Rache der Barbaren sei dir fern!
> Es ist Ventidius nicht, der mich mit Sorg erfüllt;
> Du selbst, wenn nun die Tat getan,
> Von Reu und Schmerz wirst du zusammenfallen! (1:616)

Barbarity is clearly an issue since even a German servant regards her mistress' intent as being motivated by '[die] Rache der Barbaren.' The fact that Gertrud's concern for Thusnelda's mental well-being will prove to be well founded further strengthens her credibility with the audience. Thusnelda's retort to her confidante's warning: 'Hinweg! – Er hat zur Bärin mich gemacht! / Arminius' will ich wieder würdig werden!' (1:616) echoes her parting promise to her husband: 'Du sollst mit mir zufrieden sein' (1:599). She really wants to destroy what she cannot have, but seeks to rationalize her desire for revenge as an attempt ironically to regain her husband's esteem.[95] Her response to Gertrud's refusal to be party to such cruelty divulges the full extent of her involvement which belies Hohoff's assertion of a 'gespielte Neigung Thusneldas zu Ventidius'[96] or Ryan's identification of her attitude as 'zwar nicht Liebe, wohl aber eine gewisse Sympathie.'[97]

GERTRUD *fällt ihr zu Füssen.*
    Vergebung, meine Herrscherin, Vergebung!
THUSNELDA *ihr ausweichend.*
    Die Närrin, die verwünschte, die! Sie *auch*
    Ist in das Affenangesicht verliebt!
Sie reisst ihr den Schlüssel aus der Hand und geht zu Ventidius. (1:618)

The telling word in this exchange is the 'auch.' Not only does it imply a confession that she has spontaneously made in an unguarded moment to having been in love with Ventidius, but the present tense would also suggest that she is still sexually attracted to 'das Affenangesicht,' even now as she contemplates bloody revenge. The violence with which she snatches the key from Gertrud and the determination with which she approaches her lover further underscore a degree of sexual attachment, one seconded by Ventidius' introductory speech, quite literally dripping with sensuality: 'Und wie der Waldbach fern, mit üppigem Geplätscher, / Vom Rand des hohen Felsens niederrinnt! –' (1:617). Hermann has exploited his spouse as sex bait; however, the bait has fallen in love with its catch.

The female bear performs vicariously the destructive role which Thusnelda would like to fill herself: 'Er hat zur Bärin mich gemacht!' (1:616), but for which she lacks the capability because of her female status and her physically inferior position relative to the stronger male. Kleist stresses this point by constantly insisting upon '[die] Bärin von Cheruska' (1:619), which, despite its gender, may be expected to be appropriately violent. Thusnelda even goes as far as to present the she-bear as herself:[98]

THUSNELDA Thusnelda, bist du klug, die Fürstin ists,
  Von deren Haupt, der Livia zur Probe,
  Du jüngst die seidne Locke abgelöst!
  Lass den Moment, dir günstig, nicht entschlüpfen,
  Und ganz die Stirn jetzt schmeichelnd scher ihr ab!   (1:619)

One cannot but be repulsed by the cruelty exhibited so overtly as she taunts him with the knowledge of his infidelity by paraphrasing his letter to Livia: 'Ach, wie die Borsten, Liebster, schwarz und starr, / Der Livia, deiner Kaiserin, werden stehn, / Wenn sie um ihren Nacken niederfallen!' (1:619). This represents her second allusion to her hair and the empress. (In the first reference, the formulation 'die *seidne* Locke' implies self-praise). Since she harps upon this theme – indeed, her final comment of the episode will be the third reference to her hair – we can safely assume that what really enrages her is the fact that he was prepared to exploit her source of pride in order to gain the favour of another preferred woman. In retaliation, she creates an ugly, repugnant picture of her rival in an effort to elevate herself at the empress' expense. Her conceit is further emphasized when she mocks Ventidius with his probable reward: 'Statthalter von Cheruska, grüss ich dich! / Das ist der mindste Lohn, du treuer

Knecht, / Der dich für die Gefälligkeit erwartet!' (1:619); by implication, her hair is worthy of a kingdom.

Thusnelda's final gibe and gestures of the scene are at least indicative of an excessive emotional involvement on her part:

THUSNELDA Sag ihr, dass du sie liebst, Ventidius,
   So hält sie still und schenkt die Locken dir!
Sie wirft den Schlüssel weg und fällt in Ohnmacht.   (1:620)

Although speaking sarcastically, she none the less acknowledges his sexual domination over women. The gesture of throwing away the key signifies both a death sentence and her determination to have her vengeance while the loss of consciousness is an escape from a distasteful, painful reality. In this *Liebestod*, the realization of having been spurned by a man for the sake of another woman collides with the unconscious passion for that same man. In a very real sense, however, vanity remains the main orientation involved since she unwittingly desires to gratify her thwarted love for Ventidius who has done serious damage to her self-esteem. This final act of sadistic-erotic revenge is but another manifestation of self-love: she indulges her passions.

In his interpretation of this sequence, Burckhardt maintains, 'No one is left free to abstract himself, to stand aside or above, as Thusnelda is locked in with Ventidius, as her plot is locked in with the main plot, so is Hermann with Varus and the legions, so are we with this frightful *drame à clef*.'[99] But even within this scene, someone does in fact 'stand aside or above' the action – Gertrud who reflects a 'normal' female response to the atrocity. The very key which, according to Burckhardt, includes us in this confrontation, elicits a succinct repudiation of her mistress' barbarity: 'Er [der Schlüssel] wird am Boden liegen. / – Das Ungeheu'r! Sie [Thusnelda] hält ihn in der Hand' (1:620). In designating her sovereign as a monster, she distances herself from the act and its perpetrator. One of her earlier exclamations: 'Du Furie, grässlicher, als Worte sagen – ' (1:619) and the last words of the scene further encourage the audience to share her disapproval and dissociation: 'Die Grässliche! – Ihr ewgen Himmelsmächte! / Da fällt sie sinnberaubt mir in den Arm!' (1:620). As if anticipating the moral outrage this scene would cause, Kleist included what would have to be perceived as a 'normal' recoil, thus underlining the repulsive nature of Thusnelda's revenge. It does none the less say something about the author that he chose to depict such an incident.[100]

The focal point now shifts to Marbod in what appears to be preparation for a pending power struggle between the two opposing rulers. Acting 'Arminius' Plan gemäss', the Sueven forces manage to win the 'Schlacht der Freiheit ... ehe Hermann noch den Punkt der Schlacht erreicht' (1:621).

MARBOD So traf mein tapfres Heer der Sueven wirklich
  Auf Varus früher ein, als die Cherusker?
KOMAR Sie trafen früher ihn! Arminius selbst,
  Er wird gestehn, dass du die Schlacht gewannst!
MARBOD Auf jetzt, dass ich *den Trefflichen* begrüsse!   (1:622)

Marbod's obvious interest in claiming exclusive responsibility for victory indicated by his insistence upon being confirmed as the real victor would seem at first to suggest both the deep-seated roots of the traditional rivalry and the possibility of a renewed conflict; however, as intimated by Marbod's naming Hermann 'den Trefflichen,' this dialogue anticipates a contest in German magnanimity in which each contestant will strive to outdo the other in apparent self-effacement. Also, from the relatively stronger position of being the sole victor, Marbod elevates himself by praising his rival.[101]

The final incident contributing to the play's repudiation by most commentators concerns the admirable, heroic deportment of Varus set opposite the squabbling of the German princes who argue and come to blows over the privilege of dispatching the cornered Roman commander. By concentrating upon the scene as an assault on our moral sensitivities, critics have overlooked the most important evidence of Hermann's motivation:

FUST *sich zwischen [Hermann und Varus] werfend.*
  Halt dort, Armin! Du hast *des Ruhms* genug.
GUELTAR *ebenso.* Halt, sag auch ich!
FUST   Quintilius Varus
  Ist mir, und wenn ich sinke, dem verfallen!
HERMANN *betroffen.*
  Wem? Dir? Euch? – Ha! Sieh da! Mit welchem Recht?   (1:623)

The crucial word 'Ruhm,' first mentioned by Fust, provides the basis for this clash. When the discredited princes maintain that Hermann possesses his full share, the latter is quick to defend his claim. Fust even expresses his willingness to kill Hermann, if necessary, for the right to meet Varus as a means to reinstate his reputation, but Hermann shows no sympathy for this attempt at atonement. He remains exclusively *self*-oriented and, relinquishing all rational control in the heat of the dispute, he inadvertently discloses his true feelings:

FUST Den Schandfleck wasch ich ab in seinem [Varus'] Blute,
    Das hab ich heut, das musst du wissen,
    Gestreckt am Boden heulend, mir,
    Als mir dein Brief kam, Göttlicher, gelobt!
HERMANN Gestreckt am Boden heulend! Sei verwünscht,
    Gefallner Sohn des Teut, mit deiner Reue!
    Soll ich von Schmach dich rein zu waschen,
    Den Ruhm, beim Jupiter, entbehren,
    Nach dem *ich* durch zwölf Jahre treu gestrebt?   (1:623)

Whereas in his first stage confrontation with Fust, he acknowledged the latter's noble qualities displayed in the initial fatal clash with Roman troops, he now curses him: 'Sei verwünscht' and stresses his disgrace: 'Gefallner Sohn,' something for which Fust as a victim of circumstances can not really be held accountable. Hermann hits a fellow prince while he is down. But of even greater importance is the extent to which this altercation causes Hermann, momentarily removed from the censorship of his disciplined mind, to admit that his own desire for fame has prompted his scheming against the Romans for twelve years. So adamant is he in demanding what he considers to be justly his alone that he is determined to defend his right at the most primitive level of armed combat. This involuntary confession flies in the face of statements to the effect that 'Hermann [hat] alle Ichbezogenheit überwunden'[102] or most recently, 'Hermann will seine Familie und sein Volk nicht um ruhmvoller Machtsucht willen in Kriege verwickeln, wie es z.B. Marbod tut.'[103] Moreover, at the beginning of this act, Hermann issued a categorical prohibition against the shedding of German blood: 'Es soll kein deutsches Blut, / An diesem Tag, von deutschen Händen fliessen!' (1:614), but, in this particular instance, he shows no reluctance whatever to be the first to break his own original command and engages in battle with a fellow German: 'Komm her, fall aus und triff – und verflucht sei, / Wer jenen Römer ehr berührt, / Als dieser Streit sich zwischen uns gelöst!' (1:623). As a further sign of his strong commitment to personal glory, he curses anyone who dares to touch Varus before his dispute with Fust has been settled. Even in defeat, Hermann's dominant attitude manifests itself as he tells Fust, 'Dein Schwert fällt gut. / Da nimm ihn [Varus] hin. Man kann ihn dir vertraun' (1:624). He acts as if Varus still belonged to him and, having the decision-making power of life and death, he is merely entrusting the Roman to Fust for execution. This is hardly what one would call exemplary behaviour on the part of Hermann as is asserted by Wickert when she claims, 'Hermann dagegen hat die richtige Einstellung zum Ruhm und kann daher Modell sein für die Fürsten, wie sie sich Kleist erhofft.'[104]

The pernicious influence of the drive for fame, its ability to overcome all other concerns including loyalty, obedience, and even brotherly love, is also exposed in Fust. No sooner does he wound Hermann, thus winning the right to kill Varus, then he returns, as if from a temporary alienation or delusion to his 'better' self: 'Wem? Mir? – Nein, sprich! ... / Was! Traf ich dich [Hermann]?' (1:624) and as soon as he disposes of the Roman, all of his concerns centre about the minor wound inflicted by him on his colleague: 'Hermann! Mein Bruderherz! Was hab ich dir getan? *Er fällt ihm um den Hals*' (1:624).

At the end of the scene, reason again seems to gain ascendancy as all, including Hermann, strike a note of friendship and reconciliation: 'Ich bitt euch, meine Freunde – !' (1:624). And yet, a closer scrutiny of the final conversation between Fust and Hermann reveals an underlying sour note:

FUST Hermann, du bist mir bös, mein Bruderherz,
   Weil ich den Siegskranz schelmisch dir geraubt?!
HERMANN Du bist nicht klug! Vielmehr, es macht mich lachen!
   Lass einen Herold gleich nur kommen,
   Der deinen Namen ausposaune:
   Und mir schaff einen Arzt, der mich verbindet.
Er lacht und geht ab.   (1:624–5)

Fust's query has in fact hit a responsive chord. In an attempt to simulate indifference, Hermann overreacts by resorting to laughter to conceal his anger and frustration and by magnanimously having a herald summoned to proclaim his rival's triumph. His departing laugh under the guise of nonchalance has a hollow ring and a sadistic flavour. Hermann and his fellow princes have just observed with considerable enthusiasm, if not relish, the death throes of a wounded opponent: 'DAS GEFOLGE. Triumph! Triumph! Germaniens Todfeind stürzt!' (1:624). Hermann's inappropriate laughter thus harks back to Licht's and looks forward to Hohenzollern's.

With the proclamation of Hermann as 'Germaniens Retter, Schirmer und Befreier!' (1:625) by the now united assembly of princes, Thusnelda reappears for a short but obliquely telling dialogue with her husband in the midst of this celebration. 'THUSNELDA *an seinem Busen*. Mein Geliebter!' (1:625). Both by action and word she acknowledges him only as her loved one, a further substantiation of her lack of political awareness. But, at the same time, may she not be attempting to accentuate and hence to confirm this personal relationship and ultimately to convince herself? She seeks to suppress guilt feelings since her heart has betrayed her husband, has 'committed adultery,' with a younger Roman rival. Hermann responds by addressing her as 'Mein schönes Thuschen! Heldin, grüss ich dich!' and then asking, 'Wie gross und prächtig hast du Wort gehalten?' (1:625). He has consistently used his wife solely to meet his political objectives and successfully manipulated her into a position where she had to take revenge in order to save face. Still, the punctuation is puzzling: this is not a statement but a question. Are we to assume that Hermann has not been apprised of the gruesome details which are very much in keeping with his own sadistic treatment of Septimius and, to a lesser degree, of Varus? This seems unlikely given that throughout the drama Kleist has always portrayed him as better informed than anyone else on stage. Obviously he would have no reservation in classifying her staging of Ventidius' death as 'gross und prächtig' according to his standard of permissible behaviour towards the enemy. The question mark may then imply some incipient doubt as to the purity of her motives. The conclusion of this final exchange between husband and wife tends to lend credence to a new awareness in Hermann of the fateful consequences of her involvement with Ventidius:

THUSNELDA *verwirrt*.
  Das ist geschehn. Lass sein.
HERMANN   Doch scheinst du blass?
Er betrachtet sie mit Innigkeit. – Pause.   (1:625)

Kleist added the '*verwirrt*' to the corrected, later version of the last five scenes, and by so doing, he may well have intimated his more-than-passing interest in this husband-wife-suitor triangle. Thusnelda is confused because at heart she knows that she does not deserve her husband's praise; she acted out of a sense of perverted passion and personal vengeance with no thought whatsoever for the general welfare. The 'Lass sein,' implying a reluctance to discuss an incident which she would prefer to forget, points to a loss of confidence reinforced by her physical appearance. Her 'pale' face, something over which at this moment she has no conscious control, betrays her inner turmoil. Gertrud's original warning: 'Du selbst, wenn nun die Tat getan, / Von Reu und Schmerz wirst du zusammenfallen!' (1:616) would appear to be fully justified.

The Thusnelda subplot ends here. There is every indication that Thusnelda, a pawn in her husband's game strategy, has done irreparable emotional damage to herself and one wonders about her ability to survive this crisis. Kleist does not pursue the issue any further.[105] The final stage direction, however, reaffirms Hermann's emotional dependency upon his mate. Whereas he may have some inkling of the personal cost to his wife, the 'Innigkeit' suggests that he accepts her deed as both a patriotic act and a confirmation of her love for him, a delusion shared by many, including Kurt May: 'nun erst fühlt sie sich Hermann würdig als Thusnelda, die Fürstin der Cherusker in Germanien.'[106]

'Nothing,' according to Machiavelli, 'builds up the reputation of a ruler so much as successful campaigning and proofs of his quality of leadership' (M 107). Wolf confirms the effectiveness of Hermann's exploitation of the Hally incident to unite the country behind his leadership: 'In Waffen siehst du ganz Germanien lodern, / Den Greul zu strafen, der sich ihr [Hally] verübt' (1:625), while the German princes address the Cheruskian prince as their true commander and victor: Astolf surrenders Crassus' sword to him and Wolf obediently inquires, 'Wir aber kamen her, dich zu befragen, / Wie du das Heer, das wir ins Feld gestellt, / Im Krieg nun gegen Rom gebrauchen willst?' (1:625). Despite these overt signs of respect and submission, Hermann, true to his given word, insists upon Marbod's standing as supreme commander: 'Harrt einen Augenblick, bis Marbod kömmt, / Der wird bestimmteren Befehl euch geben! – ' (1:625), and, upon the latter's entry, 'beugt ein Knie vor ihm,' exclaiming, 'Heil, Marbod, meinem edelmütgen Freund! / Und wenn Germanien meine Stimme hört: / Heil seinem grossen Oberherrn und König!' (1:626). This salutation could be sincere, but one must also bear in mind Machiavelli's admonition that a leader's 'greatness must seem to be informed by magnanimity, courage, ponderation and determination' (M 94), qualities which come to the fore in the conclusion of the drama. Also, although Hermann fulfils his part of the agreement, one which he drew up without consulting Marbod, he still sees himself in the role of king-maker. Since he has already heard from Wolf that the German tribes feel that they owe everything to him and are prepared to accept unquestioningly his leadership, he knows that Germania would indeed hear his voice. Hence, the manner in which Hermann declares his intent infers that he alone holds the real reins of power. He none the less continues to play the obedient servant, maintaining that he will not stand up until Marbod agrees to accept the contentious tribute. However, as the drama makes evident on several occasions and as is reiterated again in this scene (when told that the whole of Teutoburg lies in ruin, Hermann exclaims, 'Mag sein! Wir bauen uns ein schönres auf' [1:626]), the titular protagonist sets little store by material things.

Marbod, disclosing some reluctance to accept the title, forces Hermann to rise at which point the parts become reversed as Marbod *'beugt ein Knie vor [Hermann],'* while declaring, 'Heil, ruf ich, Hermann, dir, dem Retter von Germanien!' (1:626). Is this what Hermann secretly intended? *Die Hermannsschlacht* provides ample evidence of his being sufficiently devious and capable of setting up this scenario, but there is no direct or indirect proof other than the inference behind the conditional clause: 'Und wenn Germanien meine Stimme hört.' In this contest of magnanimity, does Marbod really have a choice? To accept Hermann's generous offer would be tantamount to appearing as an ingrate. Moreover, Hermann may be said to have set an example for his rival, one which Marbod follows to the degree of echoing Hermann's words: 'Und wenn es meine Stimme hört: / Heil seinem würdgen Oberherrn und König!' (1:626).[107] How can Marbod be expected to receive the crown from the man whose family traditionally wore it: 'Und weil die Krone sonst, zur Zeit der grauen Väter, / Bei deinem Stamme rühmlich war' (1:626)[108] and who has earned all the credit for having planned and executed the Roman defeat? If Marbod possesses any self-esteem, he has no alternative but to renounce his claim in Hermann's favour and declare him king, a choice immediately confirmed by those present: 'HERMANN *umarmt [Marbod].* / Lass diese Sach, beim nächsten Mondlicht, uns, / Wenn die Druiden Wodan opfern, / In der gesamten Fürsten Rat, entscheiden!' (1:627).

Again, one may see this speech as a noble gesture, but such an arrangement would ensure the formal ratification of his right to rule and the legitimized reunification of the tribes under his leadership, what he has been striving for from the very beginning. It is a foregone conclusion that the princes, with one exception, now support his candidacy and that the vote will constitute a mere formality. Even in the interim period, he will be expected to govern as regent.

As head of state, Hermann must forthwith deal with the exception, the rebellious unrepentant Aristan, something which he is extremely reluctant to do:[109] 'Weh mir! Womit muss ich mein Amt beginnen?' (1:627). In the case of either Septimius or Varus who tended to gain our sympathy, he displayed no compunction or indecision and may be said to have relished the administering of a death sentence. Nor did he hesitate in his willingness to sacrifice a village, his wife, or even his children to the cause. On this occasion, however, his reluctance remains consistent with his total dedication to German unification, resulting in the earlier prohibition against the taking of German lives, even those of German traitors. Hence Hermann's concern is not with Aristan the individual – he indicated his antipathy for the leader of the Ubier earlier in act three, scene five, when he addressed him in the third person – but with Aristan the symbolic head of a German tribe. The fact that this encounter takes place in a public setting witnessed by all the German princes and their followers could also have a bearing upon Hermann's behaviour, for with Machiavelli he appreciates the importance of '[being] careful about appearances' (M 92), especially since he will be making his first ruling as regent. After it becomes clear that Aristan has no remorse and persists in maintaining his short-sighted, self-centred point of view, Hermann shows himself to be the man of decisive action guaranteed to win the respect and loyalty of those present: 'Führt ihn [Aristan] hinweg und werft das Haupt ihm nieder!' or 'Führet ihn hinweg! / Was kann er sagen, das ich nicht schon weiss?' (1:628). As if written specifically as an analysis of Hermann's secret intent, Il Principe observes, 'Well-handled brutalities (if one may use the phrase about evil things) are those which are all applied sharply and simultaneously to ensure control, and not repeated, but succeeded by consideration for the welfare of the subjects' (M 59). The drastic, swift form of punishment becomes a measure of Hermann's resolve and of his absolute power over life and death, and, by its example, will undoubtedly serve as a warning for any other princes contemplating independent action. Perhaps it is by conscious design that Fust, one of Rome's former allies who stood up to Hermann a few scenes earlier, remarks in ironic support of the verdict, 'Was gilts, er weiss jetzt, wo Germanien liegt?' (1:628).

Hermann voices his concern for the 'welfare of his subjects' with his call to rise up and exterminate that predatory beast, Rome, the 'Mordbrut' in its 'Raubnest' (1:628), a choice of image which we shall pursue in the next section. Thus, Die Hermannsschlacht, in the tradition of Il Principe, furnishes a blueprint for successful rebellion against a tyrannical foreign power bent on conquest and subjugation. By an amazingly consistent display of cunning, deception, and cold calculation, Hermann, the Machiavellian schemer, has brought the German princes, his own people, his rival Marbod, his wife, and even the Romans to a point where unwittingly they have worked towards the achievement of his vision of a united

Germany under his leadership. Although Hermann has been chosen only on a temporary basis to occupy this dominant role, one which he in fact assumed from the very outset, there remains little doubt that, as in the case of Licht in *Der zerbrochene Krug*, the position will inevitably become legally permanent. Hermann has in effect gained the 'Ruhm,' 'Nach dem er durch zwölf Jahre treu gestrebt' (1:623).

THE FOX AND THE LION

Since, then, a prudent ruler must from time to time know how to handle his affairs in a bestial way, the beasts he should take as models are the fox and the lion, because the lion's strength alone will avail him little against gins, nor the wiles of the fox against the ferocity of wolves. The fox will avoid the snares and the lion will scare the wolves. Those who rely wholly on leonine qualities are fools. Deceit is essential where loyalty to a pledge would turn to his disadvantage and the reasons for giving it no longer hold good.   (M 91)

> Denn nicht ein ehrlich offner Krieg, ich denke,
> Nur eine Jagd wirds werden, wie nach Schlangen.
>
> *Die Familie Schroffenstein (1:53)*

In his description of political life, Machiavelli designates law as the proper means to regulate the affairs of men, but at the same time he recognizes that under certain conditions a reasonable approach could prove inadequate and even disastrous and hence one must be prepared to resort to the violence of the beasts. Since Kleist's political drama deals with a resistance movement against a foreign occupational force, it should come as no surprise that the protagonists on both sides, consistent with Machiavelli's pragmatic diagnosis, have recourse to bestiality to achieve their mutually exclusive aim of freedom and subjugation. As Burckhardt has aptly remarked, 'In *Die Hermannsschlacht* the beast is loose. All Kleist's works abound with animal images and metaphors; but no other is as intensely bestial as this play.'[110] One might add that in none of Kleist's works is this predominance of the animalistic element more appropriate, for a close reading of the text discloses that Kleist has consistently and consciously constructed his drama around a well-integrated poetic image based on the model of the hunt,[111] a feature which it shares with *Penthesilea*. Scene one describes the German princes as they break off from the main hunting party to discuss the fate of their country and the necessity of obtaining Hermann's leadership; the second scene provides details of the hunt, details which actually prefigure the final outcome of the play; and during the third and final scene of act one, the princes approach Hermann as part of the aftermath to the hunt: 'Das Jagen selbst ist weniger das Fest, / Als dieser heitre Augenblick, / Mit welchem sich das Fest der Jagd beschliesset!' (1:540). The sets and stage directions frequently reinforce this impression with the numerous references to the forest: '*Erster Akt. Szene: Gegend im Wald, mit einer Jagdhütte*' (1:535); '*Dritter Akt. Szene: Platz vor einem Hügel, auf welchem das Zelt Hermanns steht. Zur Seite eine Eiche, unter welcher ein grosses Polster liegt, mit prächtigen Tigerfellen* [hunting trophies] *überdeckt*' (1:563), or '*Fünfter Akt. Szene: Teutoburger Wald*' (1:600). The initial scene of the play, the very first visual impression offered to the audience, has the German princes appear before the '*Jagdhütte*' '*mit Pfeil und Bogen*' (1:535). The forest provides the fitting backdrop for not only the introductory, tone-setting hunting sequence of act one, but also for the great final hunt of act five where Hermann leads the Romans into an ambush and has them tracked down and slain like wild beasts in the '*Teutoburger Wald*.'[112] Varus lays a trap for Marbod which is ultimately intended for Hermann as well, but is caught in the snare set for him by his more cunning opponent.

In the opening speech, a character called 'Wolf' inadvertently raises the main issue:

Und Hermann, der Cherusker, endlich,
Zu dem wir, als dem letzten Pfeiler, uns,
Im allgemeinen Sturz Germanias, geflüchtet,
Ihr seht es, Freunde, wie er uns verhöhnt:
Statt die Legionen mutig aufzusuchen,
In seine Forsten spielend führt er uns,
Und lässt den Hirsch uns und den Ur besiegen.   (1:535)

Representative of the German princes, Wolf cannot comprehend why Hermann does not engage the foe in an openly declared battle: 'die Legionen mutig aufzusuchen.' Later, in a conversation with Ventidius, Hermann, in a typical example of his double-talk, explains:

Seit jener Mordschlacht, die den Ariovist vernichtet,
Hab ich im Felde mich nicht mehr gezeigt;
Die [Kleist's emphasis] Weisung werd ich nimmermehr vergessen:
Es war, im Augenblick der grässlichen Verwirrung,
Als ob ein Geist erstünde und mir sagte,
Dass mir das Schicksal hier nicht günstig wäre – .   (1:549)

Hermann portrays the decisive victory of the Romans over Ariovist at which he was present as so intimidating that he then determined not to appear again on the field of battle. Indeed, this is his intent, for as he points out to his fellow princes in that puzzling third scene of the first act:

Wie wollt ihr doch, ihr Herrn, mit diesem Heer des Varus
Euch messen – an eines Haufens Spitze,
Zusammen aus den Waldungen gelaufen,
Mit der Kohorte, der gegliederten,
Die, wo sie geht und steht, des Geistes sich erfreut? (1:544)

A primitive society of hunters would not stand a chance against a well-disciplined Roman army that is better armed: 'Gerüstet mit der ehrnen Waffe,' more skilled in the art of war: 'Die ganze Kunst des Kriegs entfaltend' and more experienced: 'In den vier Himmelsstrichen ausgelernt' (1:544). Good intentions are not enough. An open confrontation on a battle field would be suicidal: 'Nein, Freunde, so gewiss der Bär dem schlanken Löwen / Im Kampf erliegt, so sicherlich / Erliegt ihr, in der *Feldschlacht*, diesen Römern' (1:544). As in his dialogue with Ventidius, Hermann is telling the truth, but not the whole truth. When he confesses to the Roman legate that Ariovist's devastating defeat in battle convinced him 'Dass [ihm] das Schicksal hier nicht günstig wäre' (1:549), Ventidius assumes, and is meant to assume, that the disheartened German leader will be compliant to Roman wishes; however, Hermann's statement contains a veiled reference, meaningful only in retrospect, to the reasoning behind his present behaviour: since he once witnessed what would happen if he foolishly opted to meet the foe in open battle,[113] he has resolved to defeat the invaders by another strategy dictated by the pattern of the hunt and thus more suited to a 'Haufen,' 'Zusammen aus den Waldungen gelaufen' (1:544). The frequent allusion to the forest and game animals and the general prevalence of hunting vocabulary and images prove that Kleist chose to represent the German 'Horden' as a primitive society of hunters whose livelihood depends on the forest. A wise commander takes advantage of his troops' strengths and endeavours to put the enemy at a disadvantage. Moreover, hunting implies deception, stealth, cunning, baiting, and superior knowledge of the terrain, those qualities best acquired and exploited in a forest setting: 'In seine Forsten *spielend* führt er [Hermann] uns / Und lässt den Hirsch uns und den Ur besiegen' (1:535).
The present participle 'spielend' underscores another important aspect

of the dramatic model, the element of play. In the first instance, hunting is synonymous with survival but it also provides a means of entertainment, a so-called sport. In this context it should be noted that the quarry is commonly called 'the game.' Hunting as a contest – one of the central motifs in almost all of Kleist's works (*agon*) – in which one matches one's wits against the intended victim, helps to explain but does not excuse Hermann's strongly sadistic bent in the cat-and-mouse game he plays with the Romans. His lack of humanitarian or compassionate feelings towards the enemy corresponds to the pleasure of the hunter as he faces the cornered prey and slaughters it without compunction. Also the verb 'führen' singles out Hermann as the 'leading' figure of the drama, and, according to Wolf's formulation, he has others triumph over the 'Hirsch' and the 'Ur' by means of this role. Kleist associates the Romans with the buck and the Germans with the aurochs and thus a suitably selected hunting image intimates in the very first speech of the play that Hermann is in indirect control of both the Romans and the Germans, the manipulation being suggested by the causative use of 'lassen.'

In *Die Hermannsschlacht* human beings are persistently equating others and even themselves with hunted creatures. Moreover, how one sees the enemy, in terms of what beast, does in fact influence the audience's attitude towards the person being so characterized. Kleist considered human animalism to be such an important theme that he included an actual discussion of its implications in the text – in the scene where Hermann educates his wife as to the intent of their alleged allies:

HERMANN Was ist der Deutsche in der Römer Augen?
THUSNELDA Nun, doch kein Tier, hoff ich – ?
HERMANN   Was? – Eine Bestie,
  Die auf vier Füssen in den Wäldern läuft!
  Ein Tier, das, wo der Jäger es erschaut,
  Just einen Pfeilschuss wert, mehr nicht,
  Und ausgeweidet und gepelzt dann wird!   (1:570)

Since the Romans refuse to respect the customs and inalienable rights of others and assume that the world exists only to enhance their way of life, an assertion which harks back to Hermann's main criticism of the Italian character in act one, scene three, they do not treat their conquered peoples as human beings but as game animals to be hunted down and exploited. Firmly convinced that this assessment does reflect the Roman attitude towards himself and his people – and the drama furnishes sufficient proof to substantiate his claim – Hermann feels quite justified and has no moral qualms in handling the enemy in the same inhuman fashion. 'Deceit,' Machiavelli contends, 'is essential when loyalty to a pledge would turn to [one's] disadvantage and the reasons for giving it no longer hold good' (M 91), an accurate description of Hermann's policy as it relates to his alliance with the Romans. Hence, both sides of the conflict are guilty of 'die verwünschte Menschenjägerei' (1:570), and any difference is merely one of degree, for the beast figures prominently in how the Romans view the Germans and vice versa, how Hermann manipulates both the enemy and his own people, and how Thusnelda, ironically the one to curse 'Menschenjägerei,' disposes of Ventidius.

The animal most frequently mentioned in *Die Hermannsschlacht*, the 'Ur,' a slow-moving, primitive but none the less powerful creature peculiar to the German forest, is associated with the less sophisticated Germans both by Hermann: 'Die deutschen Uren!' (1:565) and by Varus who refers to the German leader as 'Fürst der Uren' (1:622). I have already noted that Wolf first mentions it in the opening speech of the play, and quite appropriately so, for in a figurative sense, Hermann must wage his real battle more against the attitudes of his own people than against the foreign invader. The 'Ur' then becomes a major concern of the second scene introduced immediately by Thusnelda's salutation: 'Heil dem Ventidius Carbo! Römerritter! / Dem kühnen Sieger des gehörnten Urs!' (1:537). This speech produces an antithesis between the gallant, chivalrous Roman 'Ritter,' a term that is employed exclusively to describe the culturally more advanced Romans, and the crude beast, both of which occur in the emphatic final position. Since the Germans are addressed only as 'Jäger' in this scene, the playwright may well be hinting at a further contrast between the warrior accustomed to doing battle in the open field from a chariot (it should be noted that the quadriga is unmanned, indicative of its alien presence in this forest where it has limited manoeuvrability) and the hunter who feels at home in this environment. On the surface it would seem that Ventidius has vanquished the 'Ur,' an insinuation of his alleged superiority over the barbarian, but as John Gearey explains, 'Deceptive appearances ... are shifted in this play to [Hermann's] side and work in his favor – indeed it is he who manufactures them.'[114] Although the Roman official receives the credit, in reality the aurochs has been cut down by Thusnelda more or less at Hermann's instigation. It was a 'set-up.' The Germans and their guests merely waited in a blind along the edge of a well-established game run ('Wo kreuzend durch die Forst die Wildbahn bricht' [1:538]), until the unsuspecting quarry arrived and was ambushed in a manner which foreshadows how the Romans will be set up by Hermann for the kill in the Teutoburg Forest. The incident also implies Hermann's willingness to sacrifice members of his own tribe to achieve his ultimate end and therefore serves as a warning that the primitive beast, the German, can turn upon the incautious hunter and destroy him.

Two additional features linked to the 'Ur' enhance its unifying function within the play. The description of the aurochs includes no less than four times a direct mention of its horns, its potentially destructive weapon: 'Dem kühnen Sieger des gehörnten Urs!'; 'Man schleppt ihn bei den Hörnern schon herbei' (1:537); 'Als es gekrümmt, mit auf die Brust / Gesetzten Hörnern'; and 'Heil ruf ich Ventidius noch einmal, / Des Urs, des hornbewehrten, Sieger' (1:538). This repetition, surely consciously done, ties in with Hermann's order which concludes this hunting scene: 'Wohlauf, ihr Jäger! Lasst das *Horn* dann schmettern, / Und bringt sie im Triumph nach Teutoburg!' (1:539) and with the final stage direction: '*Hörnermusik.*' Since the German horn was actually fashioned from the horn of the quarry, it gains the force of an acoustic leitmotif conjuring up the hunt. Although Kleist was undoubtedly aware that the Romans also made use of horns in battle, *Die Hermannsschlacht* associates the 'Hörner' exclusively with the Germans: they sound for the first time near the end of the introductory hunt scene: '*Man hört Hörner in der Ferne*' (1:537), at Hermann's command with the entry of the Roman army into Teutoburg: 'HERMANN. Holla, die Hörner! Dieser Tag / Soll für Cheruska stets ein Festtag sein! / *Hörnermusik*' (1:578), and most suitably just before the Germans ambush the Romans in the Teutoburg Forest: '*Ein Hörnertusch in der Ferne*' (1:614).

The second leitmotif linked to the 'Ur' and providing additional textual unity can be ascertained in the frequent references to the neck, a symbol both of vulnerability and servitude. A hunter often has recourse to the neck shot, one of the surest methods of felling an animal, and hence the beast of act one is brought down 'mit pfeildurchbohrtem Nacken' (1:537). Moreover, it has become a commonly recognized symbolic gesture to place one's foot upon the vanquished foe's neck, a particularly vulnerable part of human anatomy as well.[115]

Rom, dieser Riese, der, das Mittelmeer beschreitend,
Gleich dem Koloss von Rhodus, trotzig,
Den Fuss auf Ost und Westen setzet,

Des Parthers mutgen Nacken hier,
Und dort den tapfern Gallier niedertretend.   (1:535)

The neck images support the tendency to regard human beings as stalked
quarry as, for example, in Wolf's speech, combining the real with the
metaphorical:

Wie durch den Hals des Urs Thusneldens sichre Hand
Den Pfeil gejagt: o Hermann! könnten wir
Des Krieges ehrnen Bogen spannen,
Und, mit vereinter Kraft, den Pfeil der Schlacht zerschmettern
So durch den Nacken hin des Römerheeres jagen,
Das in den Feldern Deutschlands aufgepflanzt!   (1:540)

But more significantly it is the Romans who, by their design to dominate
the world, view the conquered peoples as mere animals to serve the glory
of Rome. Hence, Wolf is offended that Hermann '[beugt] den Nacken
/ Dem Joch, das dieser Römer bringt' (1:545); Septimius, although of
apparent noble disposition, must still be eliminated as 'der Halsring von
der Kette' (1:611); Hermann sees himself as the 'Befreier / Von Roms
Tyrannenjoch' (1:611); and Egbert refuses to be party to 'Die Sklavenkette,
die der Römer bringt / Den deutschen Brüdern um den Hals zu legen'
(1:609). The 'Chor der Barden' best captures this note of subjugation:

Wir litten *menschlich* seit dem Tage,
Da jener Fremdling eingerückt;
...
Doch endlich drückt des Joches Schwere,
Und abgeschüttelt will es sein!   (1:613)

Persons, degraded as beasts of burden, insist upon their *human* qualities
and upon their first right to be free.

The second animal consistently equated with the Germans is the sheep,
first alluded to in the concluding speech of the drama's initial scene: 'Es
bricht der Wolf, o Deutschland, / In deine Hürde ein, und deine Hirten
streiten / Um eine Handvoll Wolle sich' (1:537). Not only the victims but
also their persecutors, represented by Ventidius, characterize the Germans
in this uncomplimentary fashion: 'Er [Hermann] ist ein Deutscher. / In
einem Hämmling ist, der an der Tiber graset / Mehr Lug und Trug, muss
ich dir [Varus] sagen, / Als in dem ganzen Volk, dem er gehört' (1:576).

This animal image shares with the 'Ur' a sense of innocence, a low degree of intelligence, and an implied ease of manipulation. All claim this exploitable potential: the Romans, the German princes in their aristocratic attitude and especially Hermann who, in a revealing comment, asserts, 'Den Widder lass sich zeigen, mit der Glocke, / So folgen, glaub mir, alle anderen' (1:585). In addition, Hermann shows the same willingness to manipulate people in his treatment of his wife. If a hunter sets a trap for a predatory beast, it is common practice to use a defenceless creature such as a sheep or goat as bait. One detects this basic hunting technique in Hermann's aside: 'Er [Ventidius] riecht die Fährt ihr [Thusnelda] ab, ich wusst es wohl' (1:551) and it receives further substantiation when he addresses his spouse as Ventidius' 'Schäfchen' (1:569). In this hunting analogy, sustained into the second and third acts, Hermann portrays both wife and enemy as animals, the one picking up the scent of the other, and, by implication, Hermann is setting up his mate as bait to entice an unsuspecting prey into a trap as part of a comprehensively worked-out scheme.

Burckhardt has maintained, 'The noble speeches, generous acts and grand exits will be given to the "villains", while the "heroes", more often than not, will be without manliness or dignity,'[116] an assertion that appears to contradict Kurt May's evaluation: 'Unaufhörlich, wo von Römern und römischem Wesen die Rede ist, werden sie in Bildern und Gleichnissen als die Raubtiere verflucht und geschmäht, die alles Lebendige überfallen und die mit jeder erdenklichen Gewalt und List zu Tode gehetzt werden müssen.'[117] In a sense, both critics are correct. Kleist has given an appearance nobility to the enemy, while the oppressed relegate their oppressors to the bestial realm. In fact, an examination of the animal imagery uncovers a difference in degree only between the two warring factions. As we have already established, Die Hermannsschlacht soon confronts the audience with a depiction of the Roman wolf as it terrorizes the innocent German sheep, an image reinforced by Thuiskomar's simile referring to Varus' being 'gleich dem Wolf der Wüste' (1:541) and by Gueltar's metaphorical salutation of the Roman commander in his last stage appearance as 'Wolf vom Tiberstrande' (1:623). Such a comparison quite naturally prejudices the spectator against the predator and wins sympathy for the prey. The aptness of this lupine association is borne out by the exposed political intentions of the Romans and even more so by the mythical founding of Rome by a she-wolf.[118] In this connection, the last speech of the play as it appears in the generally more reliable

Pfeilschifter version (a) has Hermann allude to the Romans as 'Brut der Wölfin'[119] which in the Tieck text (b) reads simply 'Mordbrut' (1:628).

While the Germans express their pent-up hostility towards the invaders by disparaging them as the rapacious beast, the Romans see themselves as the more dignified stag. When Ventidius approaches the garden for his fatal rendezvous with all its *Liebestod* implications, he employs one of Kleist's favourite sexual images to characterize himself: 'Thusnelda! Komm und lösche diese Glut, / Soll ich, gleich einem jungen Hirsch, / Das Haupt voran, mich in die Flut nicht stürzen!' (1:618). A sexually aroused animal seeks to assuage its drive by plunging into *the* female element, water. In a letter addressed to Ulrike, dated 26 October 1803, eight years before he was to shoot himself on the banks of the Wannsee, Kleist expressed his suicidal longings in a prophetic combination of water and death: 'unser aller Verderben lauert über den Meeren, ich frohlocke bei der Aussicht auf das unendlich-prächtige Grab' (2:737). The stag theme, linking the attraction and fatal potential of water to the female principle, denotes love-Eros as being the source of death-Thanatos. This is the underlying message, one confirmed by the conclusion of the Ventidius-Thusnelda episode, but one of which the speaker is unaware, since, from his point of view, the motif connotes exuberant male domination through the exploitation of the female: he will use her to satisfy his sexual need. A certain aura of nobility,[120] none the less, surrounds this stag simile, partly because of its archetypal antecedent to which this gruesome incident in its basic outline may well be indebted. Acteon, a celebrated huntsman, happened to wander through a grove sacred to Artemis/Diana, the goddess of the hunt, usually pictured with a bow and quiver (Thusnelda first appears on stage with 'Pfeil und Bogen' [1:538]) and the goddess of the moon (Thusnelda's song depicts how an intruding male hand destroys a 'Mondesbild' [1:554] as it penetrates the surface of a pool of water). Because the young man gazed upon the goddess and her attendant as they bathed in a spring, Artemis splashed water in his face and transformed him into a stag. In this new form he fled from the scene pursued by his own dogs which eventually ran him down and devoured him.

Whereas Artemis sought her revenge by changing Acteon into the hunted animal and his dogs into the hunters, Ventidius, ironically of his own accord, regards himself as the stag which will in fact be ravaged, again vicariously, by a wild beast at the instigation of the outraged Thusnelda and, like Artemis in some representations, she witnesses the fierce destruction of her chosen victim. Both males come to the fateful meeting, one by chance, the other by previous agreement, totally unsuspecting. The myth also contains an implied emotional involvement: by one tradition Acteon is reputed to have proposed to Artemis despite her well-known abjuration of all men and marriage (cf. the Amazon myth) and the deer was her sacred animal. Both the Greek legend and Kleist's variation on the same theme point to the battle of the sexes as manifested in the common source of the hunt and warn against the danger inherent in the female species. And finally, since to look upon the naked Artemis becomes synonymous with a violent end and since Thusnelda, pretending to be her attendant, uses sex to lure Ventidius to his death: 'Im Park, dem Wunsch gemäss, den du geäussert, / Und heisser Brunst voll harrt sie auf dich!' (1:618), the siren motif comes to mind as another common component. The sirens (appropriately half woman, half beast) were also sea nymphs; hence water reappears as a feature shared by all three stories.[121]

Kleist provides adequately developed portraits of only two Romans within *Die Hermannsschlacht*, Ventidius and Varus. Because the Roman commander also likens himself to a stag, we must assume that its inclusion in the drama infers some purpose on the part of the dramatist. Surrounded by the German princes, each of whom covets the honour of the final kill, Varus expresses his indignation at being treated as a mere animal in a simile borrowed from the hunt: 'Ward solche Schmach im Weltkreis schon erlebt? / Als wär ich ein gefleckter Hirsch, / Der, mit zwölf Enden durch die Forsten bricht! –' (1:623). Whereas the Germans understandably denigrate their enemy as the predacious quadruped ('Wolf vom Tiberstrand' [1:623]) to be eliminated without second thought just as one would destroy a mad dog ('Höllenhund' [1:622]), the enemy, casting himself as the noble stag, a potential trophy with twelve points, raises himself above the squabbling 'Fürst[en] der Uren' (1:622), but an elevation solely by degree: the operative model remains the hunt as the German princes consider themselves 'die Jäger, die [Varus] fällen wollen!' (1:623).

Other animal images common to both parties further underscore this marginal difference. Septimius describes his execution at the hands of his taunting captors as '[von] Hunden in Germanien zerrissen' (1:613), while the Germans decry the Romans responsible for the rape of Hally as 'Drei'n dieser geilen apenninschen Hunden' (1:586). In both cases the speaker expresses his low opinion of the perpetrators of a dishonourable act. If an outraged character faces a seemingly desperate, perhaps even hopeless situation, he or she resorts to the simile of the wild boar in its blind charge at its tormentors. Once Hermann has partially convinced his wife of the Romans' exploitive designs, she, in her exasperation, exclaims, 'Ei, dass wir, wie die grimmgen Eber, doch / Uns über diese Schützen werfen könnten!' (1:570). This image, indicative of her desire to become the beast in order to destroy the marksmen, both looks back to the hunt scene where Thusnelda, the experienced huntress, shot down the charging aurochs but gave the credit to Ventidius, and looks forward to the garden tryst where the bear, her substitute, eliminates the hunter. But Thusnelda is not the only one to project herself into this role. When Varus learns that his forces have been led into a cleverly planned ambush, to express his determination born out of despair, he compares himself to a cornered boar which turns and meets its adversary head on: 'Lass sehn, wie er [Hermann] sich fassen wird, / Wenn ich, die Waffen in der Hand, / Gleich einem Eber, jetzt hinein mich stürze!' (1:608). Later in the conflict, the Germans use a variation of the same simile: 'Dem Varus eben doch, – der schnell, mit allen Waffen, / Dem pfeilverletzten Eber gleich, / Auf ihren Haufen fiel, erliegen wollten sie' (1:621). Now the boar, clearly in the inferior position, is even more dangerous by virtue of its being wounded.

Kleist has made extensive use of bird symbolism as well, primarily to demonstrate the changing conditions faced by the Romans. Generally they are connected with the eagle, the emblem under which each legion does battle. This association reaches a highpoint with the triumphant entry of Varus' army into Teutoburg:

THUSNELDA Septimius! Was bedeutet dieser Adler?
SEPTIMIUS Das ist ein Kriegspanier, erhabne Frau!
   Jedweder der drei Legionen
   Fleucht solch metallnes Adlerbild voran.
THUSNELDA So, so! Ein Kriegspanier! Sein Anblick hält
   Die Scharen in der Nacht des Kampfs zusammen?
SEPTIMIUS Du trafsts. Er führet sie den Pfad des Siegs. –   (1:577)

In the first three acts, the eagle stands for Rome's authority, power and victory, the invincible nature of the Roman war machine and its obvious ascendancy,[122] but as early as the first act, Hermann calls this alleged superiority into question: 'der Habicht rupft / Die Brut des Aars, die, noch nicht flügg, / Im stillen Wipfel einer Eiche ruht' (1:545). Since the Romans have appropriated the eagle emblem, it represents the exalted image they have created for themselves. However, Hermann, revealing his confidence in himself and his people, contends that the Germans have a greater potential than the Italian invaders and in fact are the true eagles. Since they have not as yet gained the use of their wings, a lesser bird of prey, a hawk, reflecting the Italian 'mindre [Anlage]' (1:544), can harass them with impunity. This well-chosen image implies both the predacious nature of the two sides and the indigenous strength of the Germans mirrored in the sacred oak, a source of national pride, appearing throughout *Die Hermannsschlacht* with the regularity of a leitmotif. Moreover, the quoted dialogue between Thusnelda and Septimius contains its fair share of retrospective ironies. Thusnelda's reference to the eagle's holding '[die] Scharen in der Nacht des Kampfs zusammen' (1:577) anticipates the confusion of the Roman army – at one point described ominously as being 'im Schatten ihrer Adler' (1:621) – in the Teutoburg Forest, while Septimius' assertion 'Er [der Adler] führet sie den Pfad des Siegs' (1:577) strikes the knowledgeable observer as particularly ironic given that Hermann has already begun to direct the Romans along the path that leads to annihilation.

The presence of three new birds in the last two acts notably enhances this note of defeat. The first of these, the raven, suggestive of death and deception, pursues the invaders and foretells their doom in the person of Teuthold, the 'Rabenvater' (1:590) who seeks bloody revenge for the rape of his daughter and the *Alraune* who 'sing[t] ja, wie ein Rabe' (1:603) and 'hat des Lebens Fittich [dem Varus] / Mit ihrer Zunge scharfem Stahl gelähmt!' (1:604). Varus comes to see in the raven his own ineluctable fate: 'O Priester Zeus,' hast du den Raben auch, / Der Sieg mir [Varus] zu verkündgen schien, verstanden? / Hier war ein Rabe [die Alraune], der mir prophezeit, / Und seine heisre Stimme sprach: das Grab!' (1:606). Just as the priest misread the future and led Varus astray, the Romans generally have misinterpreted the signs in keeping with Hermann's plan deliberately designed to deceive the enemy.

Whereas the raven is depicted as a German bird auguring destruction for the enemy, the second bird relates directly to the Romans: 'Wenn auf je hundert Schritte nicht, / Ein Blitzstrahl zischend vor uns niederkeilte, / Wir würden, wie die Eul am Tage, / Haupt und Gebein uns im Gebüsch zerschellen!' (1:600). An owl caught in daylight is a creature out of its normal habitat (cf. the quadriga of act one) and consequently an easy victim. Since the Romans are not accustomed to doing battle in such close quarters as swamp and forest, they, like the owl, find themselves disoriented and hence particularly vulnerable. The derogatory, ill-boding nature of the owl is further accentuated when employed by Varus to reprehend his ally, the German traitor Aristan: 'Dass du zur Eule werden müsstest, / Mit deinem mitternächtlichen Geschrei!' (1:607).

The ultimate fate of the invading army Kleist cleverly reflects in yet another bird appearing in a speech immediately following the owl simile:

ZWEITER FELDHERR Wir können keinen Schritt fortan,
   In diesem feuchten Mordgrund, weiter rücken!
   Er ist so zäh, wie Vogelleim geworden.
   Das Heer schleppt halb Cheruska an den Beinen,
   Und wird noch, wie ein bunter Specht,
   Zuletzt, mit Haut und Haar, dran kleben bleiben.   (1:600-1)

This particularly apt comparison contains considerable dramatic irony since it is spoken by a Roman general. The mighty eagle – the Roman army – has been reduced in status to a mere woodpecker known for making a racket but posing no serious threat. Moreover, the image, appropriated once again from the hunt, underscores the stealth and deception currently being practised by Hermann at the Romans' expense. They are in fact caught in the swamp's bird lime and will leave 'Haut und Haar' in his deviously designed trap. (The reference to the 'Haar' also anticipates a further irony: those who came to steal Cheruskian hair will pay for their audacity by forfeiting their own.) Kleist has thus skilfully charted the rise and fall of Roman fortunes by an apt choice of bird motifs:

          Du [Egbert] sollst, du Römerfeind,
   Noch heut, auf ihrer Adler einen,
   Im dichtesten Gedräng des Kampfs mir [Hermann] treffen!
   Noch eh die Sonn entwich, das merk dir wohl,
   Legst du ihn hier zu Füssen mir darnieder!   (1:610)

Analysis of the animal symbolism has disclosed a predilection common to both the Romans and the Germans to see themselves or the enemy in bestial terms. A brief survey of what one may designate lesser creatures – the spider (1:593) and the crab (1:546) connected with the Germans and the hyena (1:564) and the insect (1:593) with the Romans – also identifies a more or less even distribution of disparaging epithets. While the stag or eagle may be perceived in a more positive manner than the ponderous 'Ur,' we must bear in mind that the more favourable image linked to the Romans has been adopted by the Romans themselves, does not correspond to the attitude of their victims and does not necessarily reflect the outlook of the author. Indeed, Kleist may well be endeavouring to suggest by his consistent use of the hunt model and its derivative animalism that the differences between an advanced civilization and a barbarian horde are at best superficial and that below the surface lurks the human beast. Although we may feel some sympathy or respect for Varus and Septimius, the dramatist, in the final speech of the play, does not permit us to lose sight of the fact that the Romans belong either to the 'Raubnest' (1:628) of the Tieck version – the predatory eagle – or to the 'Brut der Wölfin' in the Pfeilschifter variant – the predatory wolf – which in either case must be 'ganz zerstört' (1:628).

The ambush in the Teutoburg Forest has all the earmarks and the atmosphere of a hunt and tends to recall several details of the introductory episode. As the trap is about to be sprung upon the still unsuspecting Romans, one of their commanders explains, 'Die Schar, auf die dein Vordertrapp gestossen, / Ist eine Horde noch zuletzt, / Die hier den Uren oder Bären jagt' (1:605). The speaker assumes that the detected Germans are merely a hunting party on the trail of the game connected with the barbarians from the first act. Ironically, he is basically correct: the Germans are hunting, a feature further evoked by the subsequent sounding of the German hunting horns, another echo of act one, but the prey is the Roman stag or eagle. Hermann derives his plan to defeat the foe from a strategy dictated not by declared hostilities on an open field of battle but by the cunning, stealth, and experience gained from the principal occupation of his people. Like the aurochs of the first act, the Romans do not sense the trap set for them until it is too late. 'Wir sind verknüpft, Marbod und ich,' Hermann informs Septimius, 'Und werden, wenn der Morgen tagt, / Den Varus, hier im Walde, überfallen' (1:612) as one would 'fall upon' cornered game.

In the quotation from *Il Principe*, employed as an epigraph to this section, Machiavelli claims that the successful leader must unite in himself the characteristics of the fox and the lion; the former by its guile will enable him to avoid the 'gins,' while the latter by its strength will shield him against 'the ferocity of wolves.' Although there is no evidence that Kleist was directly familiar with *Il Principe*, one cannot but be struck by the amazing parallels between the sixteenth-century essay and the nineteenth-century drama in which context the quoted passage distinguishes itself with particular relevance: the victims regard their oppressors as wolves, and Hermann, the prince, maintains either direct or indirect control of the political scenario by a successful combination of deceit and power, thus avoiding the trap set for him by the Romans and outwitting them at their own game. But this implicit similarity does, in fact, become explicit. In the general ethos of distrust characteristic of the political arena, Attarin cautions Marbod, 'Mein Fürst, trau diesem *Fuchs*, ich bitte dich, / Dem Hermann, nicht! Der Himmel weiss, / Was er mit dieser schnöden *List* bezweckt' (1:579). The Sueven, more familiar with Hermann than the Romans, both respect and fear his cunning epitomized in the fox. The very episode giving rise to this warning furnishes ample proof of his intellectual acumen or his insight into human motivation: he has the understanding and foresight to anticipate the actions and reactions of both the Romans – their desertion of Marbod – and the Sueven – their distrust of Hermann's motives – and to send along his children as a guarantee of his good faith without which the alliance would never have been formed.

The cunning of the fox proves totally ineffective if not seconded by the strength of the lion. From the outset of the play, Hermann possesses the vulpine but lacks the leonine qualifications (i.e., the necessary military might), and this deficiency largely explains his seemingly paradoxical behaviour towards the German princes in act one: 'Nein, Freunde, so gewiss der Bär dem schlanken Löwen / Im Kampf erliegt, so sicherlich / Erliegt ihr, in der Feldschlacht, diesen Römern' (1:544). At this stage of the struggle, Hermann recognizes quite correctly that the Romans, the lion, have superior power over the Germans, the bear, in the field of battle. In a figurative sense his goal is to become the lion himself. When Dagobert, one of his interlocutors in the same scene, disparagingly remarks, 'Gleich einem Löwen grimmig steht er [Hermann] auf, / Warum? Um, wie ein Krebs, zurückzugehn' (1:546), he unwittingly acknowledges both Hermann's leonine intent and his present cautious, crab-like behaviour prescribed by the fox. No sooner, however, does Hermann gain physical ascendancy over the cornered 'Wolf vom Tiberstrande' (1:623) than he openly appears as the lion: 'Komm her, du [Hermann] dort im Fell des zottgen *Löwen*, / Und lass mich [Varus] sehn, ob du Herakles bist!' (1:623). The symbolic value of the lion as the embodiment of strength or power Kleist further exploits by the allusion to Hercules[123] who is frequently depicted wearing the skin of the Nemean lion as a mantle. Since, therefore, Hermann may be said to have followed Machiavelli's counsel to 'take as models ... the fox and the lion' (M 91), he incarnates the ideal ruler advocated by *Il Principe*, who succeeds in destroying the wolves and, at the same time, in uniting his countrymen under his leadership: 'Heil Hermann! Heil dir, König von Germanien!' (1:626).

4

An unsung villain:
the role of Hohenzollern in
Prinz Friedrich von Homburg[1]

Men pursue their ends, which are wealth and power, by divers paths, one with caution, another at a gallop, one with brawn, another with brain, one with patience, another at a rush, and these paths may all lead to success. (M 118)

In 1970, John M. Ellis pointed out that by 1963 there had been 269 publications dealing with *Prinz Friedrich von Homburg* and that '[few] other works of German literature, and certainly no other by Kleist, have aroused as much critical interest.'[2] A brief survey of this tremendous volume of material reveals, 'quite understandably', a preoccupation with either the Elector or the Prince. As Karl Schweizer has aptly summarized, 'Gleich von welchem Aspekt man gerade dieses Drama Kleists angeht, in irgendeiner Weise umkreisen alle Interpreten doch zentrale Probleme, die den Kern des Werkes berühren: die Gestalt des Prinzen und die Funktion des Kurfürsten.'[3] Natalie has received some attention as embodying a compromise between the extreme positions allegedly held by the two chief protagonists and the role of Kottwitz has been a popular success with theatre audiences since the 1828 Berlin première. A consensus has emerged which views the Elector as the man in complete command of the dramatic action, and even John Ellis, who has done most to argue for a secularized view of the divine ruler, refers to him as 'behaving almost like an *agent provocateur*,'[4] while Eckehard Catholy in his more theatrically oriented essay calls the Elector the 'Meister eines Spiels ..., das die Erziehung des Prinzen zum Zweck hat.'[5] Although Walter Silz observed as early as 1936 that this central function belongs more correctly to Graf Hohenzollern, designating him 'the prime mover in an unhappy series of events,'[6] he outlined only cursorily and incompletely this sequence and failed in the Count's case to examine 'that conditionedness and complexity of human motives and behavior,'[7] which he called for in his article. Many commentators have subsequently met Silz's demand, but solely in their analysis of the perceived main characters, and no one seems to have attached any importance to the fact that Homburg's 'friend' actually speaks as many lines as the Elector. Since only Ellis and Reinhard Thum have devoted any noteworthy space to a consideration of Hohenzollern's function, the former including him as one of 'the spectators of the conflict,'[8] the latter seeing him as a 'malicious' manipulator in the first half of the play,[9] a need still exists to investigate the Count's involvement more closely. Whereas a majority of the critics tend to regard him almost as an embarrassing contradiction, a minor figure created by Kleist for reasons of plot expediency, it is my contention that Hohenzollern, a unique dramatic catalyst, not only initiates *all* the major actions, hence governing more of the story line than any other single individual, but manipulates consciously or unconsciously both the Prince and the Elector without ostensibly becoming directly involved himself.

If one consults the genealogy of the Brandenburg-Prussian line of the Hohenzollerns, one discovers a Christian *Heinrich* (1661–1708), but he would have been only fourteen years of age at the time of the Battle of Fehrbellin in 1675. While it has been demonstrated that Kleist took great liberties in his selection of characters and events,[10] history or legend still placed a limited obligation upon him in the portrayal of the Elector and the Prince, but with Hohenzollern, a product of Kleist's own creative mind, he could be uninhibited by any concern whatsoever for historical accuracy.[11] It follows that Kleist must have considered it significant that Homburg's confidant, his most trusted 'friend,' should trace his ancestry back to the family most intimately related to the rise of Prussia and that he would thus be directly related to the Great Elector himself. This supposition receives immediate substantiation from the list of characters which states, 'Graf Hohenzollern, von der Suite des Kurfürsten' (1:630), the only person to be distinguished in this manner; in other words, even before the curtain rises, the dramatist encourages us to associate the Count with the Elector, not the Prince, and it is surely no accident that not once in the whole work does the audience ever see Homburg as an integral part of the inner circle to which he longs to belong. Being one of the favoured few surrounding the Elector, Hohenzollern supplies the link between the seemingly objective, rational sphere of the sovereign and the subjective, irrational world of the Prince. In fact, Hohenzollern makes his initial appearance from the castle above in the presence of the court, while the titular hero remains below in isolation, a visual confirmation of this relationship.

'In the first scene,' according to Ellis, '[Hohenzollern] is characterized by emotional and intellectual insensitivity to what is going on.'[12] However, closer examination discloses no ordinary confidant but one possessed of considerable insight. In the opening speech of the play, he abstracts the essential conflict, 'Der Prinz von Homburg' versus 'Befehl' (1:631), both in an emphatic first position, establishes a degree of familiarity with his ruler, '*unser* tapfrer Vetter,' and singles out the fact that Homburg has specifically disobeyed the Elector's order: 'Befehl ward ihm *von dir*, hier länger nicht, / Als nur drei Füttrungsstunden zu verweilen' (1:631). This theme of insubordination Hohenzollern proceeds to stress even further by bringing to the Elector's attention that the cavalry is waiting for its missing leader, the Prince. Then, in an effort intended to disparage Homburg in the eyes of those present, he describes his 'friend':

> Als ein Nachtwandler, schau, auf jener Bank,
> Wohin, im Schlaf, *wie du nie glauben wolltest*,
> Der Mondschein ihn gelockt, beschäftiget,
> Sich träumend, seiner eignen Nachwelt gleich,
> Den prächtgen Kranz des Ruhmes einzuwinden. (1:632)

The Elector's previous exclamation, 'So hört ich!' (1:631) and Hohenzollern's assertion 'wie du nie glauben wolltest' indicate that in the past the Count has tried unsuccessfully on several occasions ('nie,' not 'nicht') to convince the Elector of his nephew's occasional somnambulistic trances. This excursion into the garden has therefore been instigated by Hohenzollern to confirm his previous allegations to which the Elector has apparently refused to give credence. A pattern is set which will be repeated numerous times throughout the play: Hohenzollern does not restrict himself to an objective account, but provides an interpretive description. The stage directions read quite factually '*und windet sich einen Kranz*' (1:631): he adds the crucial details, 'den prächtgen Kranz des Ruhmes,' thus furnishing a gratuitous explanation of Homburg's secret motive. Also the tortured, broken syntax utilized by Hohenzollern tends to isolate and hence underscore the worst features of the Prince's physical and mental state, features which will undoubtedly put him into a potentially damaging position, especially on the day before a crucial battle. Since we must assume that the Count was fully aware of Homburg's predicament before he brought the court into the garden, it seems reasonable to conclude that he is endeavouring intentionally, and not as Ellis maintains, 'by accident,'[13] to compromise his so-called 'friend' and to prejudice the Elector against the Prince.

Hohenzollern's delineation calculated to intrigue the ruler, even astonish him, produces the desired effect: 'DER KURFÜRST. Was! / HOHENZOLLERN. In der Tat! Schau hier herab: da sitzt er! / *Er leuchtet von der Rampe auf ihn nieder*' (1:632). As the stage directions imply, the Count assumes a managerial role: he has focused the court's attention upon Homburg's propensity to escape reality; he has aroused the curiosity of the Elector who now seeks a visual verification; he emphasizes the Prince's neglect of an order issued by a commander-in-chief who stands for discipline and obedience; and in a dramatically suggestive fashion he literally turns the spotlight upon his 'friend.' Such conduct does not meet one's normal expectations of the essentially supportive, respondent function of a confidant, for, after having initiated the incident, Hohenzollern still maintains control of it, while the Elector's surprised reaction demonstrates his ignorance: 'Im Schlaf versenkt? Unmöglich!' (1:632). Because the master of ceremonies has seen Homburg in a somnambulistic state before, he knows precisely what he is doing: 'Ruf ihn bei Namen auf, so fällt er nieder' (1:632). From the very beginning it becomes evident that Hohenzollern has an awareness denied the other principals, and by virtue of this knowledge, he occupies the dominant position in this first scene. The questionable nature of his intent is underlined by the more compassionate concern of the ladies present who assume Homburg is ill: 'KURFÜRSTIN. Man sollt ihm helfen, dünkt mich, / Nicht den Moment verbringen, sein zu spotten!' (1:632). The mockery perceived by the Electress is the key to the procedure employed by Hohenzollern: destruction through ridicule. In his response to this protest, he refuses to allow his 'friend' even the excuse of illness: 'Er ist gesund, ihr mitleidsvollen Frauen, / Bei Gott, ich bins nicht mehr!' (1:632). The Prince's behaviour does not strike the others as being normal and since the drama offers considerable proof that Hohenzollern is too securely ensconced in reality ever to be caught in such a hazardous situation, one would have to regard his insistence that Homburg is equally as healthy as he as still another indirect attempt to show the Prince in an uncomplimentary light. But if this reference to his state of mind, further minimized as 'eine blosse Unart seines Geistes,' has a derogatory connotation, then the statement: 'Der Schwede morgen / Wenn wir im Feld ihn treffen, wirds empfinden!' (1:632) would seem to counterbalance the negative effect and contradict the hypothesis that Hohenzollern willfully acts in a manner detrimental to his 'friend.' However, this alleged glorification could also be said to point out the incongruity of Homburg's reputation as a great warrior and his present vulnerability, and above all could be devised as a subtle means to annoy the Elector, assuming that there exists an underlying competitive spirit between the two main protagonists of which the Count is conscious.

Once the trap has been set, the Elector quickly manifests his interest in the bait: 'Fürwahr! Ein Märchen glaubt ichs! - Folgt mir Freunde, / Und lasst uns näher ihn einmal betrachten' (1:632). When he first heard Hohenzollern's account back in the palace, he did not believe it and may even have defended his nephew, but now his curiosity has been piqued, perhaps an unconscious response to Hohenzollern's praise of Homburg's superiority as a fighter. No sooner does the court descend to the Prince's level than Hohenzollern revokes the command to have the torches removed on the grounds that 'Der ganze Flecken könnt in Feuer aufgehn, / Dass sein Gemüt davon nicht mehr empfände, / Als der Demant, den er am Finger trägt' (1:632), further evidence of the confidant's intimate knowledge of his 'friend's' strange behaviour. This hyperbolic statement, typical of Hohenzollern's manner of speech, is only partly true. As he knows from experience, the somnambulistic Homburg does not appear to be influenced by his immediate environment because it is the function of such a dream-like state to eliminate an essentially painful or hostile objective reality in favour of a pleasing subjective illusion. Although this does not mean that his mind blots out all external provocation,[14] only when the Elector specifically interferes with the trance by removing the wreath and by offering outside stimuli - the chain of office and Natalie - which complement and extend the wish fulfilment does the Prince react directly to his surroundings.

In reply to the Elector's query: 'Was für ein Laub denn flicht er? - Laub der Weide?' (1:632), Hohenzollern, correcting the original assumption and returning to an earlier theme, retorts rather emphatically: 'Was! Laub der Weid, o Herr! - Der Lorbeer ists, / Wie ers gesehn hat, an den Helden Bildern, / Die zu Berlin im Rüstsaal aufgehängt' (1:633). For the second time, in a superficially innocent, incidental fashion, the Count emphasizes his 'friend's' drive for fame and recognition, while imputing to the Prince a source of inspiration which may or may not have been a contributing factor. Clearly, such a description with the accent upon the heroic has been designed to elicit a specific response from the listener, one which immediately follows: 'Seltsam beim Himmel! Doch, was gilts, ich weiss, / Was dieses jungen Toren Brust bewegt?' (1:633). Again, indeed for the third time, Hohenzollern insists upon the Prince's aspiration for glory as the self-evident cause: 'O – was! Die Schlacht von morgen, mein Gebieter! / Sterngucker sieht er, wett ich, schon im Geist, / Aus Sonnen einen Siegeskranz ihm winden' (1:633). The 'O – was!' and 'mein Gebieter,' syntactically located at either end of the line, would seem to counteract one another. On the one hand the interjection implies: how could you be so naïve? It is obvious what is going on in this young man's heart, whereas the conventional title denoting respect comes across in this context as an empty, meaningless form of address dictated by custom. Still occupying an intellectually superior position, Hohenzollern meets the Elector as his peer and once more goes beyond the immediately apparent to interpret or suggest his 'friend's' motive. In maintaining that 'The Prince's desire for the sun, the position of brilliance and dominance, is expressed by his initially making his "Kranz" from "Sonnen,"'[15] Ellis misses the point. Such a subjective, exaggerated image, contrived to produce a predictable reaction in the Elector and reflecting more upon its originator than its target, serves to stimulate such negative sentiments as envy, jealousy, and resentment which an older man might well feel for a younger rival. While seemingly elevating the Prince, Hohenzollern is in actual fact putting him down socially, severely damaging him in the eyes of his father figure and at the same time appealing to the worst in the Elector.

> Schade, ewig schade,
> Dass hier kein Spiegel in der Nähe ist!
> Er würd ihm eitel, wie ein Mädchen nahn,
> Und sich den Kranz bald so, und wieder so,
> Wie eine florne Haube aufprobieren. (1:633)

In yet another example of interpretive suggestion, the purpose of which is to nullify by blatant derision the high regard which Homburg enjoys, Hohenzollern gives evidence of real hostility towards the Prince, supposedly his best 'friend,' for there would seem to be no greater insult in this male-dominated society than the accusation of unmanly deportment, a prejudice amply illustrated when the Elector in the fifth act says disparagingly to the Feldmarschall: 'Das muss ein Mann mir sagen, eh ichs glaube!' (1:693). Summarizing the events of this opening scene, Ellis concludes: 'The same unwillingness to infer anything from striking incidents and the tendency to be satisfied with a superficial explanation characterize Hohenzollern's early role in the play. This allows him to maintain his view of the Prince as a hero ... a fool ..., and "eitel, wie ein Mädchen" ... without relating these conflicting impressions.'[16] Nevertheless, these 'impressions' do relate. The celebration of the popular hero cultivates the unconscious ire and jealousy of the ruler – what the Elector does not want to hear – while the foolish, unmasculine anti-hero image downgrades the Prince in the estimation of all present – what the Elector would secretly like to hear – and hence all three features, positive as well as negative, jeopardize the Prince.

Considering Hohenzollern's prompting, his insinuations and unflattering analyses, one should not be surprised by the Elector's decision: 'Bei Gott! Ich muss doch sehn, wie weit ers treibt!' (1:633). After Hohenzollern suggests a possible response if a mirror were present, the Elector wants to ascertain Homburg's behaviour if another set of circumstances were arranged. Whereas the Count remains on a theoretical, speculative level, the Elector, following his lead, creates a hypothetical-real incident: hypothetical in the sense that the ruler does not seriously offer victory, power, and love, but real in that the symbolic act does actually take place. It may therefore be maintained that the indirect incentive to trifle with a defenceless young man comes from Hohenzollern, and that this episode constitutes an additional illustration of how Hohenzollern skilfully handles an individual by planting an idea in his mind and then allowing him, so to speak, to hang himself. During the ensuing confusion engendered by the pantomime, Hohenzollern continues to reveal his duplicity by referring to his 'friend' as 'der Tor' (1:633) and 'Der Rasende' (1:634), involuntary responses which would seem to invalidate his former insistence upon the Prince's mental normalcy. He is the only one to notice that Homburg managed to snatch something from Natalie: 'Himmel und Erde! Was ergriff er da?' (1:634), and just as he opened the proceedings, he fittingly concludes them by herding the retreating Elector through the door. 'HOHENZOLLERN öffnet die Tür. Hier rasch herein, mein Fürst!' (1:634). This highly embarrassing exit, contrasting rather sharply with the more regal entrance, further demonstrates the degree to which Hohenzollern has succeeded in compromising his sovereign by bringing him down to the garden. Although the Count could not have foreseen the consequences, i.e., his behaviour is more 're-active' than 'pro-active,' he must have been aware that to take advantage of a Prussian officer in a helpless state of mind could hardly be expected to redound to a ruler's prestige. Hohenzollern's final utterance: 'Auf dass das ganze Bild ihm wieder schwinde!' (1:634) divulges again a certain amount of psychological know-how. There can be little doubt that he maintains his ascendency, not the Elector whose main concern is escape: 'DER KURFÜRST rückwärts aus-

weichend. / Öffn' mir die Pforte nur!' (1:634), and even though the latter has the final speech of the scene, the former's influence can still be felt: 'In dem Gefild der Schlacht, / Sehn wir, wenns dir gefällig ist, uns wieder! / Im Traum erringt man solche Dinge nicht!' (1:634). First he falls into Hohenzollern's highly sarcastic tone – 'wenns dir gefällig ist,' but, more important, his final reference to the impending battle and the possible prestige it may provide has been programmed by the Count who alluded twice to Homburg's key role in the 'Schlacht von morgen' and no less than four times to his inevitable victory as symbolized by the 'prächtgen Kranz des Ruhmes' (1:632).

In the next scene, the stage directions indicate that Hohenzollern reappears *'von unten, durch eine Gittertür'* (1:634), a visual representation of his ability to move freely between both camps and, if he so desires, to play one off against the other. Once he has expressed his willingness to take part in the cover-up ordered by the Elector, the need for which he has already recognized: 'Das wusst ich schon!' (1:635), and has dismissed the page in a mordacious manner, frequently reminiscent of a Mephistopheles,[17] he takes up a symbolic stance *'in einiger Entfernung hinter dem Prinzen ..., der noch immer unverwandt die Rampe hinaufsieht'* (1:635). The Count's location suggests both his determination and his devious ability to direct the Prince who gazes upwards towards the realm to which he aspires, but which, as this arrangement perceptively implies, Hohenzollern will ultimately deny him. 'Arthur! *Der Prinz fällt um.* / Da liegt er; eine Kugel trifft nicht besser!' (1:635). Kleist appears to have invented this second Christian name, perhaps as Richard Samuel[18] suggests to avoid confusion with the Elector whose first name, like Homburg's, is Friedrich. Hohenzollern is the only character in the play to use the alternative designation and this added degree of intimacy accentuates the personal relationship shared by the two men. Moreover, Homburg alone refers to Hohenzollern by his first name, Heinrich, and throughout the play, but especially during the very important third act, the Prince calls him 'Freund' (1:638).[19] Even though the Prince considers the Count to be his faithful confidant, this friendship has already been grossly violated and is called into serious question even further by Hohenzollern's cold, homicidally coloured reaction to Homburg's loss of consciousness.

Albeit Hohenzollern has superior understanding, he none the less decides cruelly to put his 'friend' on the rack for his own personal amusement:[20] 'Nun bin ich auf die Fabel nur begierig, / Die er ersinnen wird, mir zu erklären, / Warum er hier sich schlafen hat gelegt' (1:635). As this quotation suggests, it is more a case of a cat-and-mouse game played at Homburg's expense. For example, the choice of the term 'Fabel' underscores Hohenzollern's contention that whatever explanation Homburg proposes, it will be a fabrication and thus will compromise the Prince and place him indirectly even more under Hohenzollern's control. It becomes apparent in the ensuing exchange that the Count, by posing questions to which he already knows the answers: 'Wie kommst du hier zu Nacht auf diesen Platz?' (1:635)[21] and by making ironic comments: 'DER PRINZ VON HOMBURG. Welch eine Reuterei? / HOHENZOLLERN. Die Mamelucken!' (1:635), takes unfair advantage of Homburg's not fully conscious frame of mind in order to taunt him. Rather than coming to his immediate aid, he fosters and contributes to his 'friend's' inability to orient himself. In this state of almost total perplexity, Homburg discovers the glove which Hohenzollern first pretends he does not recognize, but the importance of which he acknowledges in an aside. After the Count has successfully drawn attention away from the glove, the Prince confesses: 'Ich weiss nicht, liebster Heinrich, wo ich bin' (1:636), and only at this point, several speeches into the scene, does the confidant make a serious attempt to acquaint his 'friend' with his present status. However, the extent of the dubious role the Count has assumed is perhaps best illustrated when, in reply to Homburg's query, 'Der Kurfürst weiss von nichts?' (1:637), he maintains, 'Ei, was! Der liegt im Bette längst und schläft.' As well as revealing how anxious Homburg is that others, especially his uncle, be not aware of his unfortunate habit ('Im Mondschein bin ich *wieder* umgewandelt!' [1:636]), this dialogue gives additional evidence of the reprehensible nature of both Hohenzollern's former betrayal and his present duplicity.

Because the Prince's love for Natalie, being repressed, cannot attain consciousness, on no less than three different occasions within this scene he is unable to name the third person who wore the glove. Critics have always assumed that Hohenzollern 'attempts to hide the true situation [and thus] merely heightens Homburg's confusion,'[22] and that 'he is visibly afraid that the Prince might find out what happened during his sleep-walking.'[23] On the surface, this would seem to be the case; closer scrutiny, however, brings to light certain discrepancies and ambiguities. In the first exchange produced by the Prince's mental impasse, Hohenzollern's immediate response appears quite natural. 'DER PRINZ VON HOMBURG. – Wie heisst sie schon? / HOHENZOLLERN. Wer?' (1:637). He then makes suggestions: 'Die Platen?' or 'Die Ramin?' (1:638) – women whom he knows to be out of contention, but one must not forget that the Count is under an injunction not to reveal the events of the garden, a disclosure which would undoubtedly injure the Elector. One must then ask why Hohenzollern pursues the subject of the concealed name at great length three different times?[24] Why does he not simply avoid the difficulty altogether once he has ascertained that the Prince cannot recall the glove's owner? A list of four possible candidates could indeed confuse the issue but it could also act as a means of elimination. Towards the end of this first sequence, the Count, in apparent exasperation, exclaims, 'Zum Henker, sprich! Lässt das Gesicht sich raten? / – Welch eine Dame meinst du?' (1:638). The tone supported by the oath and the imperative does not imply an attempt to conceal but on the contrary a desire to reveal. He even goes as far as to suggest an alternative means to recollect the lost identity, and it is Homburg, not Hohenzollern, who finally calls off this initial search for the name. When the Prince hesitates a second time in his narration, again his confidant does not seem to interrupt him to deflect but rather to spur him on: 'Wem? ... Nun, so sprich!' (1:638). Mercilessly pressed by his interlocutor and eager to escape further disconcerting cross-examination, the Prince resignedly maintains, ' – Es wird die Platen wohl gewesen sein' (1:638),[25] to which Hohenzollern retorts, 'Die Platen? Was! – Die jetzt in Preussen ist?' If the Count is keen on leading his 'friend' astray, why does he contradict him here, indicating that the proposal is physically-geographically impossible? Confronted by the implication, i.e., 'you can't be serious!,' Homburg now takes refuge in another name previously put forward by Hohenzollern; yet once more the latter does not let the matter rest there and casts further doubt upon the suitability of the second suggestion: 'Ach, die Ramin! Was! Die, mit roten Haaren! –' (1:638). The dash following 'Haaren' should be especially noted. In his enthusiasm, Hohenzollern has been too caught up in the cat-and-mouse game he is playing with the Prince and has almost gone too far. The dash indicates a possible recognition of the pitfall into which he could easily fall and denotes a brief time lapse during which he regains conscious control of himself and can thus continue with the concealment expected of him by the Elector. He now returns to the candidate who, by reason of her location in East Prussia, would cause the court the least amount of embarrassment. Of course, we must bear in mind that since Homburg remains convinced that he is relating a dream, Platen would still have to be given serious consideration, but a very visible, concrete object, the glove, encourages the Prince to search in his more immediate vicinity and triggers the third and last attempt to arrive at the identity of 'der süssen Traumgestalt' (1:639). Rather than passing over this crucial aspect of the incident, Hohenzollern chooses to highlight it by drawing the conclusion that the glove belongs to the unnamed female: 'Bei meinem Eid! – Und nun meinst du, der Handschuh, / Der sei der ihre?' (1:639). After he has again put forward Platen as the most likely owner and Homburg half-heartedly agrees, 'Der Platen. Wirklich. Oder der Ramin –' (1:639), Hohenzollern, unable to deny the glove, then submits that it has merely been left behind from a 'Schäferstunde' that very evening. Faced with the Prince's protestation to the contrary, he makes one last recommendation: 'Am Sonntag geht die Post nach Preussen, / Da kannst du auf dem kürzsten Weg erfahren, / Ob deiner Schönen dieser Handschuh fehlt. –' (1:639–40). Although he may ostensibly still be endeavouring to deceive the Prince, he offers counsel that contains a logical inconsistency. In view of the fact that the Count has partially succeeded in convincing Homburg to accept a safe substitute: 'Die Platen, mit den schelmschen Veilchenaugen! / Die, weiss man, gefällt dir' (1:638), 'deiner Schönen' could only refer to Platen, but she quite obviously could not be the wearer of the glove in the amorous tryst mentioned above, because, as Hohenzollern himself has noted, she is presently in East Prussia. Of even greater significance as far as the plot is concerned is the fact that Hohenzollern has inadvertently provided a way to discover the real identity of the sweet dream figure closer to home as he quite correctly singles out the glove as the key.

Throughout this scene, Hohenzollern's intentions remain at best equivocal. With the sole exception of the one outburst, 'Warum? – Ich glaube gar, der Tor –?' (1:640), induced by Homburg's allusion to Natalie in an unrelated, harmless context, the Count remains in complete command of the situation, while sadistically toying with his friend's dilemma. At times it almost appears as if he wanted the Prince to learn the identity of the unknown third person, a disclosure which would run counter to the Elector's instruction and could conceivably cause him some humiliation. Although Hohenzollern seems prepared to conceal the whole affair, why does he continually ask such pertinent questions, why does he gainsay incorrect conjectures which he made in the first place, and why, once he has established Homburg's ignorance, does he doggedly pursue the matter in two subsequent interrogations?

At the beginning of the fifth scene, we are told that the Prince appears 'den Handschuh im Kollett' (1:640) and a little later that 'Der Prinz von Homburg, Stift und Tafel in der Hand, fixiert die Damen' (1:641). Concentrating all his attention upon the discovery of the glove's owner, he is obviously following up on Hohenzollern's suggestion. Twice during the issuing of orders in almost completely similar situations, the Count exclaims 'heimlich. Arthur!'

(1:642 and 1:644). Because the Prince still dwells in a realm of subjective illusion, Hohenzollern, continuing his function of stage manager, supplies the proper cues and, as on a previous occasion, attempts to bring him back to reality by calling his name. Hohenzollern's utterances at the conclusion of these two parallel sequences: 'Bist du bei Sinnen?' (1:643) and 'Du bist des Teufels?' (1:644) intimate that he has some inkling of his 'friend's' solipsistic state. Once Homburg has successfully performed his test, his reaction: 'Der Prinz von Homburg *steht einen Augenblick, wie vom Blitz getroffen da*' (1:646), recalls the almost identical stage directions from the second scene: '*Der Prinz von Homburg bleibt einen Augenblick, mit dem Ausdruck der Verwunderung, vor der Tür stehen*' (1:634). In both cases, his fondest hopes and dreams receive confirmation as Natalie, their focal point, departs, but in the first instance a reality controlled by Hohenzollern and the Elector appears to Homburg as a dream, while in the second the dream has become reality, but a selected reality where only those features which correspond to and confirm the 'dream' are consciously recorded. In this moment of great triumphant bliss, Hohenzollern, the only one the Prince can turn to: 'O Heinrich!' (1:646), betrays him again: 'HOHENZOLLERN *unwillig*. Nun! Was gibts? Was hast du vor? / DER PRINZ VON HOMBURG. Was! Sahst du nichts? / HOHENZOLLERN. Nein, nichts! Sei still, zum Henker!' (1:646). The Count's annoyance, underlined by his curse, gives a hint that he does know what is happening to his 'friend' and the long speech he makes later in the drama to the Elector proves conclusively that he did in fact witness what occurred. How else could he have known about the glove experiment since he denies Homburg the opportunity to relate what he has just done? 'Sei still, zum Henker!' Furthermore, in reference to the final exchange between the Feldmarschall and Homburg and the Count's response to it: '*heimlich, unwillig, nachdrücklich. Fanfare! Sei verwünscht! Nicht eh, als bis der –*' (1:647), Ellis has perceptively noted, 'Hohenzollern sees that the qualifications preceding "Fanfare" are those the Prince is likely to neglect [i.e., to await the Elector's direct command before attacking].'[26] As far as the real world in its relation to the Prince is concerned, Hohenzollern remains largely in control, for he alone knows what is truly transpiring at both the subjective (Homburg) and the objective (Elector) levels.

Upon the battlefield, there are several signs that Hohenzollern still exerts a major influence over his 'friend.' Just before the hostilities commence, he remarks: 'Du [Homburg] scheinst so ernst!' (1:650), indicating that he still has the Prince under surveillance, and he admits to having knowledge of the Prince's previous frame of mind: 'Du warst zerstreut.

Ich hab es wohl *gesehn'* (1:650). Frequently, Homburg turns to his confidant for information and guidance: 'Was ich dir sagen wollte, Heinrich – / *Er führt den Grafen ein wenig vor.* / Was wars schon, was der Dörfling, mich betreffend, / Bei der Parol' hat gestern vorgebracht?' (1:650). Although the Count does correctly summarize the Elector's plan, significantly he first draws attention to the fact that Homburg's participation will be quite limited: 'Zum Glück nicht diesmal eben viel für dich' (1:650), a feature which, as he well knows, will not sit well with the Prince. As a further blow to Homburg's prestige, he then states: 'Der Truchss und Hennings, die das Fussvolk führen, / Die sind zum Angriff auf den Feind bestimmt' (1:650). In other words, the glory is to go to Truchss and Hennings, not to Homburg. 'Und dir ist aufgegeben, hier zu halten / Im Tal, schlagfertig mit der Reuterei, / Bis man zum Angriff den Befehl dir schickt' (1:650). The Prince's role is 'halten,' i.e., to hold back, but if one takes into consideration his preconditioning, can he be realistically expected to ignore the wink of fate and deny his own impulsive personality? The stage directions would seem to imply that Hohenzollern, ever observant, realizes that his words have made no impression whatsoever: 'DER PRINZ VON HOMBURG *nach einer Pause, in der er vor sich niedergeträumt.* / – Ein wunderlicher Vorfall! / HOHENZOLLERN. Welcher, Lieber? / *Er* sieht *ihn an.* – *Ein Kanonenschuss fällt'* (1:650–1). Obviously, as the fifth act amply demonstrates, very little escapes Hohenzollern's discerning eye.

No sooner does victory seem imminent without the Prince's active involvement than he issues the order to mount. Kottwitz is the first to offer resistance, insisting: 'Des Herrn Durchlaucht, bei der Parole gestern, / Befahl, dass wir auf Order warten sollen' (1:652–3). Indeed, almost all the opposition comes from the old colonel who gives evidence of harbouring true feelings of affection for the younger man. Only well into the verbal exchange does Hohenzollern support Kottwitz and rather weakly at that: 'Ich bitte dich!' and 'Lass dir bedeuten, Arthur!' (1:653). When the Erster Offizier attempts to remove Homburg from command on grounds of insubordination and is physically and verbally abused by an outraged Prince, Hohenzollern admonishes the Erster Offizier, not Homburg: 'Schweig!' Bist du rasend?' (1:653). Furthermore, considering the seriousness and the possible consequences of the act Homburg proposes and bearing in mind the Count's presence when the Elector issued his warning to his nephew (1:647), one would have to conclude that his final utterance of the scene is singularly inappropriate: 'Es war ein Rat nur, den man dir erteilt' (1:654). Surely, by virtue of his social position and his central function within the drama, Hohenzollern is the only one who at this point could effectively stand up to Homburg and make an honest attempt to dissuade him, but he does surprisingly little to avert the inevitable clash between Elector and Prince. His last words lead one to believe that he is quite prepared, if not to countenance, at least to go along with a patent case of disobedience and that he seeks to reduce even further the severity of his past opposition to it.[27]

Once the Elector places Homburg under arrest, it is primarily Kottwitz who shows concern: 'Bei Gott, ich bin aufs äusserste –!' (1:664), tries to come to the Prince's defence: 'Mein Fürst, vergönn ein Wort mir –!' (1:665), and picks up Homburg's three flags, while Hohenzollern never opens his mouth to speak up on his 'friend's' behalf. Only when an officer approaches the Prince and asks for his sword does the Count step to his side, but to counsel him not to resist and to go along peacefully: 'Ruhig, Freund!' (1:665). In his total disorientation, Homburg asks, 'Darf man die Ursach wissen?' (1:665), to which his 'friend' replies 'mit Nachdruck': 'Jetzo nicht! / – Du hast zu zeitig, wie wir gleich gesagt, / Dich in die Schlacht gedrängt; die Order war, / Nicht von dem Platz zu weichen, ungerufen!' (1:666). Hohenzollern's initial reaction expressed with emphasis is in effect the recognition that this is neither the time nor place; however, the dash signals a short pause during which he collects himself and decides what would be in his best interest and in the worst interest of the Prince. He then contradicts his first spontaneous utterance and proceeds to outline the nature of the offence, stressing the fact that 'we warned you.' Hohenzollern did inform the Prince of the battle plan, but in a consciously unpalatable fashion and with the realization that the message had failed to reach its destination, and thus his public disavowal of all responsibility amounts to an ignoble self-justification at Homburg's expense. When the latter tries to defend his actions: 'Sind denn die Märkischen geschlagen worden?' (1:666), Hohenzollern 'stampft mit dem Fuss auf die Erde. / Gleichviel! – Der Satzung soll Gehorsam sein' (1:666), a succinct expression of the Elector's position. Since the Count did very little to prevent his friend's insubordination, made no previous reference to absolute obedience to the law, and may be said to have indirectly, perhaps even consciously, encouraged the Prince's disobedience, his statements must be repudiated as hypocritical, unfeeling, and openly hostile to Homburg. By denying any personal liability and by placing all the blame squarely on the Prince's shoulders without mention of the mitigating circumstances, he follows precisely the same pattern that he will later adopt vis-à-vis the Elector. Then, as a visual confirmation of his treachery, he 'entfernt sich von [Homburg],' maintaining: 'Es wird den

Hals nicht kosten' (1:666). In his preceding speech, punctuated by his stamping foot, he underscored for the benefit of the Elector the gravity of the alleged crime, but now in his last comment, obviously meant only for Homburg's ears, he negates his public utterance in a private about-face which seeks to minimize the whole incident. This constitutes the most blatant demonstration of Hohenzollern's underlying strategy: to play both sides of the power structure to their detriment but to his own subtle advantage.[28]

The first scene of the third act, conducted at the intimate level of friend to friend, illustrates rather convincingly how Hohenzollern, tenaciously assuming the worst and playing the part of an *advocatus diaboli*, undermines Homburg's confidence and precipitates his moral decline just as he indirectly engineered his physical fall. Describing the victory celebration at the church, he prepares his case by intimating that Natalie belongs to the Elector's domain: 'DER PRINZ VON HOMBURG. – Der Kurfürst war zugegen in der Kirche? HOHENZOLLERN. Er und die Fürstin und Natalie –' (1:667). He then 'sieht *ihn bedenklich an*' (1:668), a stage description reminiscent of an earlier one: '*Er* sieht *ihn an*' (1:657), compels the Prince to review his case: 'Was denkst du, Arthur, denn von deiner Lage, / Seit sie so seltsam sich verändert hat?' (1:668) and endeavours to shake his 'friend's' confidence in his ruler and father figure:

DER PRINZ VON HOMBURG
>
> Der Kurfürst hat getan, was Pflicht erheischte,
> Und nun wird er dem Herzen auch gehorchen
>
> ...
>
> Und um das Schwert, das ihm den Sieg errang,
> Schlingt sich vielleicht ein Schmuck der Gnade noch;
> – Wenn der nicht, gut; denn den verdient ich nicht!

HOHENZOLLERN O Arthur!

Er hält inne.

DER PRINZ VON HOMBURG Nun?

HOHENZOLLERN   – Des bist du so gewiss?   (1:668)

Homburg stands by his belief that the Elector could never destroy his surrogate son: 'Das glaubt ich seinem schlimmsten Feinde nicht, / Vielwen'ger dir, der du ihn kennst und liebst' (1:669). Ironically, this rather naïve assertion proves how limited the Prince's discernment of character is, for although Hohenzollern does know the Elector quite well, it is highly unlikely that he loves him, especially since at this very moment he is impugning by insinuation the Elector's motives. Even when the Count remarks that the court martial has pronounced the death sentence, Homburg remains unperturbed, again on the basis of a purely subjective appraisal: 'HOHENZOLLERN. Und worauf stützt sich deine Sicherheit? / DER PRINZ VON HOMBURG. Auf mein Gefühl von ihm! / *Er steht auf.* / Ich bitte, lass mich! / Was soll ich mich mit falschen Zweifeln quälen?' (1:670). Here we have the first hint that Hohenzollern's doubts have none the less struck root. As the Count persists in his attempt to compel him to consider the unpropitious signs: 'Nun, Arthur, ich versichre dich –' (1:670), Homburg retorts with a second 'Lass mich, Freund!' (1:670). But his ill-founded confidence begins to crumble once Hohenzollern reports that the Elector has requested that the death sentence, not the court proceedings as Homburg first assumed, be brought to him for signature and that the Marschall fears the worst:

> [Der Marschall] fügt' hinzu, da er bestürzt mich sah,
> Verloren sei noch nichts, und morgen sei
> Auch noch ein Tag, dich zu begnadigen;
> Doch seine bleiche Lippe widerlegte
> Ihr eignes Wort, und sprach: ich fürchte, nein! (1:671)

Whereas one might expect a confidant to stress the encouraging, optimistic options, as does the Marschall, Hohenzollern persistently evaluates the intentions of others and consistently with a negative bias. Here, for example, a facial expression belies an utterance and supports the supposition that the Marschall does not consider pardon a serious possibility. Homburg, clearly affected by Hohenzollern's assessment, strives at first to overcome his doubts 'by heaping up fantastic comparisons [and by belittling] his offence once more,'[29] but ultimately his trust and faith in the Elector are completely shattered by the Count's arguments: 'O Himmel! Meine Hoffnung!' (1:672).

A critical point has now been reached which Hohenzollern has prepared for in his earlier allusion to Natalie as dwelling in the Elector's sphere of influence. As if aware of the unspoken principle of territoriality, the Count inquires, rather innocently, 'Hast du vielleicht je einen Schritt getan, / Seis wissentlich, seis unbewusst, / Der seinem stolzen Geist zu nah getreten?' (1:672). Although Ellis quite correctly emphasizes the importance of these lines, discerning in them an explicit formulation of 'the central theme of the play, the relation of conscious to unconscious motivation,'[30] I cannot agree with his evaluation of Hohenzollern as 'until now ... an extreme example of refusal to recognize the real dynamics of the relationship between two people, below the surface of their expressed attitudes.'[31] Not only did Hohenzollern suspect 'the real dynamics of the relationship' between the Elector and the Prince from the very beginning, but with amazing consistency he has manipulated and exploited a state of underlying rivalry by setting one off against the other. This crucial quotation is yet another case in point. Previously, in the officers' presence, the Count ostensibly and rather ostentatiously ('Hohenzollern *stampft mit dem Fuss auf die Erde*' [1:666]) adopted the Elector's point of view: 'Der Satzung soll Gehorsam sein' (1:666) at Homburg's expense, while now he infers an inordinate sense of self-esteem at the Elector's expense. Ellis regards the reference to the Elector's proud spirit as '[t]he reverse of an imputation of low political motivation,'[32] as a positive, proper feeling of personal dignity and worth, but pride, like Hohenzollern, is two-faced and may also signify an unwarranted feeling of one's own superiority, and hence has frequently been decried as the origin of all sin, the cause of Lucifer's fall from grace. Surely, this aspect has to be given serious consideration in the realm of power politics. Ever the cautious contriver, Hohenzollern may well have intentionally chosen an ambiguous term which lends itself to either a complimentary or derogatory interpretation on the part of his listener. It is furthermore in keeping with Hohenzollern's character always to assume or imply the least flattering alternative. Since the Prince declares his innocence, maintaining: 'Mir war der Schatten seines [Elector's] Hauptes heilig' (1:672), Hohenzollern has recourse to his final trump:

> Arthur, sei mir nicht böse, wenn ich zweifle.
> Graf Horn traf, der Gesandte Schwedens, ein,
> Und sein Geschäft geht, wie man mir versichert,
> An die Prinzessin von Oranien.
> Ein Wort, das die Kurfürstin Tante sprach,
> Hat aufs empfindlichste den Herrn getroffen;
> Man sagt, das Fräulein habe schon gewählt.
> Bist du auf keine Weise hier im Spiele? (1:672)

In his analysis of this speech, Ellis maintains that Hohenzollern 'does not suggest anything base about the Elector ... It is the Prince who now jumps to the conclusion that the Elector is annoyed because his political plans are upset.'[33] But surely the 'base' suggestion is in fact present, and rather explicitly at that. First he contradicts Homburg's protestation that he has never unwittingly annoyed his ruler; then he points out that Graf Horn has arrived with a proposed political marriage, that the Princess has already committed herself (and obviously Hohenzollern knows to whom) and that this development 'hat aufs empfindlichste den Herrn getroffen' (1:672). To what other conclusion is Homburg supposed to jump?[34] Ellis has failed to perceive a well-developed tendency on the part of Hohenzollern always to set the stage and then to manipulate the protagonist into a position or a frame of mind where he draws what appears to be his own conclusion when in actual fact he has been led surreptitiously to that very conclusion.

Is the suggestion, as Samuel contends, so 'absurd'?[35] The fourth act makes it quite apparent that the Elector feels strongly attracted to Natalie, his surrogate daughter: 'Er legt den Arm um ihren Leib,' or 'Er umarmt sie' (1:682) and seeks to win her approval: 'Mein liebes Kind! Bist du mir wieder gut?' (1:682). Ellis has made a good case for seeing in the Elector a strong, possessive ruler who unconsciously wants to keep Natalie for himself, not surrender her to a younger rival. Hence Hohenzollern may well be correct in his assumption, but not so much in the sense that the betrothal runs counter to the Elector's political plans, but rather his unconscious personal desires. The Count is not alone in assuming that the Elector is capable of such crude motivations, for the Electress does not deny this implied line of reasoning when Homburg renounces Natalie in her presence, and Natalie, appealing to her uncle, twice relinquishes her claim to the Prince: 'Ich will ihn nicht für mich erhalten wissen –' (1:679).

Homburg quickly reaches the obvious conclusion: 'Ich bins, mein Freund; jetzt ist mir alles klar; / Es stürzt der Antrag ins Verderben mich: / An ihrer Weigrung, wisse, bin ich schuld, / Weil mir sich die Prinzessin anverlobt.' (1:672). Hohenzollern, in his reaction to this confession: 'Du unbesonnener Tor! Was machtest du? / Wie oft hat dich mein treuer Mund gewarnt?' (1:672), says absolutely nothing to dispute his 'friend's' deduction made on the basis of the information supplied by the Count himself because this is the exact conclusion that he intended him to reach as part of a scheme to present the Elector in a prejudicial light and to gain further domination over the Prince. In addition, Hohenzollern's rhetorical questions are ironic from two points of view. First, they suggest: just look at the mess you have again made when I was not present to guide you! and thus imply his annoyance that the Prince would dare to take a serious step without consulting him beforehand. Second, the formulation 'treuer Mund' is, to say the least, highly hypocritical since this 'loyal' mouth would be more appropriately characterized as the 'big' mouth which set the whole dramatic action in motion by baring Homburg's Achilles' heel.

As the Prince places his fate in the hands of his confidant, thus acknowledging his dependency: 'O Freund! Hilf, rette mich! Ich bin verloren' (1:672), Hohenzollern again assumes control of the events of *Prinz Friedrich von Homburg* at a crucial stage and outlines the route his 'friend' will ultimately travel: 'Ja, welch ein Ausweg führt aus dieser Not? / Willst du vielleicht die Fürstin Tante sprechen?' (1:672). Homburg immediately acts upon this not very heroic suggestion of appealing to a woman to intercede on his behalf without further ado: '– He, Wache!' Within the realm of political realities, the Prince is mere putty in the hands of Hohenzollern. Furthermore, as Silz observed, it is Hohenzollern who first proposes 'the abandonment of Natalie ... which is the most disgraceful thing in that much-criticized scene.'[36]

> Der Schritt kann, klug gewandt, dir Rettung bringen.
> – Denn kann der Kurfürst nur mit König Karl,
> Um den bewussten Preis, den Frieden schliessen,
> So sollst du sehn, sein Herz versöhnt sich dir,
> Und gleich, in wenig Stunden, bist du frei. (1:673)

Although such a move could lead to the Prince's physical preservation, it would also signal his moral death and his social elimination as a force to be reckoned with. In his choice of the wording 'klug gewandt,' Hohenzollern may well have unintentionally exposed his mastery of those devious Machiavellian tactics used in the acquisition of political supremacy.

Despite the fact that the fourth act is the only one in which Hohenzollern does not make an appearance, his pervasive presence is felt at almost every stage. Natalie's supplication to the Elector and her subsequent intervention follow logically from Homburg's visit to the Electress, an expedient recommended by the Count. While this confrontation between the Elector and his niece does reveal a strong undercurrent of rivalry between the two main male protagonists, a sense of competition encouraged by the garden incident, it also demonstrates how the Elector is anxious 'to complete the Prince's destruction as a hero figure'[37] by having him owe his life to a woman. This practice originated, however, with Hohenzollern in the first scene of the drama. It should be noted in passing that the petition asking for mercy is drawn up by Kottwitz, the Prince's only real friend; Hohenzollern is not even mentioned in this connection. And finally it is surely significant that at the point where the Prince must make a major decision upon reception of the Elector's letter, the Count is not present.[38] But even in this instance his influence may be an important contributing factor, for it was he who successfully undermined the Prince's irrational confidence in the Elector as a father figure and the letter thus amounts to a final confirmation of rejection.

While the first four acts have concentrated primarily upon an exposure of Homburg's frailties, the final act, immediately confronting the audience with a half-dressed Elector, will largely concern itself with the latter's vulnerability as publicly uncovered by Hohenzollern.[39] Ellis, adequately summarizing the critical reception of the Count's alleged defence of his 'friend,' maintains that 'Hohenzollern first depicts what actually happened, *without interpretation*' and that he 'has *only described a sequence of events*' in which the conspicuous actions of the Elector have had a significant effect.'[40] However, a comparison of this 'sequence of events' as described by Hohenzollern with the actual occurrence brings to light notable discrepancies. Although a misrepresentation but one dictated by loyalty and love for Homburg, Kottwitz's argument is based on the premise, 'I was wrong': 'Das hatt *ich* schlecht erwogen, mein Gebieter!' (1:696), whereas Hohenzollern's reasoning infers the proposition, 'you [Elector] were wrong': '"Beweis, dass Kurfürst Friedrich, des Prinzen Tat selbst" –' (1:699). The defence is in fact a veiled attack.

In reply to the Elector's incredulous question: 'Was! Die Veranlassung, du wälzest sie des Frevels, / Den er sich in der Schlacht erlaubt, auf mich?' (1:699), Hohenzollern confidently declares: 'Auf dich, mein Kurfürst; ja, ich, Hohenzollern!' The boldness and arrogance of this address, contrasting sharply with Kottwitz's submissive plea: 'Vergönne, mein erhabner Kurfürst, mir, / Dass ich, Im Namen des gesamten Heers, / In Demut dies Papier dir überreiche!' (1:695) immediately stresses the aggressive intent behind what amounts to a public denouncement, a cunning combination of truths and half-truths. The Count, proud of his name and position, clearly views himself as on an equal footing with his ruler. Indeed, later in his speech, he tells the Elector not to interrupt him: 'Herr, lass mich vollenden! –' (1:700).

Du wirst *dich* jener Nacht, o Herr, erinnern,
Da *wir* den Prinzen, tief versenkt im Schlaf,
Im Garten unter den Plantanen fanden.   (1:700)

Hohenzollern makes it sound as if the whole incident occurred accidentally, as if the group, 'wir,' the only time he includes himself, but in a very general sense, in reference to the first crucial episode, came upon the Prince by chance, whereas in reality, Hohenzollern, aware of Homburg's embarrassingly naked state of mind and having tried unsuccessfully to convince his sovereign of its existence, deliberately and maliciously, brought the Elector and his entourage into the garden.

> Vom Sieg des nächsten Tages *mocht* er träumen,
> Und einen *Lorbeer* hielt er in der Hand. (1:700)

A subtle change has taken place. Whereas Hohenzollern had continually interpreted Homburg's somnambulistic state and actions as being unequivocally determined by ambitious aspirations: 'DER KURFÜRST. Doch, was gilts, ich weiss / Was dieses jungen Toren Brust bewegt? / HOHENZOLLERN. O – was! Die Schlacht von morgen, mein Gebieter!' (1:633), now a note of probability, 'mocht,' has crept in inobtrusively, a move designed to lessen the danger of the threat posed by the Prince. As part of the same procedure, the menacing 'prächtg[er] Kranz des Ruhmes' (1:632) has been reduced to a more innocuous 'Lorbeer.'

> *Du*, gleichsam um *sein tiefstes Herz* zu prüfen,
> Nahmst ihm den Kranz hinweg, die Kette schlugst *du*,
> Die *dir* vom Hals hängt, *lächelnd* um das Laub. (1:700)

Although Hohenzollern has his facts correct (with one exception), he has, so to speak, exploited the syntax in his endeavour to place all the blame upon the Elector. The 'Du' has become isolated, cut off from its verb 'Nahmst' by an interpolated 'gleichsam um sein tiefstes Herz zu prüfen' and appears as well at the end of the next line, 'die Kette schlugst du,' a location equally emphatic as the first 'Du' – 'You' alone were involved and the responsibility must be borne by 'you.' The Count, the psychological expert, acknowledges quite accurately that this episode did test Homburg's unconscious self. However, since there is no reference whatsoever in the text to a smile, this is but another example of Hohenzollern's technique of imputing to others motives which reflect derogatorily upon their alleged instigators. In actual fact the insinuated cavalier attitude belongs more appropriately to Hohenzollern himself, who ridiculed Homburg quite openly: 'Schade, ewig schade, / Dass hier kein Spiegel in der Nähe ist!' (1:633).

> Und reichtest Kranz und Kette, so verschlungen,
> Dem Fräulein, deiner edlen Nichte, hin.
> Der Prinz steht, bei so wunderbarem Anblick,
> Errötend auf. (1:700)

Again, this is not factually true. Only when the Elector takes the wreath from the Prince's hands does the latter blush: *'Der Kurfürst nimmt ihm den Kranz aus der Hand; der Prinz errötet und sieht ihn an'* (1:633). The realization that he had been caught, albeit unconsciously, disclosing his innermost feelings, produced the blush, but Hohenzollern suggests that the Elector's actions of putting the chain of office about the wreath and giving it to Natalie to offer to the Prince, those details of the opening scene for which the Elector alone can be held responsible, provoked the embarrassed reaction. By altering such seemingly minor details, Hohenzollern casts a more negative light upon his ruler and places him in charge of the whole 'Scherz.'

> ... so *süsse* Dinge will er,
> Und von so *lieber* Hand gereicht, ergreifen:
> *Du* aber, die Prinzessin rückwärts *führend*,
> Entziehst dich eilig ihm; die Tür empfängt dich. (1:700)

Once more Hohenzollern goes beyond mere description by enlarging upon the significance of the wreath, chain, and especially Natalie to the Prince and puts the Elector ('Du') syntactically into the leading ('führend') position despite the fact that there is no indication in the work that this actually happened. Except for Hohenzollern's presence of mind, it was every man for himself. The lengths to which the Count is prepared to go to conceal his active participation are perhaps best revealed in the formulation 'die Tür empfängt dich.' Actually, Hohenzollern directed the Elector through the door: 'HOHENZOLLERN *öffnet die Tür*. Hier rasch herein, mein Fürst!' (1:634). In order to avoid making this concession, and hence to conceal his complicity, the door itself becomes the active subject.

> Jungfrau und Kett und Lorbeerkranz verschwinden,
> Und *einsam* – einen Handschuh in der Hand,
> Den er, nicht weiss er selber, wem? entrissen –
> *Im Schoss der Mitternacht*, bleibt er zurück. (1:700)

By his choice of words and images, Hohenzollern is trying to portray

Homburg as the unwitting, sympathetic martyr of a cruel, heartless prank perpetuated by the feelingless Elector. The aim behind such a method is dictated not so much by a desire to come to Homburg's aid as by the ulterior motive of publicly exposing the Elector's indiscretion, for as we have already ascertained, Hohenzollern has treated the Prince in a much more despicable fashion than the Elector, ridiculing, deceiving, and exploiting him, all apparently prescribed by a desire to discredit both his 'friend' and his sovereign.[41]

In the opening section of Hohenzollern's narrative relating the offence committed against the Prince, the you-Elector has dominated to the complete exclusion of the I-Hohenzollern.

> Die Sache war ein Scherz; jedoch von welcher
> Bedeutung ihm, das lernt *ich bald* erkennen. (1:700)

Now, for the first time in the account, the 'I' makes its appearance as the innocent observer of the Prince's condition after the event. Of course, the Count conveniently forgets to mention how he amused himself by making sport of Homburg, but in the time reference 'bald,' he has accidentally let slip a piece of information which intimates that he actually learned of the importance of the joke right there in the garden and yet he never really acted on the basis of this knowledge to prevent any deleterious repercussions.

> Giesst die Erinnrung Freude über ihn,
> Nichts Rührenders, fürwahr, kannst du dir denken.
> Den ganzen Vorfall, gleich, als wärs ein Traum,
> Trägt er, bis auf den kleinsten Zug, mir vor;
> So lebhaft, meint' er, hab er nie geträumt –. (1:700)

Again, Hohenzollern takes great care in depicting his 'friend' in a manner calculated to arouse in his listeners pity for a victimized prince and indignation for a victimizing elector. What the Count reports here is generally true but he has intentionally failed to divulge the subjective embellishments which Homburg's description contained (1:639). Previously, in the presence of the Elector, Hohenzollern was intent upon engendering an image of the Prince as an ambitious rival and hence as a threat to the Elector, but now he deliberately overlooks or avoids this aspect.

Und fester Glaube baut sich in ihm auf,
Der Himmel hab ein Zeichen ihm gegeben:
Es werde alles, was sein Geist gesehn,
Jungfrau und Lorbeerkranz und Ehrenschmuck,
Gott, an dem Tag der nächsten Schlacht, ihm schenken.   (1:700-1)

Not once during their conversation did Homburg make a statement of
this specific nature to Hohenzollern. What we have in the above quotation
is a reasonably accurate record of the Prince's understanding of the garden
affair as expressed in his monologue addressed to 'Glück' after the 'Parole'
when Hohenzollern was absent. Again the latter, functioning as an
interpreter, analyses with amazing psychological perspicacity and accuracy what the audience alone can confirm from the Prince's first soliloquy.

At this point, the Elector interrupts Hohenzollern's narrative with a
revealing comment: 'Hm! Sonderbar! – Und jener Handschuh – ?' (1:701)
Both the punctuation and the content indicate that the Count's reasoning
has found a receptive ear. Since three out of four of the Elector's interjections
deal with the crux of the matter, the glove, it would seem safe to assume
that he has grasped the inference of the argument. (The third interruption
'Nun? Drauf?' acts as a stimulus and accentuates his eagerness to hear
the outcome.)

Dies Stück des Traums, das ihm verkörpert ward,
Zerstört zugleich und kräftigt seinen Glauben.
Zuerst mit grossem Aug sieht er ihn an –
Weiss ist die Farb, er scheint nach Art und Bildung,
Von einer Dame Hand –.   (1:701)

Hohenzollern's extraordinarily perceptive intellect has fully recognized
the degrees of complexity added to the events of the garden by the intrusion
of the glove. It both shatters Homburg's faith that the incident was a
dream – for if he had been merely fantasizing, how could the glove be
real? – and it also serves as a concrete, visual confirmation of the episode's
prophetic message. As far as the allusions to colour, style, and form are
concerned, Hohenzollern, having no way of knowing what actually went
on in Homburg's mind, indulges once more in some imaginative speculation
and neglects to point out that the Prince first threw away the glove and
only picked it up again once Hohenzollern's three pressing interrogations
had helped to focus attention upon the need to discover the identity
of the glove's owner:

> ... doch weil er keine
> Zu Nacht, der er entnommen könnte sein,
> Im Garten sprach, – durchkreuzt, in seinem *Dichten*,
> Von mir, der zur Parol' aufs Schloss ihn ruft,
> *Vergisst* er, was er nicht begreifen kann,
> Und steckt *zerstreut* den Handschuh ins Kollett.   (1:701)

While it is true that Homburg did not on the conscious level speak to any lady, Hohenzollern did none the less try to convince his 'friend,' as the only possible logical explanation, that he had indeed participated in a 'Schäferstunde' (1:639), and while the Count could be said to have 'durchkreuzt' the Prince as ordered by the Elector, he still brought him dangerously close to discovering the truth. Whereas the choice of 'Dichten' is inadvertently quite fitting, for Homburg's narrative contained many flattering adornments, both the 'Vergisst' and the 'zerstreut' are highly questionable. First, there is no mention of the Prince's putting the glove in his jerkin during this scene, although it did appear in this location at the 'Parole' and second, since Hohenzollern indirectly underlined the central function of the glove: 'Und nun meinst du, der Handschuh, / Der sei der ihre?' (1:639) and 'Da kannst du auf dem kürzsten Weg erfahren, / Ob deiner Schönen dieser Handschuh fehlt' (1:640), it can scarcely be said that the Prince overlooked its importance. Hohenzollern continues either to justify his own behaviour or to withhold any information which would reflect adversely upon the Prince or himself.

> Drauf tritt er nun mit Stift und Tafel,
> Ins Schloss, aus des Feldmarschalls Mund, in *frommer*
> *Aufmerksamkeit*, den Schlachtbefehl zu hören.   (1:701)

Nothing could be further from the truth. In fact, the stage directions specify quite unequivocally, '*Der Prinz von Homburg, Stift und Tafel in der Hand, fixiert die Damen*' (1:641), and after the Feldmarschall and Hohenzollern managed to confront him briefly with the battle orders for the first time, we read soon thereafter, '*Der Prinz sieht wieder nach den Damen herüber*' (1:643). On that occasion, Hohenzollern, aware of his 'friend's' total preoccupation with the dream and the detection of 'der süssen Traumgestalt' (1:639), was compelled no less than five times to call him back to the demands of the matter at hand.

> Doch wer ermisst das ungeheure Staunen,
> Das ihn ergreift, da die Prinzess den Handschuh,

Den er sich ins Kollett gesteckt, vermisst.
Der Marschall ruft, zu wiederholten Malen:
Herr Prinz von Homburg! Was befiehlt mein Marschall?
Entgegnet er, und will die Sinne sammeln.   (1:701)

Although Hohenzollern has in all likelihood omitted outlining the Prince's
experiment in detail since it was performed during the issuing of orders
upon which the welfare of the country depended, this statement, right
down to the quotations, is reasonably accurate in its condensed form,
but at the same time quite obviously disputes the previous adverbial
phrase 'in frommer Aufmerksamkeit.'

Doch er, von Wundern ganz umringt –: der Donner
Des Himmels hätte niederfallen können! –!   (1:701)

Hohenzollern employed a similar exaggerated image based on sight, not
sound, to describe to the court the almost total absorption of the Prince
while in his somnambulistic state: 'Der ganze Flecken könnt in Feuer
aufgehn, / Dass sein Gemüt davon nicht mehr empfände, / Als der Demant,
den er am Finger trägt' (1:632). Another comparison made by Hohenzollern:

Ein Stein ist er, den Bleistift in der Hand,
Steht er zwar da und scheint ein Lebender;
Doch die Empfindung, wie durch Zauberschläge,
In ihm verlöscht   (1:701-2)

recalls the 'Demant, den er am Finger trägt,' and further underscores
the realization that the Prince had withdrawn into a trance-like state
in which he had limited access to external reality. If Hohenzollern then
recognized the analogy between Homburg's mental attitude in the garden
and that during the 'Parole,' why then did he merely stand by and allow
the problem to arise without making a serious, concerted effort either
to apprise his 'friend' of his responsibilities or to inform the supreme
commander of the unsuitability and incapacity to exercise authority of
one of his key officers?

... und erst am andern Morgen,
Da das Geschütz schon in den Reihen donnert,
Kehrt er ins Dasein wieder und befragt mich:

> *Liebster*, was hat schon Dörfling, *sag mirs*, gestern
> Beim Schlachtbefehl, mich treffend, vorgebracht? (1:702)

Homburg posed his question *before* hostilities had begun and 'Liebster' and 'sag mirs' do not appear in the original. By inserting a term of endearment, at the very beginning of the utterance, the Count now seeks to highlight his intimate association with the Prince even though he had publicly sought to distance himself from him before, the implication being that in this instance he wishes to dissociate himself openly from the Elector. The imperative 'sag mirs' appends a note of personal urgency to Homburg's request to be informed of the battle plan while the actual inquiry was couched in less emphatic language.

At this stage the Feldmarschall intervenes to corroborate Hohenzollern's report:

> Herr, die Erzählung, wahrlich, unterschreib ich!
> Der Prinz, erinnr' ich mich, von meiner Rede
> Vernahm kein Wort; *zerstreut* sah ich ihn oft,
> Jedoch in solchem Grad abwesend ganz
> Aus seiner Brust, *noch nie*, als diesen Tag. (1:702)

This statement must be taken into consideration in any attempt to determine degrees of culpability, for if others such as the Feldmarschall have noticed the Prince's propensity to be 'zerstreut' on several previous occasions, then there would be some justification for laying most of the blame on Homburg's personality. However, according to this witness, on the day of battle the Prince was more absent-minded than ever before and this excess can only be explained in terms of the added inducement supplied by the events of the first scene. Of course, it could also-be argued that the Feldmarschall offers biased, hence unreliable, testimony, but in any event his observation does add a measure of complexity to the question of guilt.

There have been several hints that Hohenzollern's argument has begun to weaken the Elector's determination to regard Homburg's offence as a clear-cut case of insubordination which, in the interest of the state, demands the death penalty. The Elector, having instinctively singled out the glove three times, 'fällt in Gedanken' (1:701), an unmistakable signal that a seed of doubt has been successfully planted. By deleting any reference to his own involvement and by presenting a sympathetic portrayal of the Prince as an unwitting victim, Hohenzollern has fabricated an iron-clad case with only one possible verdict, which, as the Elector observes, he allows the alleged culprit to pass himself:

> Und nun, wenn ich dich anders recht verstehe,
> Türmst du, wie folgt, ein Schlussgebäu mir auf:
> Hätt ich, mit dieses jungen Träumers Zustand,
> Zweideutig nicht gescherzt, so blieb er schuldlos:
> Bei der Parole wär er nicht zerstreut,
> Nicht widerspenstig in der Schlacht gewesen.
> Nicht? Nicht? Das ist die Meinung? (1:702)

Hohenzollern's favourite practice, that of inducing someone else to draw the damaging conclusion, has again borne fruit. 'Mein Gebieter, / Das überlass ich jetzt dir, zu ergänzen' (1:702). Assuming the stance of the loyal subject, he appeals to his ruler's conscience and skilfully places the onus of decision upon the Elector just as the latter did to Homburg with the letter. Such an apparently magnanimous rejoinder, not unlike the Elector's reaction to the Prince's plea for mercy, is calculated to disparage the sovereign, no matter what his answer. His emotional response of abusing his accuser:[42] 'Tor, der du bist, Blödsinniger!' (1:702) does not speak well for his supposed objectivity or dignity of office and belies Samuel's assertion that 'The Elector's annoyance is not genuine.'[43] Who appreciates being shown up in public? Now he seeks to shift the responsibility and at the same time minimizes the importance of his 'harmless' participation:

> ... hättest du
> Nicht in den Garten mich herabgerufen,
> So hätt ich, einem Trieb der Neugier folgend,
> Mit diesem Träumer *harmlos* nicht gescherzt.
> Mithin behaupt ich, ganz mit gleichem Recht,
> Der sein *Versehn* veranlasst hat, warst du! –. (1:702)

In attempting to put the blame back on Hohenzollern's shoulders where to a large extent it rightly belongs,[44] he only does more damage to his own public reputation. But of greater consequence is the fact that he now refers to Homburg's act of disobedience as a 'Versehn,' a sure sign that the seriousness of the transgression has been lessened in his eyes and that the Prince can no longer be held one hundred per cent accountable for his behaviour. Hohenzollern may therefore be said to have achieved a double objective: he has reduced a capital offence – 'des Todes schuldig' (1:663) or 'Frevel' (1:699) – to a mere error or oversight, and he has openly compromised the Elector. At this point and only at this point can it be said with some degree of certainty that the Elector, having been made aware of the mitigating circumstances, has no intention of going through with a death sentence which would now be wholly incommensurate with the crime and which would destroy his credibility as an equitable ruler.[45] 'That Hohenzollern does have an effect on the Elector,' as Ellis notes, 'at this moment is clear … from his having the last word, an important indicator of the significance of what is said.'[46] 'Es ist genug, mein Kurfürst! Ich bin sicher, / *Mein* Wort fiel, ein Gewicht, in *deine* Brust!' (1:702). This declaration should remind one of Homburg's ambivalent reply to the news of the Elector's miraculous survival on the battlefield: '*Dein* Wort fällt schwer wie Gold in *meine* Brust!' (1:660), and while suggesting a bond between the Prince and his confidant, it also denotes a major distinction marked by the reverse position of 'mein' and 'dein.' Whereas Homburg sees everything solely in relation to himself – the 'dein' only has significance as it pertains to the 'mein' – Hohenzollern is the man who strives to manage and manipulate others – the 'mein' has power over the 'dein.' Completely in character, the Count is attributing reactions or feelings to others and, as subsequent events will prove, with considerable accuracy.

When the Prince makes his appearance before the assembled officers, Hohenzollern more or less fades into the background. Indeed, Homburg addresses his first speech to his only genuine friend, Kottwitz, and completely ignores the Count. Throughout this confrontation, Hohenzollern makes only two comments. The first, 'Er will den Tod?' (1:704), registers his astonishment at the Prince's decision to revert to the traditional heroic mould, while the second, 'Mein Kurfürst, kann dein Herz –?' (1:706) may well be determined by the desire to accommodate public opinion. It is now socially acceptable to support Homburg since the officers are clearly on his side. And finally, as soon as the Elector inquires, 'Wollt ihrs zum vierten Male mit ihm wagen?' (1:706), the involuntary, spontaneous reply 'Wie, mein vergöttert – angebeteter –?' (1:707) comes from Kottwitz and Truchss. Hohenzollern is conspicuous by his total silence throughout this scene.

The last two scenes of *Prinz Friedrich von Homburg* serve as positive proof that the Count's psychological analysis did in fact strike a responsive chord within the Elector. Now the latter, on his own initiative, leads the court back to the scene of the crime in an apparent effort to set matters straight.[47] Hence, it is singularly fitting that the instigator reappear as master of ceremonies: 'Hohenzollern tritt, mit einem Tuch, an das Geländer und winkt dem Rittmeister Stranz' (1:708). Just as he introduced the initial garden sequence which had a profound influence upon the rest of the drama, he now gives the signal to begin its re-enactment. No sooner does the overwhelmed Prince lose consciousness than Hohenzollern 'fasst ihn auf' exclaiming, 'Zu Hülfe!' (1:708) – on the surface, a demonstration of concern. In the first act, the Count not only deliberately caused his 'friend' to faint by calling out his name,[48] but also exhibited no consideration for his subsequent well-being: 'Der Prinz fällt um. / Da liegt er; eine Kugel trifft nicht besser!' (1:635). If one compares his reactions in both cases, one seems to be faced with an apparent inconsistency. There is, however, a major distinction:[49] previously, Hohenzollern was alone and unobserved with the somnambulistic Homburg; now he is playing to an audience which expects an outward show of solicitude.

In his informative analysis of the 'Tuch' image, Ellis has indicated how a waving cloth can signify, among other things, both life and death: 'This strange series of connections seems dominated by the ideas of concealment, fortune, and changeability, and shows the ironic reversal characteristic of the play.'[50] Significantly, Hohenzollern, for whom the final wave of the cloth has been reserved, marking the dénouement of the work, incarnates all of the above 'ideas' selected by Ellis. Like inscrutable fortune, he toys with the lives of men, seemingly indifferent to human suffering. For although this final gesture signals ostensibly a positive act, a granting of life, to the Prince it represents the very opposite, a denial, because he has already repudiated this dark, harsh, hostile world in favour of the brilliance of immortality[51] first promised in the garden. It is Hohenzollern who negates this ultimate escape, a development already anticipated in the opening garden episode as the Count took up a position behind the Prince who gazed longingly towards the closed 'Tor des Himmels' (1:639).

Having already created in the dramatic character Hermann a pragmatic Realpolitiker, Kleist fashioned in Hohenzollern a man who deals with realities, not ideals and who, not unlike Machiavelli, presumes the lowest common denominator or the least complimentary explanation for all human actions. On the level of underlying intent the three main contenders in the implied power struggle in Prinz Friedrich von Homburg would all seem to justify in varying degrees the Italian political theorist's unflattering view of human nature: 'For men, generally speaking, have a short-lived gratitude, are effusive in protestation, insincere, secretive poltroons, and

on the make' (M 89). Whereas both the Elector and Homburg pursue
their respective goals as dictated by unconscious self-interest, Kleist has
furnished Hohenzollern with a greater awareness and an amazing ability
to grasp the hidden mechanics of the human mind, which he fully utilizes
in his manipulation of others. Even though he is not present when
Homburg addresses Fortune, he none the less calculates with uncanny
accuracy how the Prince has interpreted the garden incident. Because
of his assumption of near equality with his sovereign and his status of
considerable intimacy with the titular protagonist, as signalled by the
exclusive use of 'Arthur' and 'Heinrich,' he occupies a unique position
between the upper and lower realms, between Elector and Prince, which
enables him to expose their weaknesses, to jeopardize their public image,
and thus to exploit both sides of the power structure for his own subtle
advantage.

Throughout the drama, he consistently has recourse to the same
methods to achieve these ends, having obviously taken to heart Machiavelli's advice that 'a ruler who wishes to survive must often forget virtue.'
(M 98). In describing an individual or an event, he goes beyond an objective
account to the prejudicial suggestion or insinuation in order to compromise
an individual, while at the same time fostering a sense of potentially
destructive competition between two rivals. He imputes to those in
authority motives which reflect derogatorily upon their supposed instigators and consequently sours their personal relationship. Another effective
weapon wielded with considerable skill is the social put-down or destruction through ridicule. Continually throughout *Il Principe*, Machiavelli
stresses the importance of preserving the respect of others, which he
rates even more highly than affection.[52] Not surprisingly, he includes a
reputation for effeminateness and cowardliness as being deleterious to
one's effectiveness as a leader of men (M 83). Hence history teaches that
the wise ruler avoids degrading himself; the Roman emperor Commodus
'went too far and lost his authority by appearances in the gladiatorial
rings, and by generally debasing his pride and the imperial dignity, so
that even the soldiers lost their respect for him' (M 100–1). Hohenzollern
displays considerable mastery at putting others into an embarrassing
plight from the first scene, where he conducts his sovereign down from
his high station to make sport of one of his commanders, through to
the underhand public denouncement of the last act. In both cases the
Elector's prestige suffers (not to mention the Prince's). As the Florentine
noted in the sixteenth century, 'Nothing builds up the reputation of a
ruler so much as successful compaigning and proofs of his quality of

leadership' (M 107). By publicly humiliating the Elector, the Count seeks to undermine his authority in the presence of those who are the very basis of his power, his officers. Illustrating the necessary 'qualities of leadership,' Machiavelli insists that 'the ruler must be deliberate in sentence' (M 88), but Hohenzollern manages to place the Elector in a position where he has to rescind a death sentence since the former has openly implicated the latter in the crime.

'Deceit,' according to Machiavelli, 'is essential where loyalty to a pledge would turn to [the ruler's] disadvantage and the reasons for giving it no longer hold good' (M 91). Hohenzollern constantly practises duplicity both in his loyalty to the Elector and above all in his alleged friendship to the Prince.[53] Although he is fully cognizant of what is taking place, he remains intentionally inactive, allowing Homburg to take a step which he knows will lead to disaster and then denies all knowledge or responsibility once the damage has been done. He changes sides whenever it suits his purpose, another expedient advocated by Machiavelli;[54] he provides harmful counsel by which he renders others dependent upon himself; he presents a duty in an unpalatable, almost incidental manner designed to encourage his listener to ignore or disobey it altogether; and he misrepresents an incident, ostensibly to help a 'friend' but in reality to conceal his own deception and to censure his superior. Recognizing that 'Generally speaking, men judge more by appearances than by realities' (M 92–3), Machiavelli recommends letting someone else do the dirty work,[55] a technique in which the Count has become quite adept. On several occasions, once he has set the stage, he adroitly manipulates the protagonist, the Elector or the Prince, into a situation or a frame of mind where he seems to draw his own conclusion, one damaging either to his unconscious rival or to himself, when in actual fact he has been surreptitiously programmed to reach this very judgment.

As far as Hohenzollern's own status within the drama is concerned, he goes to great lengths to dissociate himself from those in public disfavour, preferring to be on the winning side, even to the extent of 'hedging his bets,' i.e., he publicly supports the Elector while privately encouraging the Prince. In placing all the blame upon others by a biased, personally gratifying interpretation of an incident, he seeks to avoid all responsibility while giving the impression of standing for such altruistic virtues as obedience and submission to the state. Hence Hohenzollern follows a practice seen by Machiavelli as a major prerequisite in the acquisition and retention of power: 'We can conclude that a ruler need not be endowed with all the good qualities [mercy, fidelity to the pledged word, kindness, honesty, and devoutness] I have discussed, but he should seem to possess them. I would go so far as to say that if he did possess them, and exercised them on all occasions, it would be a mistake, while it is a good thing to seem to possess them' (M 92).

What motivates the Count in the dubious role he plays from beginning to end? To a large degree he remains an enigma beyond the strict definition of the Machiavellian power politician, but I should like to propose some possible motives for which the text offers some support. First of all, it seems particularly relevant that Kleist opted to call his schemer Hohenzollern because nothing in the historical account of the Battle of Fehrbellin would justify such a choice. The list of characters informs us from the outset that Graf Hohenzollern belongs to 'der Suite des Kurfürsten' (1:630), himself a Hohenzollern, and just before the Count's concealed attack on the Elector in act five, in response to the latter's question: 'Die Veranlassung, du wälzest sie des Frevels, / Den er sich in der Schlacht erlaubt, auf mich?' he retorts boldly, if not arrogantly, 'Auf dich, mein Kurfürst; ja, ich, Hohenzollern!' (1:699). Power resides in the very name itself, as emphasized by its final emphatic position in the verse. It designates the most celebrated, most influential German family.[56] Kleist may well have been hinting at such aristocratic omnipotence; all the major characters in *Prinz Friedrich von Homburg* have their titles consistently included in the text before their speeches – Der Kurfürst, Der Prinz von Homburg, Prinzessin Natalie, Obrist Kottwitz – but the Count, except for the opening speech of the drama, is always referred to as simply Hohenzollern. He may thus embody a law unto himself, someone who engages in play for the sake of play, because in terms of power politics, he obviously sees himself as his relative's, the Elector's, equal. Since, however, within the court hierarchy his relatively minor social position does not seem commensurate with his name, he resents the authority and acclaim enjoyed by both Homburg and the Elector[57] and out of animosity, jealousy, and pride he strives to pull them down from their pedestals. After all, the putting down of a rival, especially in public, amounts to an exhibition of one's personal power over another human being.

There are numerous indications that enmity is indeed at work in Hohenzollern's attitude vis-à-vis his 'friend' and his sovereign, but upon closer scrutiny of the text, a more specific cause would seem to suggest itself. Hohenzollern is the only person in the play to laugh. He does so twice and both times the merriment smacks of a gratuitous, diabolical cruelty. In the first instance, Homburg, in his indecision and perplexity at being unable to discern the repressed identity, becomes the butt:

'HOHENZOLLERN *lacht*. Schelm, der du bist, mit deinen Visionen!' (1:639). As I pointed out previously, Hohenzollern himself produces this painful predicament for his own amusement and displays no concern whatsoever for the pernicious effects it may have upon the impressionable Prince. The second laugh bursts forth in gleeful anticipation of the terror soon to be experienced by the unsuspecting Swedish cavalry: 'HOHENZOLLERN *lacht*. Ha! Wie das Feld die wieder räumen wird, / Wenn sie versteckt uns hier im Tal erblickt!' (1:652). When the musket and canon fire commences, unable to check himself, he cries out, 'Schiesst! Schiesst! Und macht de Schoss den Erde bersten! / Der Riss soll eurer Leichen Grabmal sein' (1:652). In this spontaneous reaction with its sexual undercurrent, he discloses his true colours, one of the few times he relinquishes self-control. The brutal nature of this hyperbolic image is further underlined by the pause which immediately follows it and by the less drastic exclamations positioned on either side of it:

GOLZ Bei Gott! Solch einen Donner des Geschützes
   Hab ich zeit meines Lebens nicht gehört!
HOHENZOLLERN Schiesst! Schiesst! Und macht den Schoss der Erde bersten!
   Der Riss soll eurer Leichen Grabmal sein.
Pause – Ein Siegsgeschrei in der Ferne.
ERSTER OFFIZIER Herr, du, dort oben, der den Sieg verleiht:
   Der Wrangel kehrt den Rücken schon! (1:652)

Clearly, Hohenzollern derives great pleasure from inflicting suffering and delights in destruction and death, his proper element. Such an attitude suggests self-indulgence in the psychological and physical domination of others and may constitute a form of revenge upon those who have denied him a status more in keeping with his own self-image: 'ich, Hohenzollern!' Seen from this point of view, all of his utterances or actions can be readily explained.

The implicit comparison of Goethe's Mephistopheles and the Kleistian Machiavellian protagonist put forward in my introduction is perhaps not as arbitrary as it may at first have seemed. A remote similarity between Goethe's devil and Hohenzollern can be perceived in terms of their relative function and their relationship to the titular hero, especially in the initial scenes. In both plays, the diabolical figure acts as the intermediary between the upper realms of light inhabited by the ultimate authority, God-Elector, with whom he is on good terms, and the lower realm of the dark study-garden occupied by Faust-Homburg whose downfall he is plotting. In the dependency of the main character upon his companion, there is a similar contrast between self-centred idealism and pragmatic cynicism. Hohenzollern also shares Mephistopheles' delight in gratuitous cruelty. Although a sadistic strain runs through most of Kleist's works and is especially noteworthy in *Die Hermannsschlacht*, nowhere has it received a more consistent treatment than in the portrayal of the Mephistophelian Graf Hohenzollern, the 'Meister des Spiels,' the true '*agent provocateur*,' and the unsung villain of *Prinz Friedrich von Homburg*.

5

The sick lion:
Robert Guiskard

In my investigation of Kleist's Machiavellian protagonists, I have chosen to deal with *Robert Guiskard* last since the fragment represented for Kleist both a beginning and, in a sense, an end: although it was one of the first themes with which he struggled so assiduously and desperately as a novice writer, it still commanded sufficient interest in 1807 for him to return to the subject at the height of his literary career. 'Die Annahme,' argues Richard Samuel, 'dass die dichterische Ausgestaltung des *Guiskard*-Fragments erst 1807 durchgeführt wurde, bedeutet allerdings noch nicht, dass Handlungsverlauf und Gehalt des Stückes ebenfalls aus dieser Zeit stammten. Es ist durchaus möglich, dass diese Elemente seit 1803 in Kleists Gedächtnis verankert blieben und dass sie 1807 nur in eine neue Stilform gegossen wurden.'[1] Many critics have recorded 'die vielfache Verschwisterung'[2] between *Penthesilea* and *Robert Guiskard*, a family resemblance, however, based more on stylistic than thematic considerations. If one bears in mind a dramatic situation where princes openly quarrel over their own particular advantage, while paying little heed to a life-and-death struggle of their own nation, where one man is regarded as the only possible key to the salvation of that nation,[3] or where a mainspring of the action lies in an underlying power conflict between an uncle portrayed as the father of his people and his nephew, a surrogate son and darling of the armed forces, one begins to see the possibility of the fragment's assuming several guises in Kleist's last two plays. Guiskard's determination to achieve his goal, if need be at the expense of his family and his people, parallels Hermann's resolve to adhere to his plan. The drive for 'Ruhm' also provides the unconscious-conscious motivation behind many actions of Hermann, the Elector, Homburg, and as I shall demonstrate, Abälard and Robert Guiskard. Finally, whereas *Der zerbrochene Krug, Die Her-*

mannsschlacht, and *Prinz Friedrich von Homburg* each include one Machiavellian protagonist, *Robert Guiskard* contains two: an older, more experienced practitioner of the art of manipulating others and a younger, up-and-coming disciple profiting from past example: 'Denn in Gestalt und Red und Art dir [Abälard] gleich, / Wie du, ein Freund des Volks, jetzt vor uns stehst, / Stand Guiskard einst, als Otto hingegangen, / Des Volkes Abgott, herrlich vor uns da!' (1:164).

Before considering the two leading personalities in the political arena, we need to evaluate the function and relative importance of the people, a designation synonymous with an army involved in a military campaign far from home. The masses are primarily significant as the instrument upon which the Machiavellian protagonist displays his leadership qualities, a view supported by Streller's study: 'Auch in *Guiskard* wird das Volk als eine von Stimmungen getriebene und bewegte Menge gezeigt, der Furcht ausgeliefert, zur Panik geneigt. Es wird ihm kein Anspruch auf eigene Meinungsäusserung zugestanden.'[4] Recent theses explaining Kleist's political position in terms of the socio-political context at the turn of the nineteenth century have endeavoured to ascertain a positive political development in his depiction of the people in *Robert Guiskard*. Typical of this approach is the following statement from Ulrich Vohland's *Bürgerliche Emanzipation in Heinrich von Kleists Dramen und theoretischen Schriften*: 'Darin, dass Kleist dem Volk der Normänner eine Mitentscheidung über die Wahl des Monarchen und weit grössere Mitsprachemöglichkeiten zuschreibt, als sie das wirkliche Volk, das diese im Verlauf des Mittelalters immer mehr verloren hatte … , besass, spiegelt sich die bürgerliche Hoffnung auf grösseren politischen Einfluss.'[5]

There is really less cause for optimism than Vohland maintains. As Iris Denneler has noted, 'Auf der Ebene des Staatssystems ist [das Volk] nur als Masse relevant und kann allein in bezug auf diesen quantitativen Aspekt Ansprüche geltend machen. Doch als substantiellen Grund bildet es die Bedingung der Möglichkeit für Herrschaft überhaupt – der Greis verweist zu Recht auf die Position des Volkes als des Herrschers "Lenden Mark."'[6] Even *Il Principe*, written in Renaissance Italy at the beginning of the sixteenth century, acknowledges the essential political strategy of maintaining popular support since 'there is no hope in adversity except the loyalty of the people' (M 63). Machiavelli repeatedly emphasizes the necessity of playing to the crowd: '[The leader] can count on support if he is in good heart and steady in emergencies, prudent in his precautions, and by the spirit and letter of his commands captures the loyalty of the masses' (M 63), and in a chapter entitled 'The Avoidance of Hatred and Contempt,' he describes contemporary and historical figures, many of whom were political upstarts, to prove that creating a good public image or gaining the loyalty of the armed forces ensures political longevity, for 'a ruler has little to fear from conspirators when he has the people on his side, whereas when they are hostile and their hatred has been aroused he must beware of everything and everybody' (M 96), a lesson also taught by *Robert Guiskard*.

As Denneler has shown,[7] one must make a distinction between the anonymous masses and their spokesmen. Indeed, even at this lower end of the social scale, an hierarchical sense of separation from and hence superiority over the people characterizes the behaviour and utterances of the committee and especially of the old man and the Norman soldier. In the latter two cases, a more direct, intimate relationship with the adulated leader may well explain their first loyalty to Guiskard. The Norman is a member of his personal bodyguard and as such may be counted upon to be particularly devoted, while the older man, whom Guiskard knows well enough to address by his first name, is called by Robert 'der wackre Hausfreund ... / Der einst die Wiege Guiskards hütete' (1:161). When putting Robert in his place, the old man stresses the personal rapport established between the ruler and the people: 'Und nicht das erstemal wärs, wenn er [Robert Guiskard] uns / In Huld es [a face-to-face meeting] zugestände' (1:162). Hence one may attribute some of the confidence and distinctiveness of the individualized representatives to their more personal contact with Guiskard himself and his ability to inspire obedience to his will.

Once Helena has made her plea that the crowd depart, the old man is quick to point out that her proffered excuse – fatigue has caused Guiskard's tardiness in rising – does not coincide with their leader's former practice. Moreover, the old man even goes as far as to imply by negation the existence of a concealed motive to send the people away: 'Wenn dich kein andrer / *Verhaltner* Grund bestimmt, uns fortzuschicken: / Für deines Vaters Ruhe sorge nicht' (1:158). This crafty formulation, despite the concluding assurance of fidelity, suggests a strong undercurrent of doubt and distrust further reinforced by the following exchange:

DER NORMANN *nachdem er sich wieder umgesehen.*
    Hört. Aber was ihr hört, auch nicht mit Mienen
    Antwortet ihr, viel weniger mit Worten.
DER GREIS Mensch, du bist fürchterlich. Was ist geschehn?

DER NORMANN *laut zu dem Volk, das ihn beobachtet.*
  Nun, wie auch stehts? Der Herzog kommt, ihr Freunde?
EINER *aus dem Haufen.*
  Ja, wir erhoffens.
EIN ANDRER   Die Kaiserin will ihn rufen.
DER NORMANN *geheimnisvoll, indem er die beiden Männer vorführt.*   (1:159–60)

The Norman's first utterance, emphasized by his furtive gesture, is only meant for the committee and not for the broad mass of the army whereas he intentionally designs his two questions (to which he already knows the answers) for public consumption, a manipulative technique frequently turned to account by the Machiavellian protagonist. As we learn from the Norman's subsequent long discourse delivered solely to the inner circle, he is convinced that Guiskard is deadly ill. Doubting the possibility of an appearance by the duke, he assumes the guise of the naïf for the sake of his general audience. The 'Haufen,' only marginally a more positive classification than the 'Pöbel' of *Die Familie Schroffenstein*,[8] is not permitted to detect the inconsistencies in Helena's speech, nor to be privy to the disconcerting revelation of Guiskard's bodyguard:

DER GREIS   Und nun
  Meinst du, er sei unpässlich, krank vielleicht – ?
DER ERSTE KRIEGER Krank? Angesteckt – !
DER GREIS *indem er ihm den Mund zuhält.*
                        Dass du verstummen müsstest!   (1:160)

Thus the leaders of the people also participate in a conspiracy of silence.

Having established the malleability of the masses, even in the hands of their own leaders, I shall turn to the younger of the fragment's Machiavellian protagonists, who, from the very outset, demonstrates his skill in the handling of the same masses. His cunning manifests itself in his initial speech: 'Mit Zürnen seh ich dich [Robert] und mit Befehlen / Freigebiger, als es dein Vater lehrt' (1:162). Since Abälard realizes that Guiskard incarnates the model folk leader, he uses the father to discredit the son by an uncomplimentary comparison. 'Und unbefremdet bin ich, nimmt die Schar / Kalt deine heissen Schmähungsworte auf' (1:162). Immediately taking the side of the crowd, he betrays his cousin with an eye to personal gain. After all, he could have spoken to Robert privately but chooses to embarrass him publicly, hoping to jeopardize whatever popular support or confidence he may enjoy: 'Denn dem Geräusch des Tags vergleich ich sie [deine heissen Schmähungsworte], / Das keiner hört, weils stets sich hören lässt' (1:162). By implication this is not an isolated occurrence born out of the present crisis but a common procedure indicative of a general arrogant attitude towards the people. This technique of pointing out a recurrent pejorative tendency prefigures Hohenzollern's efforts to disgrace his 'friend' in the opening garden scene: the Count alludes to Homburg's habit of lapsing into irresponsible day dreams such as the one Hohenzollern is in the very process of drawing to the court's attention. Also the constant, unheeded repetitions, unflatteringly compared to 'dem Geräusch des Tags,' suggests a person of little consequence, a nuisance, whose presence is merely tolerated.

Abälard then proceeds to single out Robert's major political faux pas, his insulting of the old man whose behaviour and attitude Abälard defends: 'Noch, find ich, ist nichts Tadelnswürdiges / Sogar geschehn, bis auf den Augenblick!' (1:162). All the blame rests not with the old man, but rather with Robert.

> Dass kühn die Rede dieses Greises war,
> Und dass sie stolz war, steht nicht übel ihm,
> Denn zwei Geschlechter haben ihn geehrt,
> Und eine Spanne von der Gruft soll nicht
> Des dritten einer ihn beleidigen.   (1:162)

By praising the boldness and pride of the 'Greis,' Abälard flatters him and by extension, the group that he represents. In contrast to his cousin, Abälard insists upon the respect in which one should hold an aged member of the people, a device exploited by Hermann when he agrees to act as Teuthold's avenger and, so doing, gains the full support of the masses. Since the people have traditionally honoured the aged, to humiliate or insult a venerated old man who has served so loyally in the past comes across as especially censurable.

Abälard's opening speech contains two underlying objectives: to ingratiate himself with the people and to disparage his cousin. The first goal he strives to achieve by praising the masses for their love of freedom: 'Denn seine Freiheit ist des Normanns Weib' (1:162) and by stressing the necessity of a ruler/subject relationship based upon affection: 'Durch Liebe, hör es, musst du sie [Normannskrone] erwerben, / Das Recht gibt sie dir nicht, die Liebe kanns!' (1:163). Interpreting these two verses, Denneler has argued, 'Die progressiven Tendenzen des Staatsentwurfs Abälards werden in seiner Forderung deutlich, die Herrschaft auf Liebe und Gesetz ... zu gründen.'[9] Admittedly, the quotation taken out of context could be read this way, but in context, Abälard has wittingly formulated his utterance to present himself in the best light possible and thus to sway public opinion in his favour, for in a contest between himself and his cousin Robert, only Abälard can appeal to both qualifications, 'Liebe' and 'Gesetz.' While conceding that 'the maintenance of autocratic rule in dynastic monarchies is a far easier business than it is in the newly established' (M 30), Machiavelli still emphasizes that the lasting foundation of any successful rule is 'the goodwill of the people' (M 106). Abälard is clearly playing to the crowd, telling his listeners what they would like to hear, but, at the same time, he is maligning his rival by imputing to him pusillanimity: 'Allein der glatte Nacken seines Sohnes / Der schüttelt gleich sich, wenn ihm eins nur naht' (1:162–3) and overconfidence: 'Meinst du [Robert], es könne dir die Normannskrone / Nicht fehlen, dass du dich so trotzig zeigst?' (1:163). His apparent championing of the people's cause furnishes an ideal opportunity to criticize his opponent[10] comparable to Hohenzollern's attack on the Elector disguised as a defence of Homburg in act five.

Abälard is smart enough to realize that because Robert Guiskard has assumed almost god-like status, it would be unwise in terms of his own political ambitions to denigrate the popular hero; however, he knows how to exploit his uncle's reputation to enhance his own and to lessen that of his cousin: 'Allein von Guiskard ruht kein Funk auf dir, / Und diesen Namen mindstens erbst du nicht' (1:163). The son does not at all take after his father – by inference, the nephew does – and lacks the necessary leadership quality of cunning. Ironically, by raising the issue, Abälard is demonstrating its very use against young Robert: the former has recourse to cunning to profit from a situation to the detriment of the latter. In his arrogance, Robert is none the less being more honest with his audience by exposing his true attitude, however reprehensible, than Abälard who is seeking to manipulate the masses to achieve a self-serving objective.

> Denn in der Stunde, da es eben gilt,
> Schlägst du [Robert] sie schnöd ins Angesicht, die jetzt
> Dich auf des Ruhmes Gipfel heben könnten.
> Doch ganz verlassen ist, wie du wohl wähnst,
> Das Normannsheer, ganz ohne Freund, noch nicht,
> Und bist dus nicht, wohlan, ich bin es gern. (1:163)

Again, Abälard continues his strategy of presenting himself as the defender of the people as if he had overwhelming faith in them. But of greater significance is his reference to 'Ruhm,' the second time he mentions it in the same speech (cf. 'Und heilig wäre mir das Ehepaar, / Das mir den *Ruhm* im Bette zeugt der Schlacht' [1:162]). The repetition underscores what may well be an obsession with fame, although, in context, Abälard employs it in a calculating manner to appeal to the pride of his listeners and to secure their support through flattery. This advocacy of the Norman army is also in keeping with Machiavelli's observation that to gain and to maintain power, one must be able to command the full loyalty of the army. (M 80).

Abälard has taken a major gamble in standing up to Robert, criticizing him openly, and asking those present to decide between the two princes: 'Und wenn dein [Robert's] Feldherrnwort die Schar vertreibt, / Meins will, dass sie noch bleib!' (1:163). Even in this instance, Abälard is sufficiently astute to strengthen his position by resorting to what he knows to be the final court of appeal in the eyes of the people: 'Ich will vor Guiskard es verantworten' (1:163), while displaying his leadership potential in his independence and lack of fear before Guiskard. (His later cowardly retreat in Guiskard's presence will gainsay this claim.) Robert's response: 'Dich jetzt erkenn ich, und ich danke dir, / Als meinen bösen Geist!' (1:163) indicates the irretrievable nature of the step taken by Abälard, a step avoided by Kleist's other Machiavellian protagonists until they are convinced they may attack a rival with impunity and assurance of success. Abälard has 'declared his colours' presumably only after having calculated the most opportune moment to do so. As the remainder of the fragment implies, his real opponent, the man he would like to eliminate, is not the son but the father, the true source of power from which the son derives all his authority. It would be tantamount to political suicide to attack directly the people's favourite, but persuaded that Guiskard's illness, an 'historical accident,' has created a power vacuum, he opts to make his play for the leadership at this moment. At first sight, this would seem a reasonable decision concurring with Machiavelli's contention: 'New dominions can be founded by men of gifts and ability, or by those favoured by historical accident' (M 44).

The concept of the evil mentor alluded to by Robert appears to be an especially appropriate designation not only for the Abälard/Robert relationship, but that existing between Abälard and Guiskard, Licht and Adam, Hermann and the representatives of Rome, Hohenzollern and Homburg, and Hohenzollern and the Elector. Robert is not without insight: 'Doch ganz gewonnen / Ist, wie geschickt dus führst, noch nicht dein Spiel. / – Willst du ein Beispiel sehn, wie sicher meins, / Die Karten mögen liegen, wie sie wollen?' (1:163). In an image anticipating the first speech of *Die Hermannsschlacht*, he presents the implied power struggle as a game in which he will win the final contest, no matter what cards he may be dealt. This raises the question of the role of chance in human affairs, a theme dear to Kleist. Hermann, for instance, realizes that he will be unable to fulfil his plan without the goodwill of the gods, while Guiskard, trusting in his own strength, is probably thwarted in the achievement of his goal by an unforeseen development, the outbreak of the plague. Machiavelli adopted a middle position in this debate between will and fate, a position more or less in line with Kleist's attitude as expressed in his last two plays. '[Since] there is surely a certain liberty of choice left to us,' remarks the Florentine, 'I think that it may well be true that fate determines part of our actions but allows our freedom of will to control the other' (M 117).

Robert tries to rise to the occasion, confident in his own ability to manage the people:

> Ihr Guiskardssöhne, die mein Wort vertreibt,
> Und seines schmeichlerisch hier fesseln soll,
> Euch selber ruf ich mir zu Richtern auf!
> Entscheiden sollt ihr zwischen mir und ihm,
> Und übertreten ein Gebot von zwein.   (1:163)

He flatters his listeners as 'Guiskardssöhne,' thus establishing a personal link, while reminding them of the basis of his authority. Whereas his rival sought to gain their support through false praise, he will speak to their better, more noble characters and ask them to judge for themselves. He subtly creates an admirable image of his audience and then obliges them to live up to this image by deciding in his favour. A speech from *Die Familie Schroffenstein* exposes the psychology behind this approach, one also utilized by Hermann to win over the princes: 'Weil ich [Johann] mich edel nicht erweise, nicht / Erweisen will, machst du [Ottokar] mir weis, ich seis, / Damit die unverdiente Ehre mich / Bewegen soll, in ihrem Sinn zu handeln?' (1:80). Robert then maintains, 'Und keinen Laut mehr *feig* setz ich hinzu' (1:163), the implication being that Abälard has already tried to persuade them in a reprehensible fashion. And yet he then does precisely what he said he would refrain from doing: 'Des Herrschers Sohn, durch Gottes Gunst, bin ich, / Ein Prinz der, von dem Zufall grossgezogen' (1:163). Once more he harps upon his superior claim as Guiskard's son, his greater heritage as opposed to a prince whom chance has favoured.

In fact, the conditions are reversed: Abälard should rightly be the ruler as Otto's son while Robert owes his position to the fortuitous circumstances by which his father illegally gained the crown. Robert's one and only trump in the political game transpiring before us is something for which he can claim no credit – his birth as Guiskard's son which he seeks to exploit at every opportunity.

With Abälard's reply: 'Des Herrschers Sohn? – Der bin ich so wie du! / Mein Vater sass vor deinem auf dem Thron! / Er tats mit seinem *Ruhm*, tats mit mehr Recht' (1:164), past hostilities and concealed rivalries are brought out into the open as each prince deems himself the more appropriate successor to Guiskard.[11] Also, for the third time, Abälard raises the issue of fame, evidently a primary motive in his attempt to gain the upper hand in their power struggle. At this stage, however, the conflict is reduced to a rather infantile level of debate: 'Und näher noch verwandt ist mir das Volk, / Mir, Ottos Sohn, gekrönt vom Erbgesetz, / Als dir – dem Sohne meines Vormunds bloss, / Bestimmt von dem, mein Reich nur zu verwalten!' (1:164). Abälard consistently has an eye towards popular support, presenting himself as the people's preferred candidate. This basis alone, as he has already stated publicly, will enable him to replace his uncle just as the latter illegally usurped power some thirty years ago, 'weil,' Kleist's footnote declares, 'das Volk ihn sehr liebte' (1:164). As Otto's son, Abälard has the stronger legal claim as well, and hence, from a strictly political point of view, he does have considerable justification for his intrigues to undermine Robert's and his father's influence in order to regain what he rightfully considers his heritage.

When asked to decide between Robert's command to depart and Abälard's to remain, the old man first responds by praising Abälard as a son after Guiskard's own heart. Abälard has thus managed to dupe the masses or its spokesman into believing in the sincerity of his love for the people. But the parallel which the old man draws between Guiskard when he assumed power and Abälard as he appears to the public in the present emergency: 'Denn in Gestalt und Red und Art dir gleich, / Wie du, ein Freund des Volks, jetzt vor uns stehst, / Stand Guiskard einst, als Otto hingegangen / Des Volkes Abgott, herrlich vor uns da!' (1:164) brings to mind the image of Abälard as a young Robert Guiskard, a view held by most critics.[12] When Otto died suddenly and Abälard was too young to succeed his father directly, Guiskard took advantage of his regency to steal his nephew's rightful position. Now that Guiskard himself appears to be at the brink of death and a political crisis seems inevitable, Abälard puts forward his claim with a view to excluding

Guiskard's chosen successor, his son. Abälard, by his cunning – another similarity shared with his uncle whose nickname means after all 'Schlaukopf' (1:163) – would appear to have the ability as well as the opportunity to attract wide support for his candidacy, provided, of course, that Guiskard is in fact removed as a contender. However, as the old man's speech illustrates, everything hinges upon Guiskard, and ultimately the incident serves primarily to disclose the high esteem verging on idolatry – 'Des Volkes Abgott' (1:164) – in which he is held. Even Abälard derives part of his public appeal from the fact that he enjoys the advantage of being in his uncle's presence and favour: 'Die Gunst des Oheims, lass sie, deine Sonne, / Nur immer, wie bis heute, dich bestrahlen' (1:164–5). 'Der Greis' politely but firmly puts Abälard in his place and Robert appears to win the contest, but only because the order to retire was spoken by *Guiskard's* son: 'Wenn du befiehlst zu gehn, wir trotzen nicht. / Du bist der *Guiskardssohn*, das ist genug!' (1:165)

'Conspirators against a ruler,' Machiavelli warns, 'must believe that the people will rejoice in his death' (M 95). Since Abälard knows full well that he cannot make this assumption, he must resort to clandestine means to undermine his rival's power:

> Tust du doch mit dem Heer, als wärs ein Weib,
> Ein schwangeres, das niemand schrecken darf!
> Warum hehlst du die Wahrheit? Fürchtest du
> Die Niederkunft? –
> *Zum Volk gewandt.*
> > Der Guiskard fühlt sich krank. (1:165)

The text gives no indication as to whether Abälard delivers the initial part of this utterance loudly enough for the old man or the people's representatives to hear since it is allegedly directed at Robert, but there is every reason to suspect that Abälard intends it to be overheard. While insisting upon being truthful to the people and thus implying that he treats them as equals, he exposes both Guiskard's illness and indirectly its concealment by Robert who, only in his previous speech, maintained: 'Ein ernst Geschäft hält eben / Den Guiskard nur auf eine Stunde fest' (1:165). In effect, Abälard is publicly calling Robert a liar, and the latter's vitriolic reaction: 'Dass dir ein Wetterstrahl aus heitrer Luft / Die Zunge lähmte, du Verräter, du! / *Ab ins Zelt*' (1:165) only tends to corroborate his cousin's revelation. Abälard exploits the truth to suit his purpose. Because a calculated disclosure at an opportune moment may well destroy a strong rival, a method commonly practised by Licht, Hermann, and Hohenzollern, he simply focuses attention on his uncle's vulnerability at a time when the people more than ever depend upon his leadership ability.

DER GREIS *erschrocken*.
  Beim grossen Gott des Himmels und der Erde,
  Hat er die Pest?
ABÄLARD   Das nicht. Das fürcht ich nicht –
  Obschon der Arzt Besorgnis äussert: ja.   (1:165)

It is clearly not in the best interest of the people who worship Guiskard to make this revelation at this moment since it could easily lead to panic and political chaos – we have a sampling at the beginning of the seventh scene: 'Verloren ohne Guiskard rettungslos!' (1:166). His response to the old man's question follows a typical tactic at which Hohenzollern excels. First he denies the rumour, the threat of the plague, but the dash, indicating a pause and some uncertainty, provides him with the opportunity to think and chose his words carefully. Why not plant a further seed of doubt? His next statement contradicts the first: the physician, the man who has the diagnostic expertise, has grave suspicions that it may well be the plague. The 'ja,' in the crucial final position and hence set opposite the 'nicht' of the preceding verse, is emphatically unequivocal in meaning but, in context, intentionally misleading. At first hearing, it sounds as if the doctor definitely confirms Guiskard's contraction of the sickness; however, closer scrutiny reveals that the 'ja' is merely an affirmation of the doctor's concern at the possibility. The overall effect is to suggest definitive proof of a mere conjecture. In addition, by, so to speak, using the physician to disclose the bad news, while ostensibly denying it himself, Abälard follows another lesson taught by Machiavelli 'which is that a ruler must always let others administer distasteful and corrective medicine' (M 96).

This exchange displaying the subtlety of which Abälard is capable[13] bears comparison to a similar situation in *Prinz Friedrich von Homburg*:

DER PRINZ VON HOMBURG
  Darf man die Ursach wissen?
HOHENZOLLERN *mit Nachdruck*.   Jetzo nicht!
  – Du hast zu zeitig, wie wir gleich gesagt,
  Dich in die Schlacht gedrängt; die Order war,
  Nicht von dem Platz zu weichen, ungerufen!   (1:665–6)

Both Abälard's and Hohenzollern's utterances begin with a denial: 'Das nicht. Das fürcht ich nicht – ' and '*mit Nachdruck*. Jetzo nicht!' The emphasis in Abälard's speech is intimated by repetition, while in Hohenzollern's the same effect is conveyed by the stage direction and punctuation. In both instances, the timing is crucial: the two protagonists are making a statement extremely injurious to an alleged 'friend' and in the second part, after a dash, the speaker gainsays what he maintained in his initial declaration. By striving for effect before an audience and by divulging information detrimental to the public image of a charismatic titular character, both the prince and the count are in effect attempting surreptitiously to discredit a rival.

Abälard continues to 'hedge his bets': 'Ich sagt es euch, gewiss ist es noch nicht,' while bringing to the attention of his listeners: 'Jedoch dem Arzt, der Mutter ists, der Tochter, / Dem Sohn selbst, ihr sehts, unzweifelhaft – ' (1:166). This last comment pertains to Robert's telling departure without any attempt to dispute Abälard's betrayal of the truth. Once more Abälard is exploiting others as the bearers of bad news to protect himself in the event of a reversal. Also, by citing as examples those closest to Guiskard, he reinforces the trustworthiness of his information, i.e., even Guiskard's family is convinced of his illness.

The members of the committee now ask Abälard three questions relating to the symptoms of the plague. In response to the first: 'Fühlt er sich kraftlos, Herr?' (1:166), which is repeated by the old man, a mark of its importance, Abälard reports:

> – Noch eben, da er auf dem Teppich lag,
> Trat ich zu ihm und sprach: Wie gehts dir, Guiskard?
> Drauf er: 'Ei nun,' erwidert' er, 'erträglich! –
> Obschon ich die Giganten rufen möchte,
> Um diese kleine Hand hier zu bewegen.'   (1:166)

This visual image of Guiskard stretched out on the carpet is not meant to engender confidence in the people's hero, while the reference to his loss of strength confirms the presence of the most ominous sign. 'Der erste Krieger' asks: 'Fühlt er sein Innerstes erhitzt?' to which Abälard replies, 'Er sprach: "Dem Ätna wedelst du, lass sein!" / Als ihm von fern, mit einer Reiherfeder, / Die Herzogin den Busen fächelte' (1:166). Finally, Abälard's account: 'Und als die Kaiserin, mit feuchtem Blick, / Ihm einen Becher brachte, und ihn fragte, / Ob er auch trinken woll? antwortet' er: / "Die Dardanellen, liebes Kind!" und trank' (1:166-7) may be regarded as a confirmation of the third indication singled out by 'Der zweite Krieger': 'Und Durst?' In other words, Abälard has given explicit illustrations verifying the unmistakable presence of the plague's symptoms in precisely the same order as outlined by the concerned representatives of the people and has moreover presented the evidence on a gigantic scale. While this exaggeration reflects the bigger-than-life proportions of Guiskard, it also underlines the extremely serious nature of the sickness and provides seemingly irrefutable proof of his being infected. Cunningly, Abälard again does not himself directly state that Guiskard has the plague, but does register the empress's reaction: 'mit feuchtem Blick' (1:166), a visual corroboration, and, above all, by quoting Guiskard's words in the three examples, he allows his uncle to condemn himself. This method also helps to substantiate further his claim that he is the true friend of the Norman army; one can count on him 'to deal straight' with the people – at least this is the impression he wishes to create. Abälard is appealing to the worst fears of his audience who, although they may love and respect Guiskard, are mainly concerned about their own safety and survival.

Abälard shares an additional feature with Hohenzollern: a tendency to attribute motives to another protagonist which, strictly speaking, his listeners must accept on faith. When the Elector wonders 'Was dieses jungen Toren [Homburg's] Brust bewegt?' in the first scene of the drama, Hohenzollern informs him confidently, 'Die Schlacht von morgen, mein Gebieter! / Sterngucker sieht er, wett ich, schon im Geist, / Aus Sonnen einen Siegeskranz ihm winden' (1:633). The count's conjecture sounds strangely reminiscent of Abälard's equally hypothetical assessment of Guiskard's intentions vis-à-vis Constantinople: 'Man sieht ihn still, die Karte in der Hand, / Entschlüss' im Busen wälzen, ungeheure, / Als ob er heut das Leben erst beträte' (1:167). In both cases, just before a battle upon which the fate of the nation hangs, the speakers ascribe inordinate ambition to so-called 'friends' who are not in a position to defend themselves, one because of a physical illness, the other because of 'eine bloss Unart seines Geistes' (1:632).

Taking the people further into his confidence, Abälard alludes to the fact that Guiskard has finally agreed to accept the crown of the Eastern Empire:

Nessus und Loxias, den Griechenfürsten,
– Gesonnen längst, ihr wisst, auf *einen* [Kleist's emphasis] Punkt,

Die Schlüssel heimlich ihm zu überliefern,
– Auf *einen* [Kleist's emphasis] Punkt, sag ich, von ihm bis *heut*
Mit würdiger Hartnäckigkeit verweigert –
Heut einen Boten sandt er ihnen zu,
Mit einer Schrift, die diesen Punkt bewilligt.   (1:167)

If we analyse this passage including Kleist's footnote from Abälard's standpoint and bear in mind the designation of Helena as 'Verlobte Abälards' (1:154), the prince's hostility towards his uncle becomes more understandable. Guiskard again stands in the way of his nephew; this time he prevents Abälard, as Helena's future husband, from obtaining some indemnification for the loss of the Norman crown. Abälard counts on his audience's knowing what this uncommendable condition is since he states 'auf *einen* Punkt' twice, each time stressing the 'einen.' He also repeats 'heut': it first appears in the emphatic last then in the first position. What he is endeavouring to do is to emphasize a sudden change of heart which he wants his listeners to disapprove of: Guiskard resisted before and this resistance was worthy of the man ('Mit würdiger Hartnäckigkeit'), but today, he has capitulated, agreeing to a less than honourable proposition. In light of the context in which Abälard makes this veiled censure, he may also be insinuating that, as long as Guiskard was healthy, he withstood temptation, but now that he is sick, his leadership qualities may also have been impaired. Thus, the acceptance of the reprehensible provision may be yet another indicator of Guiskard's succumbing to the plague. Since Abälard cannot find fault with the people's darling openly and still retain their good will, he must undermine their faith in his infallibility and indomitability: 'Kurz, wenn die Nacht ihn lebend trifft, ihr Männer, / Das Rasende, ihr sollt es sehn, vollstreckt sich, / Und einen Hauptsturm ordnet er noch an' (1:167). Abälard deprecates this plan as foolhardy, a criticism of its instigator, but once more, the inappropriateness of the attack may be attributed to the implied illness.

'Den Sohn schon fragt' er, den die Aussicht reizt, / Was er von solcher Unternehmung halte?' (1:167). Abälard has already gone to considerable lengths to present Robert in as poor a light as possible to the extent of maintaining, 'Allein von Guiskard ruht kein Funk auf dir [Robert]' (1:163). The old man who praises Abälard, implying that Guiskard prefers and should prefer his nephew to his own son (1:165) and who addresses Robert 'kalt' (1:165), has made amply clear to the audience his low opinion of the heir presumptive. Hence, since Abälard brings to our attention that the father has sought the counsel of that son (a decision explicable as a further symptom of Guiskard's debilitating disease) and that the plan's execution attracts this self-same son, we are encouraged to reject the 'Hauptsturm' as an ill-conceived scheme: 'Das Rasende.' However, the people, still smitten with Guiskard, express their willingness to follow him anywhere: 'O führt' er lang uns noch, der teure Held, / In Kampf und Sieg und Tod!' (1:167), a seemingly absolute trust that proves invulnerable to the prince's subtle attack. Abälard, ever the opportunist, meets this declaration of loyalty with a show of verbal support of questionable sincerity: 'Das sag ich auch!' Prudent enough to see where public opinion lies, he ostensibly upholds the majority view, including the 'mad' venture, but only if Guiskard leads the attack himself, a development which Abälard, convinced of Guiskard's elimination, deems unfeasible. Three rhetorically parallel clauses introducing a complex sentence that culminates in the most direct avowal of Abälard's intent to acquire the eastern empire for himself express his determination that Robert not be his father's successor:

> Doch eh wird Guiskards Stiefel rücken vor
> Byzanz, eh wird an ihre ehrnen Tore
> Sein Handschuh klopfen, eh die stolze Zinne
> Vor seinem blossen Hemde sich verneigen,
> Als dieser *Sohn* [Kleist's emphasis], wenn Guiskard fehlt, die Krone
> Alexius, dem Rebellen dort, entreissen! (1:167)

The images of Guiskard's clothing, perhaps intimating the physical impossibility for the man to perform the task of conquest himself, above all stress the hatred Abälard feels for his cousin, the final obstacle. One line in particular, by its very structure, captures the thrust of the dynastic rivalry: 'Als *dieser* Sohn, wenn Guiskard fehlt, die Krone ...' 'The son and the crown are consciously kept apart ...' at opposite ends of the verse, while all hinges structurally and thematically upon the middle, interpolated conditional clause 'wenn Guiskard fehlt.' This is what Abälard is relying upon: in the absence created by Guiskard's unavoidable death, not 'this son,' but the true adopted son will win the crown.

When Robert announces Guiskard's imminent arrival, Abälard is understandably '*erschrocken*' (1:168), for the impossible would seem about to transpire. He has prematurely 'tipped his hand' and, in so doing, has made an implacable and potentially dangerous enemy out of his cousin who now enjoys his revenge: 'Dir [Abälard], Heuchlerherz, / Deck ich den Schleier jetzt von der Missgestalt!' (1:168). Robert will disclose

Abälard's double-dealings to his father and thus further secure his own position. The open hostility is evident in the choice of disparaging epithets: 'Heuchlerherz' and 'Missgestalt.' However, Abälard, who lives by his wits, should not be totally discounted as his response illustrates:

ABÄLARD *mit einer fliegenden Blässe.*
  Die Wahrheit sagt ich euch, und dieses Haupt
  Verpfänd ich kühn der Rache, täuscht ich euch!
  Als ich das Zelt verliess, lag hingestreckt
  Der Guiskard, und nicht eines Gliedes schien
  Er mächtig. Doch sein Geist bezwingt sich selbst
  Und das Geschick, nichts Neues sag ich euch!   (1:169)

He initially attempts to hide behind the truth: like Hohenzollern or Licht, he has allegedly only told the truth, but has slanted it to suit his own design – to compromise, incriminate, or destroy a supposed friend. Now circumstances oblige him to wager his own life upon the veracity of his statements which, after all, were reports of what others said. In his desperate attempt to justify himself, however, and perhaps as a sign of a temporary lapse in self-control attributable to his state of shock, he mentions for the first time that he himself witnessed the ailing Guiskard, but he soon regains his old form by turning even a bad situation to some account. He praises Guiskard and the people's knowledge of their great hero: the latter is quite capable of rising above any personal calamity, and in saying this, he, Abälard, is not telling his listeners anything they do not already know. His concluding 'nichts Neues sag ich euch!' (1:168) parallels his earlier 'Ihr kennt ihn' (1:166), the establishment of a bond of common knowledge and faith between himself and the people.

The final incident of the fragment involving Abälard helps to fortify Guiskard's dominant position at his nephew's obvious expense. Once Abälard's attempt to conceal himself among the people in order to escape Guiskard's justifiable ire fails, he silently returns to the hill like a scolded schoolboy. Guiskard's last words addressed to him: 'Ich sprech nachher ein eignes Wort mit dir' (1:169), a masterfully understated threat,[14] enhance this damaging infantile impression by implying a wait-till-I-get-you-home attitude. However, Abälard's unheroic, if not cowardly, behaviour is fully consistent with his previous performance[15] and his unsuccessful ruse to avoid his just desserts merely reinforces visually his overall deceptiveness. Wisely he offers no resistance and, as ordered, takes up a position '*hinter Guiskard, während dieser ihn unverwandt mit den Augen verfolgt*' (1:169). Similarly,

when threatened by Adam with the exposure of certain financial irreg-
ularities: 'Es liesse / Von Depositionen sich und Zinsen / Zuletzt auch
eine Rede ausarbeiten' (1:182), Licht astutely assumes a compliant tone:
'Nun, also!' 'Ich weiss,' and 'Das sag ich auch' (1:182) and simply abides
his time. The fact that Guiskard keeps his eyes on his nephew suggests
that Abälard should not be taken for granted and that despite his fall
from grace, he would still have played an important part in *Robert Guiskard*,
had Kleist completed the tragedy. One wonders whether Guiskard, in
his weakened condition, would have been able to control a man of Abälard's
manipulative skills if the prince were to remain behind his back.

DER NORMANN *geheimnisvoll, indem er die beiden Männer vorführt.*
   Da ich die Wache heut, um Mitternacht,
   Am Eingang hier des Guiskardszeltes halte,
   Fängts plötzlich jammervoll zu stöhnen drin,
   Zu ächzen an, als haucht' ein kranker Löwe
   Die Seele von sich.   (1:160)

In my interpretation of *Die Hermannsschlacht* as it relates to *Il Principe*,
I noted how Hermann unites within his person the main features of the
lion and the fox, strength and cunning, a combination which Machiavelli
advocates as the prerequisite for the model leader. *Robert Guiskard* may
also be said to reflect this standard but under special circumstances:
specifically what occurs if physical illness seriously jeopardizes one's ability
to turn to account one's leonine or vulpine qualities, a scenario that also
concerned Machiavelli. Throughout the fragment, the one attribute continually associated with Guiskard is strength or authority, captured in
the image of the jungle beast, an appropriate designation given the less
than civilized nature of the political arena as depicted by both the dramatist
and the political analyst. When the Norman guard furnishes the first piece
of concrete information pointing to the likelihood of Guiskard's illness,
he has recourse to the sick lion motif, but the comparison does not stop
there as the simile becomes in Abälard's reference a metaphor: 'Das weiss
der Guiskard wohl, und mag es gern, / Wenn ihm der Krieger in den
Mähnen spielt' (1:162). In this particular instance, the prince is endeavouring to elevate the image of the folk leader not just to emphasize
his own alleged respect for his uncle and the latter's good rapport with
his army, but above all to humiliate Robert: 'Allein der glatte Nacken
seines Sohnes / Der schüttelt gleich sich, wenn ihm eins nur naht' (1:162–
3). Abälard, by his unflattering choice of imagery, implies that Robert

lacks the mane of the majestic lion and hence his father's strength, while the shaking, clean-shaven neck suggests intransigence, immaturity, and perhaps even underlying fear, all part of a very prejudicial picture Abälard tries to create in the minds of his listeners. Later, as part of a carefully executed plan not to say anything directly pejorative about the people's champion, Abälard returns to a variation of the lion motif to describe Guiskard's consuming ambition despite his sickness: 'Doch das hindert nicht, / Dass er nicht stets nach jener Kaiserzinne, / Die dort erglänzt, wie ein gekrümmter Tiger, / Aus seinem offnen Zelt hinüberschaut' (1:167). Kleist thus establishes an unmistakable link between Guiskard and the carnivorous feline.

Before the audience actually meets Guiskard, his leonine qualifications are everywhere in evidence. Helena, in her first speech, mentions her father's endurance enabling him to spend 'drei schweisserfüllte Nächte / Auf offnem Seuchenfelde' (1:157) and the old man infers his irrepressible energy by his habit of rising before the sun. Even Abälard, in his clandestine attempt to undermine Guiskard's authority, must acknowledge the bigger-than-life dimensions of his ailing rival who is thirsty enough to drink the Dardanelles dry, as hot as Mt Etna and sufficiently determined to deny even his common mortality: 'Denn weils kein andres sichres Zeichen gibt, / Als nur den schnellen Tod, so leugnet ers, / Ihr kennt ihn, wirds im Tode leugnen noch' (1:166). The young boy's visual report immediately preceding Guiskard's stage appearance best captures the heroic proportions of what Denneler defines as charisma:[16]

> Wohl, Vater, seh ich ihn!
> Frei in des Zeltes Mitte seh ich ihn!
> Der hohen Brust legt er den Panzer um!
> Dem breiten Schulternpaar das Gnadenkettlein!
> Dem weitgewölbten Haupt drückt er, mit Kraft,
> Den mächtig-wankend-hohen Helmbusch auf!
> Jetzt seht, o seht doch her! – Da ist er selbst!   (1:168)

The ecstatic tone and rhythm of this speech with its seven exclamation marks indicate hero worship in part attributed to youthful imagination, while the reference to Guiskard's physical prowess, the adverbs 'mit Kraft' and 'mächtig-wankend' and the adjective 'Frei,' the first word to describe him in the emphatic initial position, create an impression of strength and independence, the leadership qualities associated with the lion.

Whereas the tragedy contains two allusions to Guiskard as the lion, it lacks a specific reference to the balancing counterpart, the fox. However, vulpine guile forms an obvious aspect of the hero's personality. Kleist included this characteristic in the title of the drama, has Abälard draw attention to it at Robert's expense: 'Allein von Guiskard ruht kein Funk auf dir, / Und diesen Namen* mindestens erbst du nicht' (1:163) and added a footnote to explain it to his readers: '*Guiskard heisst *Schlaukopf* [Kleist's emphasis]; ein Zuname, den die Normänner dem Herzog gaben' (1:163). Cunning is regarded as a desirable, even admirable quality in a leader, one which, according to Kleist's source, Guiskard was proud of. In any assessment of the Duke's motivations, one must not lose sight of this feature which some critics, in their moralizing, have failed to take into account.

As the old man indicates, while putting Robert in his place, Guiskard has always taken care to cement a good relationship with the people: 'Geh hin zu deinem Vater, und horch auf, / Wenn du willst wissen, wie man mit mir spricht' (1:161) or 'Und nicht das erstemal wärs, wenn er uns / In Huld es [to appear before them] zugeständе, aber, traun! / Wenn ers uns, so wie du, verweigerte' (1:162). Giving these verses their most complimentary slant, Vohland interprets this policy as evidence that Guiskard respects the right of the people to present their complaints to him directly. As we noted, however, in connection with Abälard, Machiavelli stresses the importance of gaining the loyalty of the people and the support of the army, especially when power has been achieved by virtue of personal excellence or chance and not by hereditary right. Good public relations may well be part of a cunning plan to facilitate political exploitation of the masses and to assure political survival. Moreover, Guiskard's determination to take Constantinople despite the legitimate pleas of a dying army calls into serious question his supposed love for his people.

The manner in which the Duke gained the crown some thirty years ago also illustrates the crucial function of popular support: 'Denn in Gestalt und Red und Art dir [Abälard] gleich, / Wie du, ein Freund des Volks, jetzt vor uns stehst, / Stand Guiskard einst, als Otto hingegangen, / Des Volkes Abgott, herrlich vor uns da!' (1:164). Because Abälard was too young to succeed his dead father, Guiskard was appointed regent, but by demonstrating his skill as a leader and winning the confidence of the masses, he usurped Abälard's rightful position and has managed to retain it on the basis of continued popular support and even to have Robert declared his heir. By so doing, he is guilty, in Lawrence Ryan's view, of a contradiction: '[Der Widerspruch] geht darauf zurück, dass Guiskard nicht auf Grund eines rechtlichen Anspruchs, sondern auf Grund der eigenen Stärke und der offenbar überragenden persönlichen Eigenschaften die Macht übernommen hat, dass er aber zur Sicherung seiner Herrschaft sich gerade auf jenes Prinzip der Legitimität stützt, das er durch den eigenen Machtaufstieg durchbrochen und in einem gewissen Sinn ausser Kraft gesetzt hat.'[17]

Whereas from a strictly moral point of view or even in terms of logical consistency, Ryan's appraisal is correct, from a political standpoint, Machiavelli would see the dynastic urge to increase one's authority by placing one's children in positions of immediate (Helena) or potential (Robert) power as quite proper. Bearing in mind the recapitulation of history in *Robert Guiskard* which Kleist thought important enough to elucidate further by another footnote (1:164), one would have to assume that Guiskard, in his desire to expand his rule, exemplifies Machiavelli's belief: 'The urge to acquire possessions and extend dominion is normal and natural' (M 37). After all, Caesar Borgia, Machiavelli's model ruler, was the illegitimate offspring of Pope Alexander VI who did much to promote the political aspirations of his son.[18]

EINE STIMME *aus dem Volk.*
   Ihr Himmelsscharen, ihr geflügelten,
    So steht uns bei!
EINE ANDERE   Verloren ist das Volk!
EINE DRITTE Verloren ohne Guiskard rettungslos!
EINE VIERTE Verloren rettungslos!
EINE FÜNFTE   Errettungslos,
   In diesem meerumgebnen Griechenland! –   (1:166)

This dialogue illustrates the degree to which Guiskard has managed to render the masses totally dependent upon his person, for his death is viewed as being synonymous with the demise of the people and hence the nation. By skilful manipulation of public sentiment, Guiskard has been able to command absolute loyalty from his followers, even unto death: 'O führt' er lang uns noch, der teure Held, / In Kampf und Sieg und Tod!' (1:167) and thus fulfils Machiavelli's definition of the 'prudent ruler' who 'must ... so order his rule that his subjects will always have need of him and his government, whatever the political climate may be' (M 64).

A considerable amount of controversy surrounding a favourable or unfavourable evaluation of Guiskard has to do with his decision to accept the crown of Constantinople to which his daughter, the expelled empress of Greece, has legal claim. The Greek traitors set this condition as the price for the betrayal of their own city. Streller sees in Guiskard a man, 'der sich über alle menschlichen und moralischen Bedingungen hinwegsetzt,'[19] a view with which Vohland takes issue:

Guiskard, der sich nach Streller dem Volk gegenüber nicht verantwortlich fühlt, dient in seinen Plänen keineswegs 'nur seinem eigenen Ruhm' und persönlichen Erfolg ... , sondern, wie seine Zurückweisung der Vorschläge von Nessus und Loxias zeigt ..., auch dem Moral-und Rechtsprinzip. Er setzt lieber sich selbst und sein Volk den Gefahren der Pest aus, als dass er – im Widerspruch zu vielen bisherigen Anstrengungen und Opfern – das Erbfolgerecht, für das er sich lange Zeit eingesetzt hatte und um dessentwillen er jene Vorschläge mit 'würdiger Hartnäckigkeit' abgelehnt hatte ... , noch einmal bricht.[20]

From a Machiavellian perspective, one which Kleist shared on the basis of my analysis of *Die Hermannsschlacht*, such an argument comes across as politically naïve. Guiskard once broke the principle of hereditary accession in assuming power and, in a strictly legal sense, is breaking it again by now putting his son next in line both to the Norman and to the Greek crown. His determination to conquer Constantinople and thus to prejudice the welfare of his subjects is not dictated by any dedication to the law of succession, but by his own drive for fame and by his dynastic ambitions for his family. To have established Helena and Abälard upon the Greek throne would have resulted in an extension of his own regime because it would have produced a puppet state dependent upon his reputation and authority for its existence. The acceptance under duress of the title emperor to the detriment of his original obligation to his daughter's claim may well have been what he intended to accomplish in the first place and the refusals may have been prompted by a desire to disguise his true motive. 'There are,' according to Machiavelli, 'countless modern instances of ... pledges voided by the unfaithfulness of rulers and where the foxiest have come out the best. But it is important in practices of this sort to be careful about appearances' (M 92). Guiskard's play-acting before the people bears evidence of a ruler who knows how to manipulate others quite well. Are we even justified in taking this information about the proposed treachery at face value, since Abälard, a hostile witness, provides it in a thwarted, underhanded attempt to turn the crowd against his uncle? And finally, the fact that Guiskard was capable of usurping his nephew's rightful title suggests a man who does not dwell upon legal niceties, especially if they are not in his best interest, just as his efforts to deceive the people by concealing his illness do not presage well for a man allegedly acting in accordance with 'dem Moral- und Rechtsprinzip.'[21]

In the same context of Guiskard's resolve to ally himself with the disenchanted Greek princes, Ryan argues: 'Auch hier entsprechen sich äusseres Verhalten und innerer Verfall Guiskards, zu dessen Schicksal es offenbar gehören sollte, dass die alles könnende Tat, das Ziel seines ganzen Strebens, eben nicht als freie Tat, als Selbständigkeit seines Wesens, sondern nur in einem wesentlichen Sinne unfreie, auf die Hilfe anderer angewiesene Handlung und damit als Selbstzerstörung seines Wesens zu betrachten wäre.'[22] Again, I feel that this line of reasoning, although feasible, fails to take into account Guiskard's nickname: a ruler celebrated for his cunning would surely not hesitate to use others to secure a victory,[23] a policy not only endorsed but advocated by Machiavelli.[24] Also, Guiskard has no qualms of conscience in exploiting the decimated ranks of his own people to achieve the same conquest. The difference in this particular situation lies in the prevalent sense of urgency brought to a head by Guiskard's sickness and the attendant need for haste.

Even though Guiskard only appears in the final scene of the fragment, he has in his absence unmistakably dominated the dramatic action up to his arrival on stage. His triumphant entry and the authoritarian way he deals with his nephew: 'Hier bleibst du stehn, und lautlos. – Du verstehst mich? / – Ich sprech nachher ein eignes Wort mit dir' (1:169) suggest to the audience a man accustomed to command and who expects and receives unquestioned obedience (cf. Hermann). Having taken care of the traitor in his family, he *wendet sich zum Greise. Du führst, Armin, das Wort für diese Schar?'* (1:169). Addressing the old man by his first name, he establishes a link of intimacy right away, an approach contrasting with his son's rudeness and lack of respect but paralleling Abälard's taking the old man's side. This utterance directed to the people's spokesman thus shows the importance he places upon being on good terms with those who determine public opinion, while his treatment of Abälard is intended in part to inspire in the masses respect for his absolute position.[25] No matter what rumours may have been circulating, he, Guiskard, is still in control.

> Seht, als ich das hörte,
> Hats lebhaft mich im Zelt bestürzt, ihr Leute!
> Denn nicht die schlechtsten Männer seh ich vor mir,

Und nichts Bedeutungsloses bringt ihr mir,
Und nicht von einem Dritten mag ichs hören,
Was euch so dringend mir vors Antlitz führt – . (1:169)

Like Abälard, Guiskard knows how to handle people. First of all he attempts to make his listeners feel guilty: you really shocked me when I learned of your presence outside my tent. Then he praises them: since they are the best men, they must have something important to ask. Lastly, he draws attention to his direct rapport with the people, his accessibility and respect for their wishes. 'Tus schnell, du alter Knabe, tu mirs kund! / Ists eine neue Not? Ist es ein Wunsch? / Und womit helf ich? Oder tröst ich? Sprich!' (1:169). Presenting himself as eager to serve the people, he is almost shaming them into compliance by his familiar, benevolent tone, his patriarchal attitude to his children which his superior position permits him to adopt.[26] The old man, however, detects the emotional blackmail inherent in Guiskard's speech to the committee: 'Und sehr beschämen würd uns deine Milde, / Wenn du das glauben könntest von der Schar' (1:169). Samuel, apparently, taken in by what I perceive to be Guiskard's calculated manner, comments: 'Hierzu kommt ein recht ansprechender Zug seines Charakters, die Leutseligkeit gegenüber dem gemeinen Mann, die, im Gegensatz zu Abälard, eine echte Zuneigung zu verraten scheint und die sich in seinem Verhalten während der Verhandlung mit dem Volke bestätigt (10 Auftritt), so dass sein Herrschersystem auf Übereinstimmung zwischen Volk und Herrscher zu beruhen scheint.'[27] Samuel qualifies his interpretation by having recourse to 'scheint' twice, but may one speak of 'eine *echte* Zuneigung' if Guiskard is equally prepared to sacrifice it to satisfy his ambition? What particularly casts serious doubt upon the genuineness of this speech is the realization on the part of the audience that Guiskard is playing the role of the innocent with his list of questions: 'Ists eine neue Not? Ist es ein Wunsch?' (1:169). Judging from his treatment of Abälard, the spectator must assume that Robert and Helena have fully apprised their father of what has happened in his absence. In other words, from the very outset, his performance is not only a lie in appearance as the subsequent drum episode verifies, but in word as well.

Guiskard's response to the rumour: 'Du, Guiskard, seist vom Pesthauch angeweht / –!' (1:170) proves especially revealing: 'GUISKARD *lachend*. / Vom Pesthauch angeweht! Ihr seid wohl toll, ihr! / Ob ich wie einer ausseh, der die Pest hat? / Der ich in Lebensfüll hier vor euch stehe?' (1:170).[28] Once again we hear the famous Kleist laugh which, in this instance, most closely corresponds to Hermann's identical reaction when Fust proposes, 'Hermann, du bist mir bös, mein Bruderherz, / Weil ich den Siegskranz schelmisch dir geraubt?!' (1:624). In both cases it is the laughter of embarrassment at a correct diagnosis of an actual situation and hence a cover-up to conceal one's true feelings and to deceive one's listeners by a show of nonchalance. Downplaying the significance of a rumour based on fact, Guiskard intentionally misleads his own people. It could, of course, be contended that he does this in their best interest, for to know the truth here would lead to open panic and Guiskard remains confident that he will ultimately beat the plague. This approximates Hermann's realization that the masses do not possess the requisite outlook to achieve the end he has in mind and hence, for their own good, he must keep his true intent hidden from them and manipulate them to the point where seemingly, of their own accord, they adhere to his plan. But again, one can also argue that the deception occurs primarily in Hermann's and Guiskard's own best interest as part of their campaign to gain 'Ruhm,' the 'Siegskranz' mentioned by Fust, with which Kleist personally was so obsessed.[29] Can Guiskard really have the well-being of his people at heart if he persists in this charade, knowing that he may in fact be infected? His overreaction: 'Ihr seid wohl toll, ihr!' to the old man's allegation, contrasting with his conciliatory opening address, hints at his awareness:

> Ihr wollt mich, traun! mich Blühenden, doch nicht
> Hinschleppen zu den Faulenden aufs Feld?
> Ei, was zum Henker, nein! Ich wehre mich –
> Im Lager hier kriegt ihr mich nicht ins Grab:
> In Stambul halt ich still, und eher nicht! (1:170)

In a tremendous affirmation of his strength, independence, and determination, he again endeavours to shame, if not bully, his listeners into compliance, accusing them of wanting to put him prematurely into his grave. Although this whole speech is designed to convey an image of robustness, of a man who is still in full command, it remains a sham, a delineation of an amazingly strong will but one lacking the physical strength to sustain it. None the less he persists in keeping his ultimate goal before his eyes, the subjugation of Constantinople, 'das umfassende Symbol der Weltherrschaft.'[30] 'Es liegt in der Natur des Herrschers,' Meyer-Benfey remarked back in 1911, 'dass im Konfliktfalle das Herrschergefühl und der Herrscheregoismus immer stärker sind als das strenge Rechts-bewusstsein und die Sorge für das Wohl des Volkes.'[31] The predominant role of ambition or the drive for fame has subsequently been ascertained as the key to an understanding of Guiskard's psychological motivation by the secondary literature with the exception of Vohland's study.[32] Streller, for example, maintains, '[Guiskards] Pläne und Entwürfe dienen nur seinem eigenen Ruhm. Um diesen zu sichern, führt er sein Volk an den Rand des Untergangs,'[33] while most recently, Samuel has argued, 'In der Gestalt Guiskards ist die grosse Machtpersönlichkeit objektiviert, die in ihrem grenzlosen Ehrgeiz, in ihrer unersättlichen Gier nach Machterweiterung, unfähig wird, anzuhalten und der Wirklichkeit ins Auge zu sehen.'[34]

> – Zwar trifft sichs seltsam just, an diesem Tage,
> Dass ich so *lebhaft* [Kleist's emphasis] mich nicht fühl, als sonst:
> Doch nicht unpässlich möcht ich nennen das,
> Viel wen'ger pestkrank! Denn was weiter ists,
> Als nur ein Missbehagen, nach der Qual
> Der letzten Tage, um mein armes Heer.   (1:170)

The dash which begins this speech would seem to suggest that the comment was made off the cuff, but why does he even raise the issue of his health at this moment when he has just sought to convince his audience that he stands before them 'in Lebensfüll'? Does he feel that he can risk being honest with his men? There is a later indication that he sees himself as indestructible: 'Kein Leichtsinn ists, wenn ich Berührung nicht / Der Kranken scheue, und kein Ohngefähr, / Wenns ungestraft geschieht' (1:171); hence, he may be dwelling under the illusion that he is merely suffering from a slight indisposition which will pass. This diagnosis, however, does not tally with Abälard's report on the seriousness of Guiskard's illness, a report confirmed by the hasty exits of his children, Helena and Robert. The latter did not even make an effort to refute Abälard; instead, he merely heaped abuse upon his cousin, giving further credence to Abälard's claim. Thus a strong probability exists that Guiskard is deluding himself. On the other hand, he may allude to his 'Missbehagen' because he knows from Robert of Abälard's betrayal and consequently must offer a feasible explanation to put his listeners' fears to rest. Also he tries too hard to trivialize the issue, a tactic implying conscious knowledge of the true state of affairs, while, at the same time, he is clearly playing to his audience, even blaming his indisposition on his concern for their welfare. Just like Abälard, he always purports to be acting on behalf of his people.

This explanation arouses the suspicion of the old man again:

DER GREIS So sagst du – ?
GUISKARD *ihn unterbrechend*.
　　　　　　　's ist der Red nicht wert, sag ich!
Hier diesem alten Scheitel, wisst ihr selbst,
Hat seiner Haare keins noch wehgetan!
Mein Leib ward jeder Krankheit mächtig noch.
Und wärs die Pest auch, so versichr' ich euch:
An diesen Knochen nagt sie selbst sich krank!　　　　　　(1:170–1)

This additional attempt to minimize the seriousness of his illness is the reaction of a guilty man anxious to hide the truth. He does not even allow his interlocutor the time to complete his question out of fear that it may raise further doubt. Although Guiskard's hubris manifests itself in his claim to being invulnerable, the conditional clause does at least concede the possibility that he could in fact be suffering from the plague.

When the old man objects to Guiskard's associating with the infected, his immediate response to this implied admonition contains the unmistakable accent of the autocratic ruler: 'Ich habs, ihr Leut, euch schon so oft gesagt, / Seit wann denn gilt mein Guiskardswort nicht mehr?' (1:171). Moreover, confident in his mission, he has obviously convinced himself that he cannot be touched as Kleist insinuates by the allusion to Schiller's *Wallenstein*: 'Es hat damit / Sein eigenes Bewenden' (1:171).[35] Such defiance of the plague would be almost guaranteed to restore the army's faith in its leader.[36]

'Was bringst du mir?' Guiskard again innocently enquires, 'sag an! Sei kurz und bündig; / Geschäfte rufen mich ins Zelt zurück' (1:171). Since Guiskard already knows why the people have approached him, the show of ignorance is intended to downplay the seriousness of the rumour, i.e., 'how could anything be wrong when I can not even conceive of why you would desire my presence?' But, above all, the excuse for the brevity of the meeting we know to be a lie through Abälard's account and its unwitting confirmation by Robert. The proffered explanation also disputes Helena's justification for her father's inability to appear – he was indulging in a well-earned sleep after three tiring nights 'auf offnem Seuchenfeld zugebracht' (1:157). Consequently, the command 'Sei kurz und bündig,' while part of the general impression of energetic activity and control he wishes to produce, is in fact an oblique sign of a growing physical exhaustion precluding a lengthy public encounter.[37]

The old man now begins his speech which, after a mere three lines, Guiskard again interrupts, but, on this occasion, by a gesture:

Guiskard sieht sich um, der Greis stockt.
DIE HERZOGIN *leise.*
   Willst du - ?
ROBERT   Begehrst du - ?
ABÄLARD   Fehlt dir - ?
DIE HERZOGIN   Gott im Himmel!
ABÄLARD Was ist?
ROBERT   Was hast du?
DIE HERZOGIN   Guiskard! Sprich ein Wort!
Die Kaiserin zieht eine grosse Heerpauke herbei und schiebt sie hinter ihn.
GUISKARD *indem er sich sanft niederlässt, halblaut.*
   Mein liebes Kind! -
                    Was also gibts, Armin?
   Bring deine Sache vor, und lass es frei
   Hinströmen, bange Worte lieb ich nicht!
Der Greis sieht gedankenvoll vor sich nieder.   (1:171-2)

The first time Guiskard disturbed the old man's discourse, it was to insist upon his vitality and good health. Ironically, the second interruption becomes a visual contradiction of the first interruption's assertion. The short, staccato reactions of the family members underline not only their concern but also their complicity in keeping the truth from the masses. Guiskard's 'halblaut' acknowledgment of his daughter's act of loving thoughtfulness further attests to his conscious involvement and, for the spectator with a long memory, may evoke his betrayal of the one person having the presence of mind to rescue him from a potentially devastating public embarrassment. Clearly, those upon the hill are privy to knowledge being kept from those below.

This brilliantly conceived dramatic incident belies Guiskard's address, couched in energetic terms, to the old man. The latter is no longer deceived, however, by the performance put on for his benefit as indicated by the stage directions and particularly by a comment made in his subsequent speech: 'Zwar du bist, wie du sagst, noch unberührt' (1:172). This verse suggests by its very construction - a parenthetical remark in the middle of a parenthetical remark – some doubt, i.e., 'this is what *you* say but not necessarily what I believe to be the case.' The old man then outlines in a general sense the inescapable nature of the plague:

> Der Hingestreckt' ists auferstehungslos,
> Und wo er hinsank, sank er in sein Grab.
> Er sträubt, und wieder, mit unsäglicher
> Anstrengung sich empor: es ist umsonst!
> Die giftgeätzten Knochen brechen ihm,
> Und wieder nieder sinkt er in sein Grab. (1:172)

Although he depicts a typical case, he might just as well be recording the symptoms already manifested by Guiskard. The choice of 'Hingestreckt', recalls Abälard's portrayal of his uncle stretched out on the carpet unable to move his hand, while the audience, just having observed the drum episode, is encouraged to relate this information to Guiskard himself as his wife obviously does:

> DIE HERZOGIN *indem sie an der Tochter Brust niedersinkt.*
> O Himmel!
> HELENA Meine vielgeliebte Mutter!
> GUISKARD *sich langsam umsehend.*
> Was fehlt ihr?
> HELENA *zögernd.* Es scheint –
> GUISKARD Bringt sie ins Zelt! (1:172–3)

Despite the genuine concern voiced by the two women, a reluctance to disclose the real source of their alarm to the uninitiated still dictates their public persona. Significantly, Kleist supplies another clue in his stage direction: 'Guiskard *sich langsam umsehend.*' Even the smallest movement causes him immense physical effort and yet he still persists in his duplicity: realizing that his wife could inadvertently betray him, he has her removed from public scrutiny. Since the audience witnesses the foreground interplay between the main protagonists in contrast to the people who are intentionally kept in the background, the spectator gains awareness of the premeditated, conscious deception practised by Guiskard, his family, and even the old man on the Norman army. *Robert Guiskard* thus furnishes a visual, dramatic representation of Machiavelli's contention: 'The common people observe the throne from a distance, only a select few have direct contacts with it. The mass is taken in by appearances, the minority has access to the reality, and the minority [to which Abälard belongs] will not dare to be in conflict with public opinion backed by all the authority of the state [Guiskard, in this instance, equals the state]' (M 93).

Of all Kleist's dramas, with the possible exception of *Die Hermanns-schlacht*, *Robert Guiskard* comes closest to the world of political manipulation and power struggle examined in *Il Principe*. Although Machiavelli reaches as far back as Moses, Cyrus, or Romulus, he draws most of his examples from either imperial Rome or the recent history of his own native land. Both of these eras as depicted by the Florentine were periods of political crisis where gifted leaders, provided they had the determination, adaptability, and the skill to exploit others together with the good fortune to choose the opportune moment, could carve themselves out a kingdom: 'Opportunity was what these leaders required, their abilities enabled them to seize it. The states they founded became great and prosperous in consequence' (M 45). In Kleist's fragment, an older man struggles to maintain his illegally obtained title while a younger rival, waiting in the wings, makes a premature attempt to promote his own candidacy by presenting himself as the only viable alternative for a leaderless people. From a power-political point of view, Abälard's only mistake is his timing: because he underestimates his enemy's strength, he exposes his intent to his rival's supporters and thus suffers a temporary setback. Guiskard, combining within his person the attributes of both the fox and the lion, stands only hours away from achieving the conquest of Constantinople, a symbol for supreme political power, when chance, in the form of the plague, strikes him down. Machiavelli's contemporary ideal leader, one mentioned often in the pages of *Il Principe*, met a similar fate, 'a fantastically unexpected misfortune' (M 49). In the following passage, Machiavelli could just as well be describing Robert Guiskard rather than Caesar Borgia: 'If all the actions of the Duke are considered as steps in a planned policy, it is difficult to quarrel with them. In fact, I have quoted him as an example to follow by ambitious men who have risen to power by fortunate circumstances or on the backs of other people. A man of such immense ambition and breadth of vision could not have acted otherwise ... His ruthless determination and his energy, his astonishing shrewdness in the handling of friends and enemies, the soundness of the political structure which he had built in so short a time must have determined his survival, had it not been ... for his disabling illness' (M 53-4).

6

The Machiavellian
line of descent

This study acknowledges the obvious attraction the Machiavellian protagonist, however unsympathetic to our moral sensitivities, exerted upon
Kleist and has attempted to come to some appreciation of this type's
importance. One question still remains unanswered: What influences or
examples may have induced Kleist to explore the realm of 'das Gemeine'
(1:96) or 'das Schmutzge' (1:83) and thus to doubt 'das Gefühl ... der
Seelengüte andrer' (1:99)? From the outset I feel bound to concede that
two of my three proposed answers are largely hypothetical. None the
less, they still offer feasible alternatives while suggesting a sense of time
– transcending consistency as exemplified in the Machiavellian.

My textual analysis of *Die Hermannsschlacht* explored the possibility
that Shakespeare's *Julius Caesar* may have served as one of the models
for the Hally episode. I also noted the generally accepted view that
Shakespeare did influence Kleist as a dramatist. In fact, the latter even
borrowed or paraphrased lines from the former.[1] When one pauses to
consider Shakespeare's arch-villains, three come to mind: Richard III,
Edmund from *King Lear*, and *Othello's* Iago. A popular prejudice of the
Elizabethan age saw in *Il Principe* a justification for unabashed, totally
immoral wickedness: '[The Renaissance] thought of historical characters,
like Richard III and Cesare Borgia, as all bad. This doctrine was derived
wrongly from Machiavelli's *Prince*. Machiavelli himself became the symbol
of such human diabolism. Iago has the outlook and the main traits of
the Machiavel, though certainly he is more individualized than Richard
III and than Edmund in *King Lear*.'[2]

Once one has established a Machiavellian presence, albeit distorted,
in Shakespeare's plays, one is tempted to speculate as to whether or not
this presence may have inspired Kleist. In *Richard III*, Shakespeare portrays

a conflict between three brothers in which the evil brother undertakes by manipulation and prevarication to set his one brother against the other. As Clarence is being escorted to prison because of the false accusations levelled against him by his brother Richard, his alleged 'friend' promises to do all that is within his power to save him: 'Well, your imprisonment shall not be long; / I will deliver you, or else lie for you: / Meantime, have patience' (I, i, 114–6), but actually continues to plot his death. This scene depicting Richard as he trivializes the importance of the arrest while Clarence is being led away to the Tower bears some comparison with the similar event in *Prinz Friedrich von Homburg*. In both dramas, the confidant pretends to be a close friend of the accused for whose crime he is largely (in the case of Richard, totally) responsible and subsequently uses the incident to cast aspersion upon his ruler and relative: 'Meantime, this deep disgrace in brotherhood / Touches me deeper than you can imagine' (I, i, 111–2). There is, of course, a major distinction explicable in terms of different dramatic conventions. Whereas Hohenzollern does lie, as for instance in his version of the garden sequence, he does so with an amazing subtlety calculated to deceive an audience, while Richard openly confesses his dastardly design:[3]

I'll in, to urge his [King Edward's] hatred more to Clarence,
With lies well steel'd with weighty arguments;
And, if I fail not in my deep intent,
Clarence hath not another day to live:
Which done, God take King Edward to his mercy,
And leave the world for me to bustle in! (I, i, 147–52)

Edmund, the bastard son and devious schemer from *King Lear*, has recourse to techniques also turned to account by Kleist's Machiavellian protagonists. He has developed the knack of presenting himself in the most positive light possible; he attributes cunning to another (Edgar) at the very moment he is cunningly deceiving his interlocutor; and he does not hesitate to betray his father if it will serve his ambition, a betrayal rationalized as greater loyalty to the general welfare than to his own blood. (Abälard follows the same procedures.) Not unlike Hermann, he displays expertise at reading and preparing for the probable response of an individual (Gloucester) and at using someone close to himself to destroy a friend-enemy once the latter has outlived his usefulness. But a particular incident from *King Lear* seems to look forward to one of the most crucial exchanges in Kleist's last play:

EDMUND Have you not spoken 'gainst the Duke of Cornwall?
  He's coming hither; now, i' the night, i' the haste,
  And Regan with him: have you nothing said
  Upon his party 'gainst the Duke of Albany?
  Advise yourself.
EDGAR   I am sure on't, not a word.   (II, i, 25–9)

Edmund's questions and imperative together with Edgar's response bear comparison with a similar dialogue between Hohenzollern and Homburg:

HOHENZOLLERN Hast du vielleicht je einen Schritt getan,
  Seis wissentlich, seis unbewusst,
  Der seinem stolzen Geist zu nah getreten?
DER PRINZ VON HOMBURG Niemals!
HOHENZOLLERN   Besinne dich!
DER PRINZ VON HOMBURG   Niemals, beim Himmel!   (1:672)

The roles are surprisingly analogous. In both dramatic situations, a so-called friend suggests a hidden conflict which has supposedly created bad will between two groups. The Machiavellian protagonist implies that his chosen victim, innocent at least at the conscious level, represents an obstacle in forging a possible union between the inimical parties. He resorts to this tactic to shake the confidence of his listener and ultimately to destroy his rival in what amounts to undeclared hostility, undeclared in the sense that neither Homburg nor Edgar has an inkling of his 'friend's' animosity towards him.

Whereas *Richard* III and *King Lear* offer some points of contact, *Othello* provides the most striking parallels, a not surprising feature given the prominence of Shakespeare's 'greatest scoundrel'[4] within the tragedy of the Moor of Venice. In the first act, Iago expresses pleasure at the prospect of being able to exploit the gullible Roderigo for his amusement: 'For I mine own gain'd knowledge should profane, / If I would time expend with such a snipe [Roderigo], / But for my sport and profit' (I, iii, 390–2). The same could be said of Kleist's Machiavellian protagonists who regard life as a game of chance in which they attempt to gain the upper hand by controlling others. Moreover, ambition and reputation help to explain Iago's machinations; it is not simply a case of gratuitous evil. He feels that Othello has unfairly passed over him to promote Cassio and even though there is no truth to the rumour that the Moor has seduced Emilia, he insists that Othello has harmed his public image as a husband in a society where one's good name means everything: 'CASSIO. Reputation, reputation, reputation! O, I have lost my reputation! I have lost the immortal part of myself, and what remains is bestial. My reputation, Iago, my reputation!' (II, iii, 263–6).

Frequently, the relationships that develop between Othello-Iago-Cassio-Desdemona come close to those that unfold between the Elector-Hohenzollern-Homburg-Nathalie. All the time that Iago professes love and friendship for Cassio and appears to be taking the part of his 'friend' before his superior commander, he is really scheming to disgrace him. This approximates Hohenzollern's association with Homburg: on the surface the Count presents himself as the trustworthy confidant but is secretly planning to discredit both Homburg and the Elector. Iago also knows his unsuspecting victim's weaknesses just as well as does Hohenzollern: 'If I can fasten but one cup upon him [Cassio], / With that which he hath drunk to-night already, / He'll be as full of quarrel and offence / As my young mistress' dog' (II, iii, 50–3). He contrives to get Cassio inebriated and then uses Roderigo, whose love for Desdemona he also turns to account, as a willing tool in his plot to compromise Cassio and eventually to harm Othello. In the ensuing drunken brawl directed by Iago, the characters react precisely as programmed. When Othello appears upon the scene as the one accountable for upholding the law, the situation calls to mind the Elector's position as he condemns the yet unknown leader who ordered the cavalry charge:

> Give me to know
> How this foul rout began, who set it on;
> And he that is approved in this offence,
> Though he had twinn'd with me, both at a birth,
> Shall lose me. (II, iii, 209–13)

This public disorder could have had serious repercussions for the whole community:

> What! in a town of war,
> Yet wild, the people's hearts brimful of fear,
> To manage private and domestic quarrel,
> In night, and on the court and guard of safety! (II, iii, 213–16)

Like the Elector, Othello becomes a captive of his public pronouncement and, despite the strong personal inclination he may feel for Cassio, must deny the private – 'Shall lose me' – in favour of the general good.

In the ensuing dialogue, Iago, by seemingly minimizing both the importance of the disturbance and Cassio's (Homburg's) complicity, achieves two objectives: he retains Cassio's trust and he elevates himself in the eyes of his commander (Elector) who assumes, as he is intended to assume, that 'his ancient' is speaking out of loyalty to a comrade. No sooner is Othello (Elector) out of earshot, however, than Iago further downplays the seriousness of the offence and assures Cassio that he will be eventually reinstated: 'What, man! there are ways to recover the general again: you are but now cast in his mood, a punishment more in policy than in malice; even so as one would beat his offenceless dog to affright an imperious lion: see to him again, and he's yours' (II, iii, 272–7).

When Iago questions Cassio about the details of the public uproar, the situation looks forward to Hohenzollern's interrogation of Homburg after the garden incident. 'CASSIO. I remember a mass of things, but nothing distinctly; a quarrel, but nothing wherefore' (II, iii, 289–90). Homburg, in his somnambulistic trance, may be said to achieve a state of emotional inebriation, with some external prompting, reminiscent of Cassio's actual drunkenness. Similarly both victims cannot remember the specific details but are asked to do so by the very man who concocted their public embarrassment in the first place. Cassio, who, incidentally, has the reputation of cutting a dashing figure with the ladies, shares Homburg's dependence upon his 'friend' in his moments of despair: 'I'll [Iago] tell you [Cassio] what you shall do' (II, iii, 319). Just as Hohenzollern urges Homburg's appeal to the Electress, Iago counsels the disgraced lieutenant to seek Desdemona's intervention: '[Confess] yourself freely to her; importune her help to put you in your place again: ... this broken joint between you and her husband entreat her to splinter' (II, iii, 324–9). Iago also practises with Hohenzollern the art of imputing unflattering motives to others: 'Cassio, my lord [Othello]! No, sure, I cannot think it, / That he would steal away so guilty-like, / Seeing you coming' (III, iii, 38–40), and, ever the opportunist, he knows how to plant a seed of doubt in the mind of his unsuspecting, ingenous listener.

Because almost all the analogies I have drawn are based more upon comparable psychological techniques and general situation than upon precise similarities in wording, they tend to underscore a more general affinity in Shakespeare's and Kleist's acknowledgment and effective theatrical exploitation of the Machiavellian protagonist. However, whereas the Elizabethan believes in the possibility of total human depravity, of a conscious, willing self-dedication to evil: 'I [Iago] have't. It is engender'd.

Hell and night / Must bring this monstrous birth to the world's light' (I, iii, 409–10), Kleist casts his schemer in more subtle, greyer tones with the possible exception of the enigmatic Hohenzollern, who, at times, does act and sound like a cousin not that far removed from the arch-fiend Iago.

For my second hypothesis, I am proposing a model who clearly had a contemporary relevance and could be said, perhaps more than any other single individual, to have influenced the specific path that Kleist's career was obliged to follow. I offer by way of introduction three evaluations of this model from quite different historical perspectives:

Mais ses discours indiquaient le tact des circonstances, comme le chasseur a celui de sa proie.[5]

[Il] met du calcul dans tout ce qu'il fait, dans ses expansions apparantes et jusque dans ses explosions sincères; quand il s'y abandonne, c'est de parti pris, avec prévision de leur effet, afin d'intimider ou d'éblouir; il exploite tout d'autrui, et aussi de lui-même ... il exploite tout pour l'avancement de l'édifice qu'il bâtit.[6]

The urge to dominate, to dare, to play for the highest stakes was as instinctive to him and as irresistible as the urge of the mountaineer to climb Everest.[7]

All three quotations, the first from a contemporary of Kleist's, Mme de Staël, the second from the noted French historian of the second half of the nineteenth century, Hyppolyte Taine, and the last, from a relatively recent study by the English historian Felix Markham, could be describing one of Kleist's Machiavellian protagonists, Hermann, Robert Guiskard, or Hohenzollern, but, of course, refer to, in Nietzsche's words, 'Napoleon, diese Synthese von Unmensch und Übermensch.'[8]

In the Introduction, I outlined a basic similarity between the lives of the Florentine Machiavelli and the Prussian Kleist and, strangely enough, the same fundamanetal pattern, at least in the initial stages, may also be discerned in Bonaparte's earlier career. At the time of his birth in 1769, the struggle for Corsican independence from French rule had caught the imagination of several European writers. Raised in a country notorious for political strife and committed to a strong sense of family loyalty, young Napoleon, not unlike Machiavelli[9] or Kleist, embraced the independence movement of his native land against the foreign oppressor. 'Napoleon's heroes remained,' to quote Markham, 'Rousseau and Paoli [the leader of the Corsican independence party]. For him the [French] Revolution meant a great opportunity of freedom for Corsica.'[10] However, in the eyes of many, he came to betray the ideals of the French Revolution in the pursuit of his own personal ambition.

There exists an even more direct link between Machiavelli and Napoleon. Taine, in his hostile portrait of the French despot, proposes that Corsican society, being founded on anarchy, promoted the development in Napoleon of an immoral outlook harking back to fifteenth-century Italy: 'De là les premières impressions de Bonaparte, semblables à celles des Borgia et de Machiavel.'[11] In point of fact, the Bonaparte family traced its lineage as far back as the eleventh century to a noble Florentine family which had moved to Corsica about two hundred years before Napoleon was born. Hence, 'il descend des grands Italiens, hommes d'action de l'an 1400, des aventuriers militaires, usurpateurs et fondateurs d'États viagers; il a hérité, par filiation directe, de leur sang et de leur structure innée, mentale et morale.'[12] Attempting to establish an image of Napoleon as an anachronistic Renaissance figure, Taine offers an interesting, admittedly imaginative, parallel between the two most illustrious artists of the Italian Renaissance and the nineteenth-century man of action, a parallel which, as I shall demonstrate later (Kleist's glorification of the *vita activa*), suggests an affinity with Kleist the artist and frustrated *homme d'action*: 'On le [Napoleon] reconnaît pour ce qu'il est, pour un frère posthume de Dante et de Michel-Ange; ... il est un des trois esprits souverains de la Renaissance italienne. – Seulement, les deux premiers opéraient sur le papier ou le marbre; c'est sur l'homme vivant, sur la chair sensible et souffrante que celui-ci a travaillé.'[13]

Not the first to see the relationship between Renaissance Italy and Napoleon, Taine acknowledges his debt to Stendhal and especially to Mme de Staël.[14] In her writings we can ascertain one of the first significant attacks on the heroic cult that began to evolve and was substantially encouraged and exploited by Napoleon during his lifetime. For the purposes of my hypothesis, it is thus worth noting that a famous Kleistian contemporary known for her personal hatred of the French leader (he exiled her from Paris in 1802) interprets the negative manifestations of the Napoleonic phenomenon in terms of his having read and taken to heart *Il Principe*: 'Bonaparte s'est enivré de ce mauvais vin de machiavélisme; il ressemblait, sous plusieurs rapports, aux tyrans italiens du quatorze et quinzième siècle; et, comme il avait peu lu, l'instruction ne combattait point dans sa tête la disposition naturelle de son caractère

... il y [in *Le Prince*] a cherché ce qui passe encore pour de la profondeur parmi les âmes vulgaires: l'art de tromper les hommes.'[15]

Throughout Kleist's literary active years from 1801 until 1811, Napoleon dominated European society. His influence, as Kleist discovered as early as March 1802 in Switzerland, could not be avoided: 'Mich erschreckt die blosse Möglichkeit, statt eines Schweizer Bürgers durch einen Taschenspielerskunstgriff ein Franzose zu werden' (2:719). The secondary literature has concentrated almost exclusively on what could be called Kleist's negative portrayal of the 'allgemeinen Wolf' (2:718), the dominant, most obvious mode perhaps best captured in a section from the 'Katechismus der Deutschen' entitled 'Von der Bewunderung Napoleons':

FRAGE Was hältst du von Napoleon, dem Korsen, dem berühmten Kaiser der Franzosen?

...

ANTWORT Für einen verabscheuungswürdigen Menschen; für den Anfang alles Bösen und das Ende alles Guten; für einen Sünder, den anzuklagen, die Sprache der Menschen nicht hinreicht, und den Engeln einst, am jüngsten Tage, der Odem vergehen wird. (2:354)

This vituperation represented a minority response, for Napoleon was generally celebrated as the saviour not only of France but of Europe, including even Prussia: 'Als Napoleon diese Errungenschaften [die Vernichtung des Feudalsystems, die Abschaffung der Rechtsungleichheit und des Gewerbezwangs, und die Religionsfreiheit] auch den süddeutschen Staaten aufzwang, wurde er als der Retter des deutschen Reiches und Volkes stürmisch begrüsst und seine Siege über die Österreicher und Russen als Befreiung der Menschheit gepriesen. Bis in die höchsten Kreise und die nahe Umgebung des Königs reichte die Napoleonverehrung in Preussen.'[16]

Since even Mme de Staël, Napoleon's most tenacious detractor, had to concede, 'Que Bonaparte fût un homme d'un génie transcendant à beaucoup d'égards, qui pourrait le nier?'[17] it would be unreasonable to assume that Kleist was able to remain totally isolated from and unaffected by the dominant public attitude of the time. When Kleist went to Dresden from France in August 1807, there were, in Richard Samuel's words, 'Anzeichen ..., dass sich eine positive Wendung gegenüber dem Napoleonischen System anbahnte.'[18] By 'Anzeichen,' Samuel alludes to Kleist's renewing his association with Wieland and his desperate attempt to gain an endorsement from Goethe, two well-known *Napoleon-Verehrer*. His obvious dislike did not prevent him from revising and publishing a flattering anecdote in the *Berliner Abendblätter* glorifying the emperor's compassion and the tremendous loyalty of his wounded troops at the Battle of Aspern (2:283). Of course, this may have been dictated by the necessity of remaining on the right side of the censorship, a tactic which Machiavelli would have approved of.

One of the most revealing passages calling into question Kleist's purported blind hatred for the Corsican occurs in the very same dialogue 'Von der Bewunderung Napoleons' quoted earlier in which the latter is repudiated as a diabolic, unnatural spirit. (If Napoleon is rejected on the grounds of anti-nature, could not the same be said of Hermann who uses people to serve his ends and drives Thusnelda, 'Das Ungeheu'r' [1:620] to her unnatural act?) The father maintains, 'Gleichwohl, sagt man, soll er viel Tugenden besitzen. Das Geschäft der Unterjochung der Erde soll er mit List, Gewandtheit und Kühnheit vollziehn, und besonders, an dem Tage der Schlacht, ein grosser Feldherr sein' (2:355). As I remarked in my discussion of *Die Hermannsschlacht*, except for the subjugation of the world, all of these 'virtues' apply equally well to Hermann. This would seem to suggest that Kleist sought someone who could beat Napoleon at his own game and hence that he used the emperor as his standard for the type of political leader, the despot, necessary to succeed in the political arena.[19] The exchange goes on to insist that the Corsican should not be shown 'Bewunderung' and 'Verehrung': 'Das wäre ebenso feig, als ob ich die Geschicklichkeit, die einem Menschen im Ringen beiwohnt, in dem Augenblick bewundern wollte, da er mich in den Kot wirft und mein Antlitz mit Füssen tritt' (2:355). In other words, it all depends upon one's point of view. There is a strong inference in this analogy that Kleist would like to be on the giving side, not the receiving end of the defeated Germans. Hermann may be said to realize vicariously this ambition.

The dialogue between father and son ends with the concession that people may admire Napoleon, 'Wenn er vernichtet ist' (2:355), specifically when he no longer poses a threat, but again by implication, despite his cunning, his devilish, unnatural ways singled out in the first half of the dialogue, the father finds nothing wrong in acknowledging the emperor's greatness provided the personal danger to one's self or one's country has been eliminated. Such reasoning supplies ample justification for a Hermann-type figure, a German Napoleon. Hence, to employ an appropriate cliché, Kleist's attitude to *the* political figure of his age may well have been based upon a love-hate relationship. Kleist always longed to perform 'eine grosse Tat' that circumstances, largely created by Napoleon, prevented him from achieving, while no less a figure than Goethe was extolling the subjugator of the German states as the man of deeds.[20] Napoleon, driven by ambition, was enjoying a career crowned by success and fame, the elusive 'Siegeskranz' (1:633), the 'Ruhm ... / Nach dem [Kleist-Hermann] durch zwölf Jahre treu gestrebt' (1:623).

Many commentators have substantiated the claim that Kleist proved unusually perceptive about the political situation in Europe. Samuel, for example, asserts: 'Kleist war der einzige *Dichter* [Samuel's emphasis], der das Problem seiner Zeit in seiner ganzen Tiefe erfasst und gestaltet hat, soweit die negative Seite Napoleons in Betracht kommt,'[21] and in fact, Kleist did recognize Napoleon's dynastic ambitions and their European repercussions as early as December 1805 when he wrote to Rühle von Lilienstern: 'Die Zeit scheint eine neue Ordnung der Dinge herbeiführen zu wollen, und wir werden davon nichts, als bloss den Umsturz der alten erleben. Es wird sich aus dem ganzen kultivierten Teil von Europa ein einziges, grosses System von Reichen bilden, und die Throne mit neuen, von Frankreich abhängigen, Fürstendynastien besetzt werden. Aus dem Östreichschen, bin ich gewiss, geht *dieser glückgekrönte Abenteurer, falls ihm nur das Glück treu bleibt*, nicht wieder heraus' (2:761). In much the same vein, but *after* Napoleon's new imperial rule based upon his family had been instituted, Mme de Staël queried, 'Bonaparte ne faisait rien en Allemagne que dans le but d'y établir son pouvoir et celui de sa famille: une telle nation était-elle faite pour servir de piédestal à son égoïsme?'[22]

The designation of Napoleon as 'dieser glückgekrönte Abenteurer' with his new 'Fürstendynastien' would also suit Robert Guiskard, 'falls ihm nur das Glück treu bleibt.' Many critics, most notably Streller, Denneler, and Samuel, have seen in Robert Guiskard an image of Bonaparte. In Streller's view, 'Es ist also die Problematik des Usurpators, der auf Grund seiner Tüchtigkeit das Herrscheramt übernommen hat und mit dem Prinzip der Legitimität in Konflikt gerät.'[23] He assumes that the remarkable topicality of *Robert Guiskard*, as it relates for instance to Napoleon's crowning himself emperor in 1804, is either fortuitous or based upon Rousseau's treatment of usurpation in *Le Contract social*; however such a thesis fails to take into consideration that the fragment, written down in 1807–8 may reflect a more mature, later version coloured by recent historical events.[24] Denneler emphasizes the 'naturgewaltig[en] "Zauber" und die ans Göttliche grenzende Verehrung des Helden'[25] as points of similarity between Guiskard and Napoleon and draws an analogy between the report of Guiskard's visiting those infected by the plague and a widely publicized incident from the Egyptian campaign.[26] During the siege of Acteon, Bonaparte paid his respects to his plague-stricken soldiers in a Jaffe hospital and allegedly helped care for the sick and bury the dead, 'but on the retreat there is little doubt,' according to the historian J.M. Thompson, 'that, unable to carry a number of incurably sick with him, and unwilling to leave them to the vengeance of the enemy, he gave orders that they should be given a fatal dose of opium.'[27] Questioning some of Denneler's correspondences since 'das Fragment in der Hauptsache Ende 1807 geschrieben wurde und es deshalb nicht möglich war, aktuelle politische Fragen des Jahres 1808 zu behandeln,' Samuel contends that Kleist based his Robert Guiskard on the 'Bonaparte von 1803 und 1804, an dessen Unternehmung gegen England Kleist zweimal, im November und Dezember 1803, teilzunehmen versuchte, [den] Napoleon, der – gegen alles Völkerrecht – im März 1804 den Herzog von Enghien entführen und hinrichten liess und der sich im Mai 1804 – als Kleist wiederum in Paris war – zum Erbkaiser "wählen" liess.'[28]

Other historical events may have found their way indirectly into Kleist's characterization of the Machiavellian protagonist. Robert Guiskard knew how to profit from a situation, the untimely death of his brother and his nephew's minority status, to usurp the crown just as Napoleon took advantage of the revolution to become First Consul and eventually emperor. Also, on 24 December 1800, while on his way to the opera, the First Consul narrowly missed being assassinated by an 'infernal machine' that exploded on the street killing several innocent bystanders. Napoleon used this attempt on his life to purge the left opposition: one hundred and thirty die-hard republicans were condemned as terrorists without proper legal defence and deported to Guiana (cf. Hermann's exploitation of the Hally episode). Only a few days later, the real perpetrators, royalist extremists, were arrested and guillotined, but Napoleon refused to set free the deported Jacobins since, anticipating this eventuality, he had cunningly had them proscribed as a threat to the welfare of the state. 'He laughingly pointed this out to a member of the Council of State who had the courage to come and plead for the innocent victims,'[29] most of whom died in exile. (Licht, Hermann, and Hohenzollern exhibit this same sadistic trait.)

During the Italian campaign, 'Bonaparte was already adopting the useful device of misrepresenting the relative strength of the forces engaged on each side'[30] and resorting to the exaggeration of the perfectly normal resistance of the local inhabitants to the occupation in order to have a grievance against the Venetian government[31] (cf. Die Hermannsschlacht).

He also had the reputation of being capable of creating an event to serve his own devious ends. When the Venetians fired upon and boarded a French ship and a clash between two rival forces resulted in the death of a number of French troops, the two incidents came at such a convenient time that they were 'said to have been instigated by [Napoleon's] agents.'[32] But above all, Napoleon had an earned reputation as a skilled military leader who inspired an almost fanatical sense of loyalty and devotion in his men. The following appraisal by Markham could relate to Robert Guiskard: 'His surest touch was, of course, with his soldiers. A record of victory and professional skill is the first requisite for a commander in gaining the confidence of his soldiers; but to this Napoleon added an uncanny insight into the psychology of the soldier. As he said, "The military are a freemasonry: and I am its Grand Master." His constant reviews, and his presence on the battlefield, enabled him to establish an extraordinary degree of personal contact, particularly with the guard.'[33] Moreover, from Vendémiaire to Waterloo, his political base, that which made it possible in the first place and which sustained it throughout, was victory in the field achieved without regard to the cost in human lives. 'La vieille doctrine de la perfidie,' according to Mme de Staël, 'n'a réussi à Bonaparte que parce qu'il y joignait le prestige de la victoire.'[34] Military success and a commitment to total warfare form the basis of the political policy espoused by both Guiskard and Hermann.

All of the preceding similarities between Napoleon and Kleist's Machiavellian protagonists may be purely accidental; none the less, a survey of Kleist's correspondence and essays reveals an awareness of the French ruler's strengths and tactics. The 'Katechismus der Deutschen' makes it clear that Napoleon cannot be trusted to tell the truth:

FRAGE Also, wenn zwei Angaben vorhanden sind, die eine von Napoleon, dem Korsenkaiser, die andere von Franz, Kaiser von Österreich: welcher glaubst du?
ANTWORT Der Angabe Franzens, Kaisers von Österreich.
FRAGE Warum?
ANTWORT Weil er wahrhaftiger ist. (2:352)

Nor can he be expected to respect international conventions such as neutrality: 'Napoleon, Kaiser der Franzosen, hat [Deutschland], mitten im Frieden, zertrümmert, und mehrere Völker, die es bewohnen, unterjocht' (2:351). The 'Katechismus' deplores as well those Germans who 'reflektieren, wo sie empfinden oder handeln sollten,' who 'meinten, alles durch ihren Witz bewerkstelligen zu können' (2:356). Early in his life, Kleist adopted from his friend Ludwig von Brockes a new life directive: 'Handeln ist besser als Wissen' (2:620) and since throughout the dramatist's lifetime, Napoleon was celebrated as the Faustian man of action,[35] it would not be unreasonable to suspect that Kleist secretly admired the French emperor because he acted while expressing a marked scorn for abstract speculation. '[Napoleon's] aversion pour les fantômes sans substance de la politique abstraite,' in Taine's words, 'va au delà du dédain, jusqu' au dégoût; ce qu'on appelle en ce temps-là l'idéologie est proprement sa bête noire; il y répugne non seulement par calcul intéressé, mais encore et davantage par besoin et instinct du vrai, en praticien, en chef d'État.'[36] One is reminded of Hermann's emotional repudiation of the German princes:

> Die Schwätzer, die! Ich bitte dich [Eginhardt];
> Lass sie zu Hause gehn. –
> ...
> Meinst du, die liessen sich bewegen,
> Auf meinem Flug mir munter nachzuschwingen?
> Eh das von meinem Maultier würd ich hoffen.
> ...
> Es braucht der *Tat*, nicht der Verschwörungen.   (1:585)

Both *Robert Guiskard* and *Die Hermannsschlacht* bear evidence of an aristocratic contempt for the broader masses.[37] Whereas some critics see a vestige of political progress in the fact that Kleist's totalitarian leaders must seek public support for their rule, political experience as recorded in *Il Principe*[38] has taught that a head of state, regardless of the form of government, can only hope to remain securely in office provided that he has some measure of popular backing. The image that comes to mind, especially in reference to *Die Hermannsschlacht*, is that of the mindless herd which the ruler must tolerate and cajole to secure his objectives. It is no accident that the '[Rat] der gesamten Fürsten' (1:627), i.e., an aristocratic body, will determine Hermann's election as '[Germaniens] würdgen Oberherrn und König' (1:626). Furthermore, in the 'Lehrbuch der französischen Journalistik,' Kleist ascribes to Napoleon in his control of the press[40] an equally low opinion of the people. Although the tone of the proverbial-like statements is ironic: 'Was das Volk nicht weiss, macht das Volk nicht heiss' or 'Was man dem Volk dreimal sagt, hält das Volk für wahr' (2:361), one still senses an underlying scorn for a so easily manipulated mass. As for the task 'Dem Volk eine gute Nachricht vorzutragen,' the 'Lehrbuch' offers the following advice: 'Ist es ein blosses Gefecht, wobei nicht viel herausgekommen ist: so setze man in *Moniteur* eine, im *Journal de l'Empire* drei Nullen an jede Zahl, und schicke die Blätter mit Kurieren in alle Welt' (2:364). Hermann also practises statistical misrepresentation to dupe his people with the one distinction that the news – Roman atrocities – constitutes 'good' news only for the German leader but not for his suffering subjects. When faced with the necessity of dealing with bad news, one should adhere to the proposition, 'Zeit gewonnen, alles gewonnen' (2:364). 'Dieser Satz ist so klar,' notes the commentary, 'dass er, wie die Grundsätze, keines Beweises bedarf, daher ihn der Kaiser der Franzosen auch unter die Grundsätze aufgenommen hat. Er führt, in natürlicher Ordnung, auf die Kunst, dem Volk eine Nachricht zu verbergen' (2:365). And finally, if one is obliged 'Dem Volk eine schlechte Nachricht vorzutragen,' 'Man schweige davon ..., bis sich die Umstände geändert haben' (2:366). Kleist had already demonstrated much earlier than the 'Lehrbuch' this same deceptive strategy in Robert Guiskard who tries to keep bad news from his subjects in an effort to gain time and in the hope that circumstances will change.

Kleist further displays his knowledge of Napoleon's manipulative tactics in the 'Aufzeichnung auf Gut Friedensdorf' written only two months before his suicide: '(1) Der Krieg zwischen Napoleon und Fr. Wilhelm bricht binnen hier und vier Wochen aus: (2) Die Franzosen fangen den Krieg nicht an; sie setzen den König so, dass er den Frieden brechen muss; und dann erdrücken sie ihn' (2:879). This matches to a large degree Hermann's plan of allowing the Romans to enter Cheruska: he is confident that the enemy forces by committing the inevitable excesses entailed by an occupation will arouse public opinion against them and thus grant him the needed pretext to wage war on a foreign enemy. Like Napoleon he consciously sets up a situation where his opponent is obliged to act in a way anticipated by the instigator so that the latter has ample justification and the ensuing public support to destroy his foe.

Kleist conceived the 'Katechismus der Deutschen' as a piece of propaganda to raise support for the German-Austrian resistance to Napoleon, and yet, as previously indicated, several of the positive values put forward may be justifiably applied to 'dem berühmten Kaiser der Franzosen' (2:354). In answer to the father's question: 'Und welches sind die höchsten Güter der Menschen?,' the son responds: 'Gott, Vaterland, Kaiser, Freiheit, Liebe und Treue, Schönheit, Wissenschaft und Kunst' (2:356). Ironically, the French emperor, at various stages of his reign, managed to associate himself in the minds of many with all of these 'höchsten Güter der Menschen.' By signing the Concordat with Rome, he re-established Roman Catholicism as the state religion and was even lauded by some as the defender of the Roman Catholic faith. (The Pope came to Paris to anoint Bonaparte at his coronation as emperor in 1804.) In his frequent proclamations or bulletins from the line, he never failed to appeal to the patriotism of his fellow Frenchmen and he successfully created the desired image of himself as emperor both at home and abroad. When he came to power as First Consul or when he invaded Europe, many regarded him as the promoter and protector of the values, especially freedom, championed by the French Revolution, while the love and fidelity he was able to instil in his troops became legendary (Heine's 'Die Grenadiere'). Although he viewed art and science as means to an end and strictly regulated their production, Napoleon astutely cast himself in the role of patron of the arts and sciences as indicated by his homage to Goethe and by the inclusion of the scientific community in the Egyptian campaign. Summarizing Napoleon's achievements in the years 1799 to 1804, Samuel writes: 'Der Wiederaufbau Frankreichs, seine soziale Gesetzgebung, die einheitliche Rechtskodifikation, die straffe administrative Zusammenfassung des Landes, der Aufbau des Heeres auf der allgemeinen Wehrpflicht, die Regelung der religiösen Frage, die umfassenden Bestrebungen in Kultur und Wissenschaft hatten ihn zum Vorbilde des Herrschers und Staatslenkers erhoben.'[40]

To conclude my examination of Kleist's familiarity with Napoleon's Machiavellian machinations, I shall focus on what may well be a 'Nietzschean slip' from the 'Katechismus':

FRAGE Wer hat ein solches Recht [ein Reich wiederherzustellen], sag an?
ANTWORT Jedweder, dem Gott zwei Dinge gegeben hat: den guten *Willen* dazu
und die *Macht*, es zu vollbringen. (2:353)

Kleist designates *Wille* and *Macht* as the two forces required to resurrect the defeated German-Austrian empire, but as in the case of the wrestler image interpreted earlier, these values can obviously be operative on both sides of a conflict and must have been equally present in Napoleon who destroys the 'Reich' in the first place. Once the will is directed towards the achievement of power for its own sake, will and power unite to form a Nietzschean will to power as exemplified in Licht, Hermann, Hohenzollern, Abälard, and Guiskard or in Kleist's most obvious prototype, Napoleon himself. Mme de Staël emphasizes '[la] force de sa [Napoleon's] *volonté*[41] and both she: 'Bonaparte a dit de lui-même, avec raison, qu'il savait jouer à merveille de l'instrument du *pouvoir*[42] and Taine: 'Ma [i.e., Napoleon's] maîtresse, c'est le *pouvoir*[43] see in power one of the strongest motivations behind the emperor's phenomenal success on the military and political battlefield.

'Wen vertritt Hermann – das Wunschbild eines Anführers, der Napoleon gewachsen war.'[44] Most critics, myself included, agree with Samuel's evaluation of Hermann as an anti-Napoleon. However, when Samuel tries to assign a specific role-model to Hermann: 'Wenn angenommen werden darf, dass Kleist die Pläne des Triumvirates kannte und nicht nur völlig von ihnen überzeugt, sondern auch aktiv in ihre Durchführung verwickelt war, dann kann Hermann nur ein Porträt des Freiherrn vom Stein darstellen,'[45] I have some difficulty with his hypothesis. In his earlier article 'Goethe-Napoleon-Heinrich von Kleist,' Samuel observes, 'Man hat Kleist eine Lust für Grausamkeiten vorgeworfen, und doch kann nachgewiesen werden, dass alle die den Römern zugeschriebenen Gewaltakte, welche die Deutschen schliesslich zur Verzweiflung trieben, den Tatsachen der Jahre 1806 bis 1808 entsprechen.'[46] But what about the 'Gewaltakte' for which Hermann alone bears responsibility? 'Es hat lange gedauert, bis Stein zu dem angeführten Entschluss kam: "Soll es dem Kaiser Napoleon allein erlaubt sein, an die Stelle des Rechts Willkür, der Wahrheit Lüge zu setzen?"'[47] Only with extreme reluctance did Stein reach this position. He obviously did not approve of dishonesty, deception, and intrigue even if dictated by necessity, but could see no other alternative under the circumstances. In fact, there is every indication that he sincerely regretted having to resort to such unethical means. The same may not be said of Hermann who actually enjoys inflicting destruction upon both friend and foe and shows no sign of remorse or regret.

'Hermann,' Samuel goes on to argue, 'ist durchaus nicht skrupellos. Immer muss er sich gegen das Menschliche in sich wehren, das sein Amt, ein höheres Menschliches zu erreichen, zu unterdrücken ihm gebietet. "Du bist so mild, o Sohn der Götter, / Der Frühling kann nicht milder sein." So wird Hermann von den Barden charakterisiert.'[48] When Samuel concurs with this assessment by the 'Chor der Barden,' he does not take into account that this scene, written primarily in praise of art, immediately follows one of the drama's most brutal episodes where Hermann baits and has executed the defenceless, decent Roman Septimius. I also take issue with the designation of 'das Menschliche' as a category peculiar to or practised by the Cheruskian ruler. My interpretation of *Die Hermannsschlacht* has shown that Hermann fails to extend this quality not only to the Romans but also to his own people and his wife. Whereas he may conquer his desire for revenge on the German traitors, his driving ambition to secure national unity determines this conquest, not 'humanitarian' concerns.

In outlining the goals of the Triumvirate with which Kleist allegedly sympathized, Samuel includes 'die Bildung eines innerlich freien Staates auf der Grundlage parlamentarischer Regierungsform und sozialer Gleichberechtigung' and, to support his contention, he points out, 'Auch bei Kleist legt Hermann nach der Niederwerfung des Feindes die Führung nieder und verlangt die Entscheidung in einer freien Wahl durch den Fürstenrat, während er in einem seiner Pamphlete sagt: "Nach Beendigung des Kriegs soll ein Reichstag gehalten, und von den Fürsten des Reichs, nach der Mehrzahl der Stimmen, eine Staatsverfassung festgesetzt werden."'[49] It would, of course, be possible to explain the free vote 'in der gesamten Fürsten Rat' (1:627) as an attempt to conform to the drama's pseudo-historic flavour, but the pamphlet advocating the same solution and *only* applicable to nineteenth-century Germany does not presage well for social equality since the parliamentary form of government recommended will be founded upon a class principle. Only the princes, not the people, are to decide by majority vote the nature of the constitution. May one realistically expect meaningful participation by the people in the parliamentary process or 'die Bildung eines innerlich freien Staates' if a conservative aristocracy, to which Kleist, despite his efforts to renounce his title, belonged, were to formulate a constitution? At heart, he shared with Goethe a distrust of the masses. Although Kleist was sufficiently pragmatic to recognize the necessity of courting their favour, he demonstrated in *Robert Guiskard* and *Die Hermannsschlacht* that the people can be easily misled and manipulated.

Because Kleist sympathized with the group who out of incipient feelings of German nationalism desired or were plotting Napoleon's downfall, it would not be out of place to consider the portrait of the French emperor painted by his most famous disparager, Mme de Staël. Even though her *Considérations sur les principaux événements de la Révolution Française* was first published in 1818 one year after her death, one may assume that much of the anecdotal material relating to Bonaparte was common knowledge among the anti-Napoleon faction. The general public would quite naturally have an understandable curiosity about and insatiable appetite for any information, whether complimentary or otherwise, relating to the personality dominating all of Europe. Mme de Staël passed through Dresden at the beginning of June 1808 and contributed an article, 'Le Retour des

Grecs,' to *Phöbus*.[50] At the time of her visit, Kleist actively participated in the cultural life of the city and it would be difficult to imagine his not having come in contact with her or his not having at least been made aware of their common dislike of the French leader. I have also chosen to include several details provided by Taine's depiction of Napoleon since the historian was a 'spiritual heir, if a bitterly disillusioned one, of Mme de Staël. The hundred and forty pages of [Taine's] chapter on Napoleon belong to literature.'[51] Moreover, Taine derived much of his material from the memoirs and personal reminiscences, in a word, gossip, recorded by hostile parties close to the emperor, the sort of rumours and salon tales which would undoubtedly have found favour with the resistance movement.

The image that emerges is very negative indeed. Both writers agree upon egoism as Napoleon's key motivating force:

Il regarde une créature humaine comme un fait ou comme une chose, mais non comme un semblable. [Hermann?] Il ne hait pas plus qu'il n'aime; il n'y a que lui pour lui; tout le reste des créatures sont des chiffres. La force de sa volonté consiste dans l'imperturbable calcul de son égoïsme; c'est un habile joueur d'échecs dont le genre humain est la partie adverse qu'il se propose de faire échec et mat [cf. the game image of *Die Hermannsschlacht*].[52]

[Sur] le trône, comme dans les camps, général, consul ou empereur, il reste officier de fortune et ne songe qu'à son avancement. Par une lacune énorme d'éducation, de conscience et de coeur, au lieu de subordonner sa personne à l'État, il subordonne l'État à sa personne [cf. Robert Guiskard].[53]

With a mind 'réduisant tout au calcul,'[54] he fully comprehends the psychological motivation of his adversaries, possesses the uncanny talent of reading their intent from their external appearance (the Machiavellian protagonist is always looking at his victim), and subsequently draws personal profit from their faults. '[Il] s'est montré grand psychologue autant que stratégiste accompli.'[55] In describing Napoleon's concentration of all his energies upon the attainment of one goal, Taine could just as well be characterizing Hermann with a metaphor straight from the pages of the drama: 'Pendant qu'il est occupé d'un objet, le reste n'existe pas pour lui; c'est une espèce de chasse dont rien ne le détourne.'[56] His calculation even includes the conscious control of his emotions. Once, after one of his verbal explosions, he reportedly confided in l'abbé de Pradt, '"Vous m'avez cru bien en colère: détrompez-vous; chez moi, la colère n'a jamais dépassé ça." (Il montrait son cou.)'[57] Since he appreciates the importance of good public relations to safeguard his authority, he knows how to use language to secure the loyalty of his followers and to captivate the masses: 'Mais ses discours indiquaient le tact des circonstances, comme le chasseur a celui de sa proie,'[58] a quotation singularly applicable to *Die Hermannsschlacht*. Analysing this special gift, Markham comments, 'He had the art of increasing devotion towards him by a familiarity which possessed the knack of behaving towards his inferiors as if they were his equals. The charm which Napoleon could turn on at will was used unscrupulously to fortify his mastery over men's minds [cf. the final scene from *Robert Guiskard*].'[59] As for Napoleon's ethical values or lack thereof, his two French critics depict him as a liar, as '[cet] homme, si habile dans l'art de dissimuler'[60] and as a leader lacking all respect for laws and treaties.[61] 'Il ne croyait ni à la vertu, ni à la probité; il appelait souvent ces deux mots des abstractions; c'est ce qui le rendait si défiant et si immoral.'[62] He takes advantage of the weaknesses of others in order to control them: 'Selon lui, on tient l'homme par ses passions égoïstes, par la peur, la cupidité, la sensualité, l'amour-propre, l'émulation,'[63] the private vulnerabilities so effectively turned to account by the Machiavellian protagonist – fear by Licht and Abälard, greed for recognition and fame by Hohenzollern, sensuality and self-love by Hermann, and rivalry by Hohenzollern or Hermann.

Blessed with an uncanny sense of timing, Napoleon has the faculty of making the best out of any opportunity which circumstances offer him: his role during the siege of Toulon (the chance wounding of the artillery officer enabled Bonaparte to display his professional competence), his handling of the Vendémiaire crisis of 1795 (the whiff of grape-shot), the propaganda value of his successful Italian campaign, and his eventual seizure of absolute power in 1799.[64] Driven by ambition: '[L'ambition] est le moteur premier de son âme et la substance permanente de sa volonté, si intime qu'il ne la distingue plus de lui-même et que parfois il cesse d'en avoir conscience'[65] and by the pursuit of fame: '[Bonaparte] resta seul, comme il le voulait, en possession de la gloire militaire de la France,'[66] he pays constant court to his 'maîtresse ... le pouvoir.'[67] And finally, to put the finishing touches to the portrait, both nineteenth-century writers paint Napoleon as a man given to cruelty and even sadism. In connection with the Egyptian campaign, Mme de Staël insists, 'Toutes les fois qu'il a trouvé quelque avantage dans la cruauté, il se l'est permise ... [Ce] qu'il appelle la nécessité, c'est son ambition; et, lorsque cette ambition était compromise, il n'admettait pas même un moment qu'il pût hésiter à sacrifier les autres à lui,'[68] while Taine reports, 'Il était même doué d'une espèce de sourire satanique qui venait involontairement se placer sur ses lèvres, toutes les fois que l'occasion se présentait ... de conclure à la nécessité d'une rigueur, d'une condamnation quelconque.'[69]

On the one hand it is remarkable how this biased portrait matches Kleist's Machiavellian protagonist, especially Hermann, but on the other hand, Mme de Staël and Taine, like Machiavelli or Kleist before them, are describing the typical features of the eternal despot, unfortunately equally valid and verifiable in their twentieth-century manifestations. Still I would argue that although Hermann does not necessarily represent Baron vom Stein, he could incarnate an anti-Napoleon Napoleon with one major mitigating distinction: 'D'autres chefs d'État [in whose ranks one could include Hermann] ont aussi passé leur vie à violenter les hommes; mais c'était en vue d'une oeuvre viable et pour un intérêt national ... Quand ils saignaient la génération présente, c'était au profit des générations futures, pour les préserver de la guerre civile ou de la domination étrangère.'[70]

In my pursuit of the Kleistian Machiavellian's lineage, I have so far proposed two hypothetical sources: Shakespeare's three villains whose personalities are indebted to a popular Elizabethan misconception of *Il Principe* and the contemporary model, Napoleon, who, to use Mme de Staël's image, 's'est enivré de ce mauvais vin du machiavélisme.'[71] Taine, attributing Napoleon's basic psychological makeup to his 'premières impressions ... semblables à celles des Borgia et de Machiavel'[72] dwells at length upon Bonaparte's talent for discerning the secret motives of others: 'Effectivement, nul ne l'a surpassé dans l'art de démêler les états et les mouvements d'une âme et de beaucoup d'âmes, les motifs efficaces, permanents ou momentanés, qui poussent ou retiennent l'homme en général et tels ou tels hommes en particulier, les ressorts sur lesquels on peut appuyer, l'espèce et le degré de pression qu'il faut appliquer.'[73] We have already ascertained the same capacity to read others and to benefit from this knowledge in Kleist's Machiavellian protagonists, but what does this imply about their creator, the dramatist himself? Taine poses a similar question in connection with Napoleon whom he regards as a military artist: 'Mais comment, sauf par divination, atteindre les passions qui sont des sentiments intimes, et comment, sauf par conjecture, calculer des forces qui semblent répugner à toute mesure?' and concludes: 'Dans ce domaine obscur, glissant, où l'on ne peut marcher qu'à tâtons,

Napoleon opère presque sûrement, et il opère incessamment, d'abord sur lui-même; en effet, pour pénétrer dans l'âme d'autrui, il faut au préalable être descendu dans la sienne.[74]

A letter written on 31 January 1801 to Wilhelmine von Zenge discloses that Kleist, like Machiavelli or Napoleon, had descended into the slippery, dark realm of his own soul with almost the same devastating consequences. He deplores the fact that nature has granted him *'jene traurige Klarheit,* die [ihm] zu jeder Miene den Gedanken, zu jedem Worte den Sinn, zu jeder Handlung den Grund nennt' (2:621), the perspicacity to recognize the hidden, uncomplimentary motivations of humanity. 'Sie [jene traurige Klarheit] zeigt mir alles, was mich umgibt, und mich selbst, in seiner ganzen armseligen Blösse, und der farbige Nebel verschwindet, und alle die gefällig geworfnen Schleier sinken und dem Herzen ekelt zuletzt vor dieser Nacktheit' (2:621). This 'traurige Klarheit,' a literal negation of *Aufklärung,* would result in the creation of 'ein dunkles Licht,' the Machiavellian protagonist, a denial of the basic optimism characteristic of Kleist's age as exemplified in Goethe's *Faust*:

DER HERR Wenn er [Faust] mir jetzt nur verworren dient,
　So werd' ich ihn bald in die Klarheit führen.
　. . .
　Ein guter Mensch, in seinem dunklen Drange,
　Ist sich des rechten Weges wohl bewusst.[75]

Whereas Licht may indeed bring light into chaos in *Der zerbrochene Krug,* it is at best a 'sad' and ironically illuminating commentary on the human condition that the bearer of enlightenment stands more closely allied to the prince of darkness than to the 'God [who] is light.'[76]

Notes

CHAPTER ONE

1 *Heinrich von Kleist. Sämtliche Werke und Briefe*, ed. Helmut Sembdner (Munich: Carl Hanser 1961), 1:95–6. All subsequent references to Kleist's works will be drawn from the two volumes of this edition and parenthetical citations in the text include volume and page numbers. Italics for emphasis are mine in all quotations except where otherwise noted. Italics are also used for stage directions in Kleist's plays in conformity with the edition cited. In addition, foreign words are italicized as usual, e.g., *drame à clef*.

2 Niccolò Machiavelli, *The Ruler*, trans. Peter Rodd (London: The Bodley Head 1954), 83. I have chosen to quote from this translation because of its admirable readability. All subsequent references to *Il Principe* will be drawn from this translation and parenthetical page references, preceded by M, are to this edition.

3 Robert E. Helbling, *The Major Works of Heinrich von Kleist* (New York: New Directions 1975), 187

4 Georg Büchner, *Sämtliche Werke*, ed. Hans Jürgen Meinerts (Gütersloh: Siegbert Mohn 1965), 391

5 Machiavelli's family belonged to the landed gentry or lesser nobility, which, having fallen upon harsh economic times, had allied itself with the city authorities of Florence.

6 In this respect, Machiavelli's dedication of *Il Principe* to 'His Magnificence Lorenzo de Medici' (M 120) bears comparison with Kleist's dedication of *Prinz Friedrich von Homburg* to 'Ihrer Königlichen Hoheit / der Prinzessin / Amalie Marie Anne / Gemahlin des Prinzen Wilhelm vom Preussen / Bruders Sr. Majestät des Königs / geborne Prinzessin von Hessen-Homburg' (1:629). Ironically, the results were similar: *Il Principe* did not help Machia-

velli regain favour with the Medici family and the historical Homburg's descendant was instrumental in preventing Kleist's final drama from being performed.

7 Walter Elliot, 'Introduction' to Machiavelli's *The Ruler* (London: The Bodley Head 1954), 7

8 This anticipates Hermann's argument in I/3, although ironically the Germanic leader ascribes to his own people 'ein[e] grösser[e] Anlage,' while 'der Italier doch hat seine mindre / In diesem Augenblick mehr entwickelt' (1:544).

9 Peter Rodd, from the 'Translator's Note' to *The Ruler*, 15. Kleist's Hermann, of course, possesses all of these characteristics.

10 Kurt May, *Form und Bedeutung* (Stuttgart: Ernst Klett Verlag 1957), 254. May even goes as far as to designate 'dieses Drama als Vorbild eines aktivistischen Dramas, [das] bis heute nicht übertroffen ist' (255). In the same vein, Beda Allemann sees in *Die Hermannsschlacht* 'ein geradezu minutiös realistisches Bild der Situation des Jahres 1808': 'Der Nationalismus Heinrich von Kleists,' in *Nationalismus in Germanistik und Dichtung*, ed. Benno von Wiese and Rudolf Heuss (Berlin: E. Schmidt 1967), 310.

11 Hermann August Korff, *Geist der Goethezeit*, Part IV (Leipzig: Koehler & Amelang 1953), 278. Ernst Stahl even claims that Kleist is 'the first important political dramatist in modern German literature': *Heinrich von Kleist's Dramas* (Oxford: Blackwell 1948), 100.

12 Sigurd Burckhardt, *The Drama of Language. Essays on Goethe and Kleist* (Baltimore/London: The Johns Hopkins Press 1970), 160

13 *Goethes Werke*, ed. Erich Trunz (Hamburg: Chr. Wegener 1957), 3:17

CHAPTER TWO

1 The text of this chapter first appeared under the same title as an article in *The Germanic Review*, 58 (1983): 58–65.

2 Manfred Schunicht, '*Der zerbrochene Krug.*' *Zeitschrift für deutsche Philologie*, 84 (1965): 550–62

3 Ilse A. Graham, 'The Broken Pitcher: Hero of Kleist's Comedy,' *Modern Language Quarterly*, 16 (1955): 99–113

4 Oskar Seidlin, 'What the Bell Tolls in Kleist's *Der zerbrochene Krug*,' *Deutsche Vierteljahrsschrift*, 51 (1977): 78–97

5 'His [Licht's] function in the play is to justify his name, to bring light into a hopelessly confused situation': Introduction to *Der zerbrochene Krug*, ed. R.H. Samuel (London, Melbourne, Toronto: Macmillan 1968), xxviii.

6 'The exposure of Adam's guilt is brought about by the testimony of Brigitte, Walter's watchfulness and Licht's interventions': E.L. Stahl, *Heinrich von Kleist's Dramas* (Oxford: Blackwell 1948), 70

7 Samuel, xxxvii–xxxviii

8 Hans Joachim Schrimpf, '*Der zerbrochene Krug*,' in *Das deutsche Drama*, ed. Benno von Wiese (Düsseldorf: Bagel 1958), 1:350. Writing in a similar vein, Schunicht maintains: 'Licht versucht aus krassem Egoismus, die Wahrheit so lange aufzusparen, bis ihre Enthüllung dem Dorfrichter tödlich sein muss, gedenkt er ihn doch in seinem Amte zu beerben' (557).

9 Cf. 'In komischem Kontrast assistiert dem hektisch aufgestörten Adam ein bedrohlich gesammelter, überlegener Schreiber Licht, dessen böses Doppelspiel hinter aller scheinbaren Hilfe und hinterhältigen Freundlichkeit leicht zu durchschauen ist.': Schunicht, 552.

10 For example, Stahl comments, 'If this is the story which the picture [Le Veau's engraving] tells, Kleist has completely altered it both in his description and in his play' (70).

11 Schrimpf, 342. This critic feels that Kleist's description is based on Salomon Gessner's idyl *Der zerbrochene Krug*.

12 John Milfull makes this point in his article 'Oedipus and Adam. Greek Tragedy and Christian Comedy in Kleist's *Der zerbrochene Krug*,' *German Life and Letters*, 27 (1973–4): 7.

13 Schunicht assumes that Licht has no possible knowledge of Adam's nocturnal escapade and explains these striking coincidences in terms of the autonomous existence and power of language; 'die Sprache selbst enthüllt noch von allem Wissen des Sprechenden, noch gegen seinen Willen die Wahrheit über Vergangenheit und Zukunft' (560).

14 Sheep are traditionally associated with innocence and hence the comparison is doubly ironic if one considers its object and its creator. However, since sheep are easily manipulated and the image originates with Licht, the metaphor does possess a certain validity in hindsight.

15 Samuel, I feel, misses the point of this exchange. 'Adam insinuates that Licht wants to unseat him and succeed him ... and that he was an accomplice in the former's dubious practices ..., but whether the latter is true is not revealed' (xxxviii), while Schrimpf recognizes the secretary's complicity: 'Er [Licht] ist unredlich genug, um seinen Vorteil zu erlangen ("Es liesse von Depositionen sich und Zinsen ..."), aber zu kraftlos, um zu sündigen' (350). The latter part of Schrimpf's assessment fails to take into consideration Licht's complex motivation.

16 The full significance of this scene has either been ignored or largely misrepresented by the secondary literature. Samuel, for instance, writes: 'The

audience as well as Licht receive a glimpse of the truth through the innocently made statement of one of the maids [actually, the collaborating statements of two maids] that he had returned home late the night before,
injured and bald ..., although his cocksureness is able to gloss this over'
(xxxi). Schunicht also does not see how Licht has backed Adam into a
corner: 'Mit derbem Behagen, das durch Lichts hintergründige Unter-
brechungen kaum zu stören ist, berichtet Adam genüsslich ausmalend zahl-
reiche Details' (555).

17 In reality, 'der Bediente' announced: 'Der Gerichtsrat Walter / Lässt seinen
Gruss vermelden, gleich wird er hier sein' and to this Adam exclaimed: 'Ei,
du gerechter Himmel! Ist er mit Holla / Schon fertig?' (1:182). In other words,
Adam, not the servant, was the only one to mention Holla.

18 Schunicht, 559

19 Schrimpf detects a 'dunkle Ahnung des Schreibers' which becomes 'zu
immer stärkerem Verdacht' in the exposition, but which 'sich spätestens mit
Beginn der eigentlichen Verhandlung zur Gewissheit verdichtet hat ("Das ist
ja seltsam"),' 352. The Licht quotation (1:204) is still ambiguous, for it could
indicate honest puzzlement; it could, however, be merely intended for public
consumption.

20 No one seems to have recognized what motivates Licht's devious tactics
during the trial. Samuel states: 'He [Licht] realises the link between Adam's
injuries and the happenings of the previous night, but keeps his gradual
recognition of these interconnections to himself' (xxxviii).

21 Schrimpf, 352

22 Hence I am in partial agreement with Günther Blöcker's conclusion: 'Der
Dorfrichter Adam wird nicht durch Worte überführt, sondern dadurch, dass
ihm die strittige Perücke über den Kopf gestülpt wird': *Heinrich von Kleist oder
das absolute Ich* (Berlin: Argon 1960), 231. Schunicht disagrees with Blöcker
and feels that Eve's declaration, 'Der Richter Adam hat den Krug zerbrochen!' (1:241) is the real key (557–8). However, it is clear that Frau Marthe:
'Ei, solch ein blitz-verfluchter Richter, das!' (1:240) and Ruprecht: 'Ei, du Blitz-
Pferdefuss!' (1:240) are convinced of Adam's guilt by the wig test.

23 When Adam is supposed to show his club-foot to Walter to demonstrate its
normalcy, he does in fact, according to the text, exhibit the disfigured left
foot and not the healthy right. The district judge then proceeds to act as if
the incriminating limb were indeed whole. Most directors and critics have
assumed that either Walter was inattentive in this instance or that Kleist
simply made a mistake. However, Franz Peter Wirth in a 1974 production for
German television (Zweites Deutsches Fernsehen) opted to take Kleist at his
word and thus suggested a degree of complicity between Adam and Walter

and the attempt at a cover-up by the latter. Cf. *Mannheimer Morgen*, 28/29 June, 1975. At the other extreme, Schrimpf maintains, 'Gerichtsrat Walter ... vertritt die weise Vernunft. Er steht jenseits der Ereignisse und auch der Komik als der leidenschaftslose Anwalt der Gerechtigkeit' (351), a point of view which the text does not fully substantiate.

24 Wolfgang Schadewaldt's appraisal may be quoted as being typical: 'Mit dieser Vitalität hat Richter Adam in all seiner Verschmitztheit einen Grundzug des Naiven und ist und bleibt so etwas wie ein Kerl, der uns trotz allem nicht widerwärtig wird, sondern mit seinen unerschöpflichen Einfällen und zu seinem Teil sogar unsere Sympathie hat': '*Der zerbrochene Krug* und *König Ödipus*,' in *Heinrich von Kleist*, ed. Walter Müller-Seidel (Darmstadt: Wissenschaftliche Buchgesellschaft 1967), 321.

25 Schrimpf in part misses the point when he asks, in reference to Licht's statement, 'Und schliesslich, ist das noch Mensch, noch Tier?, was im Munde des Schreibers so geschildert wird' (362). Licht's observation is more a reflection on its originator than on its object.

26 Cf. Samuel: 'On the other hand it should be observed that he [Licht] does not get it all his own way: he will only be acting judge ..., pending further investigation' (xxxviii), or Schrimpf: 'Wer wünscht ihn [Licht] auf dem Richterstuhl zu sehen? Ausdrücklich betont Walter am Schluss, dass er das Amt nur vorläufig verwalten soll' (361).

27 Even structurally their roles are similar. They both have the first lines and tend to dominate intellectually the opening and closing episodes, whereas their control throughout the rest of the play is more indirect and subtle. Of course, significant differences do exist, but they are determined by the disparity in social status and Licht's pedantry. Hohenzollern considers himself to be on an equal footing with the Elector and Homburg, while Licht, a subaltern, resorts to the language of the sycophant in Walter's presence: 'vergebt mir, gnädger Herr' (1:239), or 'verzeihn Euer Gnaden' (1:237). The behaviour of both Licht and Hohenzollern is, however, determined by a will to power which in the case of the Count is more artfully expressed.

28 Their absolute confidence is betrayed by the fact that both Hohenzollern and Licht tell their respective superiors (Elector and Walter) not to interrupt. Licht lets Frau Brigitte narrate her story and only intercedes to collaborate or to interpret her testimony, whereas Hohenzollern repeats the whole dream episode and aftermath, but from an extremely biased point of view, designed to incriminate or embarrass the Elector, while concealing his own involvement.

29 Marjorie Gelus, 'Laughter and Joking in the Works of Heinrich von Kleist,' *The German Quarterly*, 50 (1977): 452–73

30 Ibid, 453

CHAPTER THREE

1 H.A. Korff, *Geist der Goethezeit*, Part IV (Leipzig: Koehler & Amelang 1953), 276. Korff sees this new trend in the fact that *Die Hermannsschlacht* and *Prinz Friedrich von Homburg* '[dringen] mit gleichem leidenschaftlichen Willen in die Welt, wie [Kleists Dichtertum] bis dahin immer tiefer eingedrungen war in sich selbst' (277). In a similar vein, Hans Joachim Kreutzer has commented: '[*Die Hermannsschlacht*] eröffnet die letzte Phase in [Kleists] Entwicklung als Dramatiker, die Hinwendung zum vaterländischen Drama. Wenn man gemeint hat, dass in ihr Kleists zentrale Thematik in den Hintergrund gedrängt werde, so wäre das eher ein Hinweis, dass wir unsere Kleistauffassung erweitern müssen': *Die dichterische Entwicklung Heinrich von Kleists* (Berlin: Erich Schmidt 1968), 233. Such an assessment fails to take into consideration Kleist's continual preoccupation with what I have called the Machiavellian protagonist. In *Die Hermannsschlacht* a secondary interest becomes the prime interest carrying the complete dramatic action from beginning to end.

2 In a recent reappraisal with which I mostly concur, Jeffrey L. Sammons has noted: 'Hermann not only thinks out his rebellion, he *stages* [Sammon's emphasis] it ... He oversees the action and directs it to its climactic conclusion': 'Rethinking Kleist's *Hermannsschlacht*,' in *Heinrich von Kleist-Studien*, ed. Alexej Ugrinsky (Berlin: Erich Schmidt 1981), 35.

3 Ernst Stahl, *Heinrich von Kleist's Dramas* (Oxford: Blackwell 1948), 99

4 In referring to the princes as 'German,' I am simply following Kleist's practice which consistently makes use of the adjective 'deutsch' but designates the nation indiscriminately as both 'Deutschland' (1:537) and 'Germanien' (1:537).

5 Karl Federn, for example, notes that, with the exception of Hermann, the drama contains few well-rounded characters. *Das Leben Heinrich von Kleists* (Berlin: Brückenverlag 1909), 242

6 Of the several productions of the period, by far the most enthusiastically received was that offered to Berlin (10 March 1875) by the Meininger troupe, a triumph which enjoyed eighty-three performances and thereby ensured the inclusion of *Die Hermannsschlacht* in the German theatrical repertoire. Cf. W. Kühn, *Kleist und das Deutsche Theater* (Munich: Hans Sachs 1912), 103–4.

7 Rolf Busch has fully documented this development in *Imperialistische und faschistische Kleist-Rezeption 1890–1945* (Frankfurt a.M.: Akademische Verlagsgesellschaft 1974).

8 Robert E. Helbling, *The Major Works of Heinrich von Kleist* (New York: New Directions 1975), 186

9 Kurt May, *Form und Bedeutung* (Stuttgart: Ernst Klett 1957), 261

10 Helmut Sembdner, 'Anmerkungen' to Hanser edition. *Heinrich von Kleist. Sämtliche Werke und Briefe* (1:942).

11 Sigurd Burckhardt, 'Kleist's *Hermannsschlacht*: The Lock and the Key,' in *The Drama of Language. Essays on Goethe and Kleist* (Baltimore and London: The Johns Hopkins Press 1970)

12 'Die Hermannsschlacht was written in 1808, the year after Kleist's imprisonment at Fort de Joux, at the time when he was at the height of his literary ability. That fact alone should give us pause before we discuss the work as inferior and an aberration': R.K. Angress, 'Kleist's Treatment of Imperialism: *Die Hermannsschlacht* and "Die Verlobung in St. Domingo,"' *Monatshefte* 69 (1977): 20.

13 '[On] its deeper levels it [*Die Hermannsschlacht*] is concerned with the inevitability of large abstractions degenerating into bestiality in the process of realization': Ilse Graham, *Heinrich von Kleist. Word into Flesh: A Poet's Quest for the Symbol* (Berlin, New York: de Gruyter 1977), 201.

14 Lawrence Ryan, 'Die "vaterländische Umkehr" in der *Hermannsschlacht*,' in *Kleists Dramen. Neue Interpretationen*, ed. Walter Hinderer (Stuttgart: Reclam 1981). Ryan notes, for example: 'Zumindest seit dem Zweiten Weltkrieg hat die Kleist-Forschung Die Hermannsschlacht fast einhellig an die Peripherie des Kleistschen Werks gedrängt' (188) but concludes: 'Im Kontext des Gesamtwerkes hat dieses Stück vielmehr seine Bedeutung als Fortsetzung wie als Abwandlung einer sich bei Kleist durchgehend ausprägenden Thematik. Einerseits ist Die Hermannsschlacht auf das übrige Werk hin zu relativieren, insofern die früheren Motive nun im politisch bestimmten Kontext wiederkehren: die Auflehnung des Herzens gegen die Vernunft, der Spontaneität gegen das sie beherrschende Gesetz' (209)

15 Hans-Dieter Loose, *Kleists 'Hermannsschlacht'* (Karlsruhe: von Loeper 1984). Loose makes an extensive, fully documented historical argument to justify seeing the drama as, to quote a sub-title notation, 'Ein paradoxer Feldzug aus dem Geist der Utopie gegen den Geist besitzbürgerlicher und feudaler Herrschaft.' His model does cast light upon many problems critics have had with this puzzling work, but largely ignores the scheming of the Machiavellian protagonist. Unfortunately, certain lessons which may be drawn from *Die Hermannsschlacht* were valid in the Florentine's sixteenth-century Italy and have not lost their relevance for our present century.

16 Walter Müller-Seidel, *Versehen und Erkennen. Eine Studie über Heinrich von Kleist* (Cologne: Böhlau 1961), 53. More recently, Gabriele M. Wickert has remarked:

'*Die Hermannsschlacht* gilt nicht als eines der dichterisch oder gedanklich bedeutsamsten Dramen Kleists, obwohl man im Gegensatz zur unmittelbaren Nachkriegszeit wieder bereit ist, darüber zu sprechen': *Das verlorene heroische Zeitalter* (Bern/Frankfurt a.M./New York: Lang 1983), 79.

17 Ernst von Reusner, *Satz. Gestalt. Schicksal. Untersuchungen über die Struktur in der Dichtung Kleists* (Berlin: Walter de Gruyter 1961), 108.

18 Helbling, 189

19 Ibid, 183

20 Friedrich Gundolf, *Heinrich von Kleist* (Berlin: Bondi 1932), 126–7

21 Korff, 286

22 Rolf L. Linn, 'Comical and Humorous Elements in Kleist's *Die Hermannsschlacht*,' *Germanic Review* 47 (1972): 165

23 Burckhardt, 116

24 Joachim von Kürenberg, *Heinrich von Kleist* (Hamburg: Robert Mölich Verlag 1948), 189

25 Helbling, 188

26 Kürenberg, 190

27 Helbling, 186

28 Sammons, 35

29 To quote a few examples of the danger of taking Hermann at his word: '[Hermann] ist schaffend ohne jede Hoffnung auf positive Erfolge, der Hinterhalt, den er vorbereitet, ist ein Fanal der Verneinung': Walter Muschg, *Kleist* (Zurich: Seldwyla 1923), 281; 'Denn Hermann will ja nicht das Vaterland. Er will überhaupt nichts auf Erden erringen, sondern im Gegenteil alles aufgeben, um in einem freien Tod über seine Feinde zu triumphieren': Günter Blöcker, *Heinrich von Kleist oder Das absolute Ich* (Berlin: Aragon 1960), 33; 'So kann man auch Hermanns Bereitschaft zum "schönen Tod der Helden", seine "einzige Sorge, wie er geschlagen werde", sein Ziel, "alles zu verlieren", als Leiden, als Willen zum Leiden verstehen': Reusner, 108. Loose sees in Hermann's desire to die an heroic death 'im Schatten einer Wodanseiche,' 'Hermanns (Kleists) Topos seiner erhofften noch utopischen Menschheitsgemeinschaft' (84), and not the performance of a skilled actor. One critic, however, has recognized the importance of language as a means to conceal one's true intent: '"La parole est [*sic*] été donné [*sic*] à l'homme pour déguiser ses pensées." Dieses Wort Talleyrands könnte man als Motto über die *Hermannsschlacht* schreiben, als Leitmotiv für das Verhalten in einer Umwelt, in der der Schwache nur durch Trug stark ist, weil es in der Politik kein Recht, sondern nur ein gegenseitiges Übervorteilen gibt': Hans Heinz Holz, *Macht und Ohnmacht der Sprache* (Frankfurt a.M./Bonn: Athenäum 1962), 79.

30 Cf. 'Hermann durchschaut vielmehr die warnend gemeinten Einwände Thuiskomars – repräsentativ für alle Fürsten – als Argumente, welche im Grunde nur dem eigenen Sicherheitsinteresse und dem Erhalt ihrer Eigenmacht gelten, obwohl sie sich formal wie Anzeichen der freundschaftlichen Besorgtheit über das Schicksal der potentiell Verbündeten hören lassen': Loose, 79. This is a fair assessment except that Loose goes too far when he sees in Thuiskomar a representative for all the princes. Wolf is clearly an exception. Also Linn argues that 'No one suffers defeat unless he fights first, and in the fight resides fame rather than in the victory; not to accept the yoke is greatness, whether it is shaken off or not. From this thought Hermann derives the self-assurance and lightheartedness which accompany him on his perilous path' (165). However, the real joke played on the princes is the fact that Hermann has no intention whatsoever of suffering defeat. He wants to win!

31 Burckhardt, 147

32 When interpreting Hermann's claim that he intends to be defeated by the Romans, Angress argues: 'This turns out to mean that he is ready to die fighting them' (20).

33 Cf. 'Katechismus der Deutschen': 'FRAGE. Wer sind deine Feinde, mein Sohn? / ANTWORT. Napoleon, und solange er ihr Kaiser ist, die Franzosen' (2:352).

34 Ernst Fischer, 'Heinrich von Kleist,' in *Heinrich von Kleist*, ed. Walter Müller-Seidel (Darmstadt: Wissenschaftliche Buchgesellschaft 1967), 524

35 Helbling, 188

36 Siegfried Streller, *Das dramatische Werk Heinrich von Kleists* (Berlin: Rütten & Loening 1966), 190. I am indebted to Streller for drawing my attention to the conditional nature of Hermann's hatred.

37 Kleist utilizes the same image of the sea to describe the 'Volk' in *Robert Guiskard*. Interestingly enough, the unifying force that would enable the masses to realize a political goal is in both cases the leadership of a great aristocratic ruler.

38 Hence I cannot fully endorse Graham's interpretation of this scene: 'All along, Hermann has been in earnest. He is resolved to forfeit everything, every material possession and every emotional bond to gain – freedom' (204). In my view, she underestimates the important function of *Ruhm*.

39 Sammons, 35. Cf. also: 'Er kann seine Aufgabe als Einzelgänger nur lösen, indem er alle anderen durch List über seine wahre Absicht täuscht': Streller, 179.

40 '[Thusnelda] is realistic enough to accept intrigue and war as facts of life, but she believes that there is a personal sphere transcending the sordid arena of politics – a republic of the human spirit in which every gentle soul holds

immediate citizenship. And this sphere she wants to keep out of Hermann's schemes – "aus dem Spiel"': Burckhardt, 127. Burckhardt's formulation strikes me as a little too idealistic for the very vain, self-centred Thusnelda.

41 Burckhardt, 131. Loose has declared even more recently: 'Das von Hermann angeregte Verhältnis zwischen Ventidius und Thusnelda erweist sich nach dem Textverlauf nicht als notwendig für Hermanns politisches Konzept' (114).

42 Linn, 162

43 Burckhardt attaches particular importance to this song and proposes a possible final wording: 'Drecken is, I suggest, the only conclusion that would fit the stanza's sense, meter and rhyme scheme. It points to Ventidius' final reward for his theft (which he commits during the singing); but more threateningly it points to Thusnelda herself. The birth of a nation cannot be celebrated within the aesthetics of "schöner Schein"; a very different baptism is required – a total immersion into the unredeemed physicality of man's origins' (160). Although I agree that mud would indeed fit the poem's and the drama's context, I still harbour a few reservations: the word 'Drecken' does not really exist, except by poetic licence, and this interpretation runs counter to another motif found in 'Die Marquise von O,' where again a 'Knabe,' disturbing a beautiful, pure image, throws mud upon a female swan, 'worauf dieser [Schwan] still untergetaucht, und rein aus der Flut wieder emporgekommen sei' (2:116). Here, immersion leads to rebirth of purity in the tradition of baptism.

44 Helbling, 186

45 Burckhardt, 123

46 In reference to this conversation between husband and wife, Gabriele Wikkert has commented, 'Die sympathisierende Weichheit Thusneldas, die in diesem Gefühl beispielhaft für die milde Natur der Germanin ist, ist für die Manipulation durch die betrügerische Antinatur [i.e. Ventidius and Rome] besonders anfällig': Das verlorene heroische Zeitalter (Bern/Frankfurt a.M./New York: Lang 1983), 102. This statement discloses the vulnerable aspect of Wickert's thesis which she, in my view, imposes somewhat arbitrarily upon Die Hermannsschlacht. She does not recognize Thusnelda's exclusively self-centred motivation behind all her statements and actions, and if 'die milde Natur der Germanin' may be called into question in this instance, it certainly stands totally refuted by the 'Bärin' episode, the 'natural,' psychologically consistent follow-up to this exchange. I also find it ironic that Wickert speaks of Thusnelda's being a victim of 'Manipulation durch die betrügerische Antinatur,' by which she means Roman civilization, at a point in the drama where it becomes especially evident that she is being obviously manipulated

by her husband who, in Wickert's interpretation, represents a 'Beispiel zur Besserung' (110).

47 The stage directions at this point in the conversation: 'Hermann sieht sie an' (1:556) parallel a similar notation made in connection with another of Kleist's Machiavellian protagonists, Hohenzollern: 'Er sieht ihn [Homburg] an' (1:651). In both instances, the stare implies an awareness that the individual being observed is out of touch with reality and essentially deluding him- or herself.

48 Angress is only one of many critics who tend to take Thusnelda at her word while ignoring the underlying implications. In connection with these lines, she contends, in my view, incorrectly, 'Thusnelda, who is not the little goose [a quote attributed to Kleist] she is sometimes presented as but rather the spokeswoman for humanitarianism (of course only until she herself is caught up in her revenge), asks him to see the Romans as human beings and not in the mass' (26). Although Angress quite perceptively notes in reference to 'Die Verlobung in St. Domingo,' 'Erotic love is the antithesis of political engagement' (27), she fails to see the full applicability of this observation to the Thusnelda-Ventidius relationship: 'When she is betrayed as a woman, Thusnelda turns rabidly anti-Roman' (29), whereas in actual fact she merely turns rabidly anti-Ventidius. Throughout the play she is too caught up in her narrow world defined primarily by her vanity to show any sincere concern for the national crisis.

49 Richard Samuel also emphasizes Hermann's sense of religious mission but does so in the general Kleistian context of total surrender to an idea: 'Kleist ist hier, wie immer, von dem Glauben der rückhaltlosen Hingabe an eine grosse Idee besessen; wenn sie einmal erfasst ist, dürfen persönliche und materielle Bedenken keine Rolle spielen' (414).

50 I take issue with an interpretation made by Rolf Linn of a line from the first scene of the third act: 'Hermann issues orders to the effect that the foreign guest be given whatever law and gratitude demand. The first elder assures him that he will be obeyed, to which the second elder comments, "Warum soll er warten, bis mans nimmt?" ... Here speaks the wit of an uncomplicated realist who knows that things are bad, but who is neither pained nor subdued. The present evil, so he seems to understand, is but a brief moment of darkness before the dawn' (164). As far as the people are concerned, Hermann, their only hope, has capitulated completely, and there remains no hope whatsoever for the future, only Roman domination. Hence the humour in this instance is a defence mechanism to conceal a widely prevalent sense of despair.

51 Streller, 183

52 Although the National Socialist regime misrepresented or chose to ignore those features of Kleist's opus which did not conform to the party line, one must none the less acknowledge, however reluctantly, that *Die Hermanns-schlacht's* position as the most performed play of the Nazi era was to a large extent warranted. The incident involving the Roman who used a woman's own child to club her to death, enlarged upon by Hermann's addition of the gratuitous cruelty of the father's living interment smacks of concentration-camp mentality, while Eginhardt's eagerness to serve ('Du [Hermann] sollst die Leute haben. Lass mich machen' [1:566]) and his blind dedication to the cause (after each of the three reports, it is Eginhardt who takes the messenger aside and convinces him to give credence to Hermann's fabrications) anticipate the absolute obedience expected and received by the *Führer* even if his commands entailed obviously immoral acts. One should not close one's eyes to a clearly discernible sadistic bent in Kleist's psychological makeup that also comes to light in the narratives, as, for example, in his propensity for smashed brain matter.

53 Fischer also acknowledges Hermann's use of psychology on his wife and hence his indirect complicity in Ventidius' violent end. However, Fischer does tend to state his case a little too categorically: 'aber vor allem war es doch die von Hermann heraufbeschworene Vorstellung, sie werde aussehen wie ein Totenkopf, die sie zur "Bärin von Cheruska" machte' (524). Her vanity is her main motivating force, as here suggested by Fischer, but the reference to the 'Totenkopf' appears in act two, scene three. Only when she learns that it is her alleged admirer Ventidius who intends to reduce her to such a state does she assume responsibility for his death in act four, scene ten.

54 Burckhardt, 120

55 Korff, 282

56 A passage from *Prinz Friedrich von Homburg* reveals Kleist's obvious disdain for rumourmongers as the Elector puts one in his place:

> DER KURFÜRST *finster*. Wer hat dir das gesagt?
> FELDMARSCHALL   Wer mir das sagte?
>   Die Dame Retzow, der du trauen kannst,
>   Die Base meiner Frau! Sie war heut abend
>   In ihres Ohms, des Drost von Retzow, Haus,
>   Wo Offiziere, die vom Lager kamen,
>   Laut diesen dreisten Anschlag äusserten.
> DER KURFÜRST Das muss ein Mann mir sagen, eh ichs glaube!   (1:693)

57 Blöcker, 34

58 In her interpretation of *Die Hermannsschlacht*, Wickert examines in greater detail what she considers to be the essential conflict between the decadence of civilization and the heroic ideal of nature: 'Während die germanischen Stämme als organisch gewachsene Völker geschildert sind, wird die Ordnung der Römer als künstlich gezeigt: Sie stellen wohl eine höhere Stufe der Entwicklung dar im Sinne von Wissenschaft und Kultur, doch fehlt ihnen die innere Verankerung in der Natur, auf der die Einheit der Germanen fusst' (81). Although her analysis does contribue to a greater appreciation of the drama, her thesis has a tendency to indulge in questionable speculation beyond the text, as for example: 'Hermann selbst lehrt seinem Volk die betrugsbereite Schläue und Härte, die ihrem von Natur aus sanften und offenen Wesen sonst fremd seien.' [Hermann in fact conceals from his people his deceptive ways; after all they are on the receiving end.] Sobald ihnen der Sieg gewiss ist, wollen sie diese fremden Attribute wieder ablegen, um wieder ganz zu sich selbst zu kommen. Es sei nur eine vorübergehende Tarnung' (87). The scene describing the slaughter of Varus *after* the victory has been decisively won does not presage well for a return to Teutonic 'gentle' being.

59 Judges, 19: 16–30. Helmut Sembdner indicated this source in the notes to his 1961 edition *Sämtliche Werke und Briefe* (1:945). In fact, the Hally episode replicates the biblical prototype quite consistently in terms of the grotesque details. A concubine is cut up into twelve pieces, one of which is sent to each of the twelve tribes of Israel, while in Kleist's adaptation the violated daughter's remains are to be divided among the fifteen German tribes. One should bear in mind this derivation in any evaluation of the incident. Kleist may be held accountable for the inclusion of this morbid tale, but not for what Helbling calls its 'pathological elements' (190) since Kleist merely borrowed them. It is also of some interest to note that this passage, although universally deplored by the critics, does have its apologist: 'Die Szene der entehrten Hally ... könnte von dem grossen Engländer sein': Joachim von Kürenberg, 192.

60 'Es ist in der *Hermannsschlacht* auffällig, dass der Befreiungsimpuls nicht von einer breiten Basis im Volk oder im Fürstenadel mithin nicht von der "Nation" getragen wird. Von der "Horde" – wie das germanische Volk mehrmals genannt wird – sehen wir überhaupt sehr wenig: sie scheint in dumpfer Ohnmacht zu verharren, bis Hermann sie aufrüttelt. Für ihn ist das Volk nur manipulierbare Masse, die er der eigenen Zielsetzung zu unterwerfen weiss': Ryan, 195. In dealing with Hermann's attitude to his people, Angress tends to contradict herself partly out of her failure to see *Die Hermannsschlacht* as an apology for despotic absolutism. Whereas she recognizes

that Hermann '[wishes] for harm to come to his people from the Romans so that they will rise against them' (25), she also argues, 'Like Hermann, Hoango ['Die Verlobung in St. Domingo'] is shown as fair-minded towards his own people' (24). In a sense, Kleist depicts Hermann as an even more committed fanatic in that he is prepared to risk the lives of his two sons proffered as hostages, while Hoango places his children held as hostages before the demands of his people's rebellion.

61 Shakespeare, *Julius Caesar*, act III, scene ii, line 213

62 Although the sixth scene, act four, of *Die Hermannsschlacht* lacks the full rhetorical impact or response of the equivalent scene from *Julius Caesar*, one none the less hears echoes of Shakespeare's tragedy, albeit somewhat distorted given the different context. (In an unrelated situation, Katharina Mommsen has observed appropriately, 'Überhaupt ist zu berücksichtigen, dass sich Shakespeare-Anspielungen in Kleists Dramen in Fülle finden': *Kleists Kampf mit Goethe* [Heidelberg: Stiehm 1974], 188–9.) The lines: 'DAS VOLK. Empörung! Rache! Freiheit! / TEUTHOLD. Auf! Greift an!' (1:591) recalls the verse 'ALL. Revenge! About! Seek! Burn! Fire! Kill! Slay!' (line 208), while Hermann's final 'Komm, Eginhardt! Jetzt hab ich nichts mehr / An diesem Ort zu tun! Germanien lodert' (1:591) approximates Mark Antony's self-congratulatory concluding comment: 'Now let it work. Mischief, thou art afoot, / Take thou what course thou wilt' (lines 205–6). The near ritualistic use to which the respective cadavers are put is quite analogous: 'FIRST CITIZEN. ... Come away, away! We'll burn his body in the holy place, / And with the brands fire the traitors' houses / Take up the body' (lines 258–9). And last, in terms of the general situation, other parallels come to mind: in both dramas, the orator profits from the good will and gullibility of alleged friends (the conspirators: Varus and the Romans) whom he is secretly determined to eliminate and whose generosity and trust place him in the position of being able to deliver a call for bloody revenge in the guise of a funeral oration.

63 In his analysis of this monologue, Ryan expresses a view typical of that held by most commentators: 'In diesem Augenblick wird spürbar, dass Hermann in seiner Skrupellosigkeit nicht etwa einer hemmungslosen Mordlust frönt, sich einem Zwang unterwirft, den ihm die "grosse Sache" auferlegt' (198). the subjective element, the attitude of the despotic 'L'état, c'est moi' is ignored.

64 Nietzsche, *Also sprach Zarathustra*, in *Nietzsches Werke*, kritische Gesamtausgabe, ed. G. Colli and M. Montinari, Part 6, vol. 1 (Berlin: de Gruyter 1968), 81

65 Burckhardt, 128

66 Ibid, 148

67 May, 257

68 In a parenthetical comment, Holz questions the authenticity of the letter '(von dem man nie wissen wird, ob er nicht eine Zweckfälschung ist, wie die zur Steigerung des Grässlichen ausgestreuten Gerüchte)' (83). Although I concede Hermann's ability to stoop to such a measure, the evidence of the lock would seem to support the genuineness of the letter. A vain woman such as Thusnelda would be expected to recognize a lock of her own hair of which she is especially proud. Just before his departure with his purloined token, Ventidius declared to her, 'Doch selbst der Tod nicht trennt mich mehr von [dieser Locke]' (1:555). Hence, to find that very lock together with the letter is a very convincing and damning piece of evidence. The drama also demonstrates that Ventidius is quite prepared to exploit people.

69 For example, May's comment: 'Denn Thusneldas befreiendes Rachewerk geht schliesslich mit dem Hermanns auf das gleiche Ziel hin zusammen' (258), although partially true, fails to take into account that Thusnelda is a mere puppet in the hands of the skilled manipulator, Hermann, who sets the whole revenge sequence in motion. Also her ultimate goal, as I shall establish, remains a purely personal one and thus only indirectly may be said to serve the common purpose.

70 Holz also recognizes Thusnelda's strong emotional commitment to Ventidius. '"O Hertha! Nun mag ich diese Sonne nicht mehr sehn." – Das ist ein Ausruf echter Verzweiflung, und wenn darauf Thusnelda sich *auch* [Holz's emphasis] von Hermann abwendet, ihn auffordert: "Geh, lass mich sein" und gleich darauf nochmals: "Geh, geh, ich bitte dich! Verhasst ist alles, Die Welt mir, du mir, ich: lass mich allein" – so zeigt sich darin echte, unaussprechliche Erschütterung des Gefühls an, mit dem Hermann leichtfertig gespielt hatte' (83).

71 Cf. '[Ventidius] degradiert den "geretteten Menschen" in Thusnelda zum materialen Tausch-Objekt, das seinen eigenen Aufstieg in der Hierarchie der Günstlinge in Rom "finanzieren" soll': Loose, 115.

72 Bertolt Brecht ('Die Ballade von der Sexuellen Hörigkeit'), *Die Dreigroschenoper, Stücke für das Theater am Schiffbauerdamm* (Berlin: Suhrkamp 1955), 73–4

73 This interpretation contradicts Loose's evaluation: 'Hermanns notwendiger Erziehungsprozess seiner Gattin angesichts des römischen Weltprinzips' (116), which fails to take into account Hermann's premeditated sexual exploitation of his wife for political gain and Thusnelda's almost total preoccupation with herself from beginning to end.

74 Stahl has also noted that Hermann intentionally keeps his master plan a secret, except in the case of Marbod, until its disclosure furthers the accomplishment of its ultimate purpose (99).

75 This interpretation disputes that offered by Gabriele Wickert in her thesis
Das verlorene heroische Zeitalter, which does not take sufficient cognizance of
the autocratic attitudes expressed in *Die Hermannsschlacht*: 'Wenn sich Hermann auf die Freiheit beruft, so meint er damit auch das Prinzip der inneren
Gleichheit, dessen sich Germanien im Gegensatz zur römischen Autokratie
rühmen kann. Es ist eine Gleichheit der Blutverwandtschaft, die nur eine
einzige Aristokratie, die des Mutes, d.h. der persönlichen Eigenschaften,
kennt. Sie nährt sich nicht von dem demütigen Verhältnis eines Herrschers
zu seinen Untertanen. Frei, stolz und selbstbewusst wünscht sich Hermann
seine Stammesgenossen' (89). As an example of Hermann's egalitarian attitude towards his subjects, Wickert cites the incident where Egbert, on behalf
of the army, refuses to obey Hermann in his alleged campaign against Marbod: 'Hermann spielt nur mit ihnen, um ihre Gesinnung auf die Probe zu
stellen. Nichts ist ihm natürlich lieber als diese mutig stolze und selbstbe-
wusste Haltung seiner Leute' (90). Hermann is indeed 'playing' with his
people, but on a grander scale than Wickert realizes. Because he has successfully engineered this confrontation by the cunning deception of his tribe, the
incident confirms more than anything else his expertise in programming a
desired response at precisely the desired moment. As an aristocrat, he never
articulates the desire to have 'free, proud and self-assured' subjects and he
even disparages his people privately as '[die] deutschen Uren' (1:565) or as
sheep: 'Den Widder lass sich zeigen, mit der Glocke, / So folgen, glaub mir,
alle anderen' (1:585), two creatures known for a low level of intelligence and
the latter for an amenable disposition. Moreover, one would also have to
question the most recent claims made by Hans-Dieter Loose: 'Die Realutopie
einer menschheitsumfassenden Gemeinschaft hat Hermann im Blick, die frei
ist vom Geist der Gewalt [What about the emotional violence done to his
wife or the desire to set fire to his own encampment?], der Unterdrückung
von Einzelmenschen durch andere Menschen [Hermann's treatment of his
own people?], die frei ist von der Ausbeutung von Menschen durch andere,
die nach Besitz und Macht streben [Hermann's sadistic pleasure in exercising power over others and his drive for personal fame?]' (92). I remain
unconvinced that Hermann sincerely strives for a 'Realutopie' since the
drama cautions against taking him at his word and even if he does, would
not the means preclude the end?

76 Linn, 166

77 Burckhardt, 122

78 In view of this explicit command which signals the additional slaughter of
the three Roman cohorts left behind by Varus, I find the following statement
very puzzling indeed: 'Kleist zeigt seinen Hermann an keiner Stelle im

Drama in eine kriegerisch-aggressive Handlung gegen die Römer verwikkelt': Loose, 93. Perhaps Hermann is not directly involved, i.e., he does not wield the club himself, but the annihilation of the Romans occurs solely at his instigation, and only because Fust proves to be the better fighter does Hermann lose the coveted privilege of killing Varus.

79 Cf. 'Septimius is led away to be killed, but he also has the last word, lamenting that he is being [sic] torn to death by dogs, a Penthesilean image for a barbarous death': Angress, 28.

80 Koch, 188

81 Streller, 182

82 Stahl, 102

83 Burckhardt, 160. I cannot agree, however, with his attribution of 'moral superiority' to the Romans (148), but have already dealt with the issue.

84 Burckhardt, 146f

85 Quoted in Sembdner, 1:945

86 Korff, 286

87 Hence I disagree with Ryan's interpretation of this famous quotation: 'Das Wort "Gefühl" lässt hier aufhorchen. Es ist aber nicht so zu verstehen, dass der Hass eines Hermann eine unbeherrschte Aufwallung wäre, den schon ein "Moment des Besinnens" vergehen liesse. Er ist vielmehr eine konzentrierte Sammlung aller Kräfte auf ein bestimmtes Ziel hin, die aber – als "Gefühl" im Kleistschen Sinn – gerade wegen ihrer starken Zielgerichtetheit der Gefahr ausgesetzt ist, sich durch Unerwartetes und Ambivalentes beirren – "verwirren" – zu lassen' (198). Ryan does not distinguish between Hermann's hatred of the Romans based on 'eine konzentrierte Sammlung aller Kräfte' and the implied hatred of the German traitors to which the 'Verwirre das Gefühl mir nicht!' applies more directly.

88 Ibid, 286

89 Gundolf, 135. Cf. also: 'Sie will ihre ideale Moralordnung wieder herstellen': Loose, 131.

90 Fischer, 524. Cf. also: Streller's evaluation, 'abstossend, aber begründet motiviert' (190).

91 I should add to this list Burckhardt who writes, '[Thusnelda] lacerates her moral self – and ours – almost as much as she does Ventidius; it is not just the Roman whom she punishes for having betrayed what used to be Kleist's highest value [trust], but herself for having held it' (128). I would agree that her revenge is quite consistent with her vanity from the beginning of the relationship to its conclusion.

92 Federn, 243

93 Fischer, 523

94 Burckhardt, 129

95 Ryan's discussion of Thusnelda's 'Abstieg in die Bestialität' (205) contains many useful observations, but generally his analysis does not take into account her main motivation, her excessive female conceit. 'Auf die Klage über ihre tiefe persönliche Erniedrigung ("Er hat zur Bärin mich gemacht!") folgt sofort der Satz, in dem sie ihr neugewonnenes Bewusstsein der von ihm vertretenen Sache bekundet: "Arminius' will ich wieder würdig werden!"' (206). Nowhere in the drama does she show an interest in the fate of her country unless it relates directly and personally to herself. Even the reference to becoming worthy of her husband, in addition to being a rationalization, is still couched in domestic (husband), not national ('der von ihm vertretenen Sache') terms.

96 Curt Hohoff, *Heinrich von Kleist in Selbstzeugnissen und Bilddokumenten* (Hamburg: Rowohlt 1958), 95. Kürenberg also does not perceive the full extent of Thusnelda's emotional involvement with Ventidius: 'Dieser junge Römer spielt ihr vor, sie zu lieben, und aus Mitleid lässt sie ihm einige Hoffnung' (190).

97 Ryan, 197

98 Kleist raises the issue of human bestiality as early as *Die Familie Schroffenstein* in a passage which foreshadows the psychological motivation of the *Bärin* episode: 'Ich [Rupert] erwarte, dass ein Bär / An Oheims Stelle tritt für Ottokar. / Und weil doch alles sich gewandelt, Menschen / Mit Tieren die Natur gewechselt, wechsle / Denn auch das Weib die ihrige – verdränge / Das Kleinod Liebe, das nicht üblich ist, / Aus ihrem Herzen, um die Folie, / Den Hass, hineinzusetzen' (1:53).

99 Burckhardt, 143

100 Many critics, having singled out the similarity between the *Bärin* episode and the concluding calamity of *Penthesilea*, regard the former as a parody of the latter, a view abetted by Kleist's description of Thusnelda as 'brav, aber ein wenig einfältig und eitel, wie heute die Mädchen sind, denen die Franzosen imponieren' (quoted in Sembdner, 1:943–4). The parallels are more extensive, however, than the secondary literature has indicated. In both dramas, the male is portrayed as a gallant warrior (although Ventidius as the intriguer educated in the drawing rooms of Rome has a more subtle, polished approach despite his questionable sincerity). Unarmed and thus not in a position to defend himself, he enters the arena naïvely convinced of the female's love for him, a fatal source of overconfidence. A wild animal or animals destroy the unsuspecting male, while the female participates either actively or vicariously in the kill: 'Während sich Penthesilea ihren Hunden zugesellt und "den Zahn schlägt [...] in seine [Achilles'] weisse Brust", ist

Thusnelda zwar äusserlich gesehen nur Zuschauerin beim Todeskampf des
Ventidius, lässt aber keinen Zweifel daran, dass die "zottelschwarze Bärin
von Cheruska" ... nur stellvertretend für sie selbst die Tat ausführt': Ryan,
204. In each case the female feels deceived by her suitor and reacts primarily
on the basis of damaged pride. In the earlier drama, the outcome hinges on a
fatal misunderstanding; in the second case, an actual betrayal has taken
place. Both women attempt to escape the painful realization of what they
have done, the one by repressing the memory of her bloody revenge, the
other by fainting. In their defence, it should be noted that the two protagonists are being used by their respective societies: Penthesilea falls victim to
an unnatural social code embodied in the high priestess and Hermann consciously manipulates his wife as bait to trap an enemy. Kleist encourages his
audience to be more sympathetic to Penthesilea than to Thusnelda, in part a
product of the latter's minor billing in the cast of Die Hermannsschlacht. The
German princess comes across as more childish and considerably more vain
than her Amazon predecessor, while, most significantly, her premeditated,
deliberately sadistic revenge contrasts sharply with the spontaneous slaughter of Achilles by an enraged Penthesilea: 'What Penthesilea did in a trance
and delusion, Thusnelda does knowingly and by design. What in Penthesilea
we experience through the merciful and even ennobling medium of tragic
poetry, we are now made to witness with brutal directness and to the
accompaniment of vile sarcasms': Burckhardt, 123.

101 On the basis that Hermann's forces arrive too late to take an active part in
the defeat of Varus, Loose maintains, 'Hermann ist in Wahrheit nicht an
einem militärischen Krieg interessiert' (107). This is true, but not in the sense
that Loose intends, as Hermann advocates the equivalent of guerrilla tactics.
Moreover, Loose tends to take at face value Hermann's claim to Ventidius:
'Dagegen mir [as opposed to Marbod], du weisst, das sanftre Ziel sich
steckte: / Dem Weib, das mir vermählt, der Gatte, / Ein Vater meinen süssen
Kindern, / Und meinem Volk ein guter Fürst zu sein' (1:548). Again, this
reveals the danger inherent in Loose's general approach. By ignoring the
psychology of the characters, he is deceived by this histrionic display almost
as much as is Ventidius. The drama demonstrates that one should exercise
extreme caution when taking Hermann at his word. As for Hermann's late
arrival, this may well represent another of those ironic twists of fate which
constantly plague Kleist's protagonists. No joy is complete. It also sets the
stage for the confrontation at the end of the drama since Marbod, although
the official victor, was, after all, following Hermann's plan when he vanquished the Romans.

102 Streller, 188. Cf. also: 'Kleist hat nach zehn Jahren den Weg aus der ichbefangenen Natur des Selbst zum Du, zur Gemeinschaft gefunden,' Hohoff, 108; 'Es spricht für seine reine und völlig selbstlose Gesinnung, dass er den eigenen Ruhm dem ruhmvollen Weiterbestehen des Germanenreiches unterordnet': Wickert, 90; or 'From the beginning he [Hermann] is willing to give up all he has for that cause': Angress, 20. This conflict over 'Ruhm' also contradicts another of Angress' contentions: 'He is a revolutionary who wants to be successful, not a hero who wants to be admired' (25). But, most surprisingly, she regards Hermann's 'final willingness to allow a near-traitor, Fust, to take from him the glory of killing Varus,' as an example of his 'suppressing his subjectivity' (28), a view not substantiated by the text.

103 Loose, 108

104 Wickert, 96

105 There would appear to be a failure to recognize the devastating effects of the Ventidius incident upon Thusnelda after her revenge. In this context, Burckhardt's comment is revealing: 'The horror which in the earlier play [*Penthesilea*] had to be, and was atoned for is now itself the "atonement"' (123).

106 May, 258

107 As Sammons so aptly put it, 'With Marbod, [Hermann stages] a classical drama of heroic renunciation' (35).

108 Wickert would seem to have overlooked this line underscoring an hereditary aristocracy when she maintains, 'Die einfache militärische Ordnung der Germanen, die sowieso nur auf einem Adel der persönlichen Fähigkeiten beruhte, bedurfte keiner inneren Reform' (93). The drama emphasizes tradition and it remains doubtful whether one can derive the concept of 'personal ability' from the mere mention of 'rühmlich.'

109 Burckhardt has provided an excellent analysis of this episode: 'Kleist points with the utmost hardness to the fact that [the state] is a legal structure and thus, like every new state or jurisdiction, caught in the paradox of *ex post facto* law. Its founding is signalled by an act of law – the execution of Aristan.' Burckhardt goes on to argue that 'the first and most basic law, being constitutive of a new sovereignty, is an act of force, a naked assertion of authority' (154).

110 Burckhardt, 126–7

111 Burckhardt was the first to comment upon the presence of this theme: 'This is a hunting play; there is an open season not only on bisons and Romans, but on all kinds of sentimentality, more particularly on patriotic sentimentality' (119–20). However, he failed to follow up on this observation as it relates thematically and stylistically to the hunt. Moreover, I hope to demonstrate

that Kleist's skill in exploiting this poetic image refutes Federn's claim, one echoed by many critics, that the emphasis on *Realpolitik* has been accomplished largely at the expense of art (242). More recently, Loose has observed, 'Das Thema "Jagd" durchzieht als Leitmotiv in Situationen, Anspielungen, Vergleichen, Bildern, Redewendungen – ähnlich wie in der *Penthesilea* u.a. – die *Hermannsschlacht*. Von der ersten bis zur letzten Szene bleibt das Thema vorder – oder hintergründig angesprochen, wechselt in konnotativen Anspielungen zu "Krieg" und tendiert wieder zu "Jagd" zurück' (173). Cf. also: 'Das abenteuerliche Stelldichein zwischen Thusnelda und Ventidius, bei dem die Bärin aus den deutschen Wäldern den römischen Jüngling zerreisst, hat eine szenische und metaphorische Vorgeschichte, die von der Jagdszene des Eingangs bis zur römischen Katastrophe im Teutoburger Wald reicht': Norbert Miller, 'Verstörende Bilder in Kleists *Hermannsschlacht*,' *Kleist Jahrbuch-1984*, ed. Hans Joachim Kreutzer (Berlin: Erich Schmidt 1984), 103.

112 Loose also outlines the important supportive role of the sets. In reference to the first *Bühnenbild*, he writes, 'Es entsteht der Eindruck einer natureingebetteten Kultur der Germanen, gegen die das später aufgeführte Gegenstandssymbol und römische Siegeremblem der Quadriga ... als ein Sinnbild aus einer anderen Welt absticht' (68).

113 Samuel has noted that the Spanish resistance to Napoleon taught how an open war could end in disaster, while little wars or guerrilla warfare could paralyse a vast enemy army: 'Kleists *Hermannsschlacht* und der Freiherr vom Stein,' in Walter Müller-Seidel, *Heinrich von Kleist*, 423. Loose also observes: 'Einen Krieg in der traditionellen militärischen Weise hält [Hermann] als Mittel zur Bekämpfung der Bedrohung durch die Römer für hoffnungslos unwirksam und für verderbenbringend' (86).

114 John Gearey, *Heinrich von Kleist. A Study in Tragedy and Anxiety* (Philadelphia: University of Pennsylvania Press 1968), 14

115 'Den Fusstritt will er [Achilles], und erklärt es laut, / Auf deinen [Penthesilea's] königlichen Nacken setzen' (1:347), or 'Lasst ihn [Achilles] kommen. / Lasst ihn den Fuss gestählt, es ist mir [Penthesilea] recht, / Auf diesen Nacken setzen' (1:363). This image of total subjugation becomes a near obsession with Penthesilea who at one point exclaims, 'Er [Achilles] soll den Fuss auf meinen Nacken setzen!' (1:377).

116 Burckhardt, 117

117 May, 257

118 Cf. 'Hier sind die Römer die wilden Wölfe, die in die friedliche germanische Herde einbrechen. Dieses kalkulierte Bild des Wolfes ist nicht nur durch sein Anspielen auf die Gründerlegende Roms zu beachten, sondern es charakteri-

siert auch die Römer als Raubtiere, als Plünderer, vor denen sich ganz
Europa zu fürchten hat' Wickert, 82.

119 Sembdner, 'Anmerkungen' (1:946). Horst Dieter Schlosser, among others, has
made a good case for seeing the Pfeilschifter version (a) as 'die allerletzte
Bearbeitung, die das Stück überhaupt erfahren hat.' 'Zur Entstehungsge-
schichte von Kleists *Hermannsschlacht*,' *Euphorion*, 61 (1967): 174.

120 Kleist did not necessarily view this image in a pejorative light since he has
Graf vom Strahl use it in reference to himself (1:527) and in an earlier letter to
Wilhelmine von Zenge, dated 21 July 1801, he saw himself as the stag (2:671).

121 In his study *Kleists Penthesilea* (Bonn: Bouvier 1976), Albrecht Sieck has documented in considerable detail the analogies between the titular protagonist
and Artemis/Diana: 'Auf das artemische Jagdmotiv trifft man in Verbindung
mit der Hauptfigur immer wieder. Der Bericht Moroes über die Tragödie, die
sich an Achilles vollzieht, ist ein Jagdbericht' (96). Although he recognizes
the importance of the hunt and its relationship to the goddess, he overlooks
completely the direct parallels *Penthesilea*'s final calamity offers to the Acteon
myth. Like his huntsman forebear, Achilles approaches his death in innocence and without the least suspicion of his impending fate. In both instances, familiar, apparently friendly creatures (Acteon's own hunting dogs and
Penthesilea and her dogs) which the male would not normally suspect of
harbouring violent intentions against him (cf. 'Achilles *in den Bart*. Die
[Hunde und Elefanten] fressen aus der Hand, wahrscheinlich – Folgt mir! / –
O! Die sind zahm, wie sie [Penthesilea]' [1:409]) turn on him and tear him to
pieces. Achilles is referred to as a stag, once by the narrator Meroe: 'Und eilt
entsetzt, und stutzt, und eilet wieder: / Gleich einem jungen Reh' (1:412) and
a second time by Penthesilea herself: 'Ha! sein Geweih verrät den Hirsch'
(1:413). His desperate efforts to escape the released dogs and his violent demise correspond to Acteon's fate although what was performed vicariously in
the Greek legend by the animals is, in Kleist's version, shared by woman and
beasts: 'Und stürzt – stürzt mit der ganzen Meut, o *Diana*! / Sich über ihn,
und reisst – reisst ihn beim Helmbusch, / Gleich einer Hündin, Hunden
beigesellt' (1:413). It is thus fitting, both in terms of the drama's inner logic
and the Acteon myth, that Penthesilea make gestures indicating 'Den
Peleïden sollte man ... / Vor der Dianapriesterin Füssen legen' (1:416) since it
could be argued that she has appeased Diana, the patron goddess of
Amazon civilization. Cf. also 'Das Niederschiessen des Achill dann und,
zusammen mit den Hunden, das Einschlagen der Zähne in sein Fleisch ist,
wie man weiss, den Bakchai des Euripides und dem (auch dort verwen-
deten) Aktaion-Mythos nachgestaltet. In beiden Fällen werden Menschen
durch Gewalt eines Gottes ihrer Identität enthoben: die von Dionysos beses-

sene Agaue erkennt, ihn zerfleischend, ihren eigenen Sohn nicht; und Aktaion wird durch Artemis seiner menschlichen Gestalt beraubt, so dass die eigenen Hunde ihn fressen': Peter Michelsen, 'Der Imperativ des Unmöglichen: Über Heinrich von Kleists *Penthesilea*,' in *Antike Tradition und Neuere Philologien*, ed. Hans-Joachim Zimmermann (Heidelberg: Carl Winter 1984), 143.

122 Loose sees a political-social message in Kleist's exploitation of the eagle. 'Indem sich das "System Napoleon" in der Emblemanalogie mit dem römischen Legionsadler u.a. diese Identifikation ... zulegt, entlarvt Kleist in seiner *Hermannsschlacht* ... diese Emblemanalogie als Vorzeichen der zum Untergang verurteilten zeitgeschichtlichen (französischen) imperialen Realität, die an der Handlungsweise seines Hermann zerbricht' (42).

123 The reference to Hercules is particularly appropriate on several counts. In his first recorded feat at age eighteen, he delivered the neighbourhood of Mount Cithaeron from a huge lion which preyed on the flocks of his supposed father Amphitryon. Hercules fulfilled his first labour by strangling the Nemean lion, thereafter wearing its skin, and he even laid himself upon it in his final earthly act of self-immolation. Moreover, the Greek hero's name is also linked to a stag. As Hercules' third labour, Eurystheus required him to capture the stag of Oeneo, a task which took a year to accomplish and for which Artemis/Diana severely reprimanded him since the deer was an animal sacred to her.

CHAPTER FOUR

1 The text of this chapter first appeared under the same title in *The Germanic Review* 56 (1981): 95–110.

2 John Martin Ellis, *Kleist's Prinz Friedrich von Homburg* (Berkeley, Los Angeles, London: University of California Press 1970), 1. All future references to Ellis will be taken from this 1970 study unless otherwise indicated.

3 Karl Schweizer, *Heinrich von Kleist. Prinz Friedrich von Homburg* (Munich: Oldenburg 1968), 7

4 Ellis, 33–4

5 Eckehard Catholy, 'Der preussische Hoftheater-Stil und seine Auswirkungen auf die Bühnen-Rezeption von Kleists Schauspiel *Prinz Friedrich von Homburg*,' *Kleist und die Gesellschaft* (Berlin: Erich Schmidt 1965), 80

6 Walter Silz, 'On the Interpretation of Kleist's *Prinz Friedrich von Homburg*,' *The Journal of English and Germanic Philology* 35 (1936): 505

7 Ibid, 502

8 Ellis, 47–52

9 Reinhard Thum, 'Kleist's Ambivalent Portrayal of Absolutism in *Prinz Friedrich von Homburg*,' *The Germanic Review* 56 (1981): 3. Thum's article, appearing in the same year as my article on Hohenzollern, states in note 15: 'Surprisingly, no previous critic has pointed out Hohenzollern's important role as the conscious and often manipulative observer' (12). Generally, Thum and I are in agreement, except for our interpretations of the latter half of the drama.

10 Fontane emphasized Kleist's complete disregard for historical accuracy in the *Wanderungen durch die Mark Brandenburg* (Munich: Nymphenburger 1960), where we read: 'Prinz Friedrich von Hessen-Homburg ... war vor allem nicht der, der er uns in dem Heinrich von Kleistschen Schauspiel entgegentritt' (1:380).

11 E.G. Fürstenheim has put forward the view that Kleist's *Prinz Friedrich von Homburg* and its anomalies can be explained as an attempt to combine the historical Homburg incident and the Katte episode. Since K.H. Krause, Kleist's major source (*Mein Vaterland unter den Hohenzollerschen Regenten*), presented Katte in a negative light, Fürstenheim feels that this 'may well account for the somewhat dubious role which the prince's friend, Hohenzollern, plays in the *Prinz von Homburg*': 'The Source of Kleist's *Prinz Friedrich von Homburg*,' *German Life and Letters* 8 (1954–5): 106.

12 Ellis, 47

13 Ibid, 84. Although disagreeing with Ellis's evaluation of Hohenzollern, I am none the less greatly indebted to his excellent study and its disclosure of the 'competitive undercurrent' (41) in the relationship between the Prince and the Elector.

14 'Hohenzollern is mistaken in his certainty that the Prince is not receiving any more impression from what is happening about him than the diamond on his finger': Ellis, 77.

15 Ibid, 81

16 Ibid, 47

17 Interestingly enough, Mephistopheles' famous image of the grasshopper: 'Er [der kleine Gott der Welt] scheint mir, mit Verlaub um Euer Gnaden, / Wie eine der langbeinigen Zikaden, / Die immer fliegt und fliegend springt / Und gleich im Gras ihr altes Liedchen singt' (*Goethes Werke*, ed. Erich Trunz [Hamburg: Christian Wegener 1957], 3:17) finds a distant echo in Hohenzollern's angry response to the page in this scene, although formulated for a specific rather than general context: 'HOHENZOLLERN *unwillig*. / Still! die Zikade! – Nun? Was gibts? / PAGE. Mich schickt – ! / HOHENZOLLERN. Weck ihn mit deinem Zirpen mir nicht auf!' (1:634–5).

18 *Prinz Friedrich von Homburg*, ed. Richard Samuel (London, Toronto, Wellington, Sydney: Harrap, rev. ed. 1962), 160

19 The Prince refers to Hohenzollern three more times as his 'Freund' in the first scene of the third act. The only other person to be designated a friend by Homburg is Kottwitz, but significantly in the formulation 'alter Freund' (1:703). Clearly, this is more a case of a father-son relationship than friend to friend as Kottwitz himself later makes clear: 'Mein Sohn! Mein liebster Freund! Wie nenn ich dich?' (1:704).

20 Hohenzollern displays very little of the embarrassment to which Ellis alludes, 48.

21 In his second speech of the play, Hohenzollern provides a rather explicit answer to this question: 'Glock zehn zu Nacht, gemessen instruiert, / Wirft er erschöpft, gleich einem Jagdhund lechzend, / Sich auf das Stroh um für die Schlacht, die uns / Bevor beim Strahl des Morgens steht, ein wenig/ Die Glieder, die erschöpften, auszuruhn' (1:631).

22 Samuel, 161

23 Ellis, 47–8

24 Cf. 'Hohenzollern does not avoid discussion of the Prince's dream as the Elector's orders had surely implied. On the contrary, he probes and questions the Prince to see what extent his friend can remember, while awake, the events which took place in his dream': Thum, 4.

25 In his more recent book, a more concise formulation of his 1970 study, Ellis maintains: 'What this exchange really shows is the Prince first trying to remember, finally succeeding in line 164 ['– O Lieber!'], now realizing it is dangerous to admit the name, and covering up what he has remembered': *Heinrich von Kleist. Studies in the Character and Meaning of His Writings* [(Chapel Hill: University of North Carolina Press 1979)], 95. If, as Ellis proposes, the Prince has recalled the name and then seeks to conceal it, why does he engage in the third interrogation concerning the identity of 'der süssen Traumgestalt' (1:639)? The same degree of perplexity as in the first two exchanges is present. Also, if he knows the name, why then does he perform the glove experiment in the subsequent scene and give evidence of extreme surprise at discovering its owner? 'Herr meines Lebens! hab ich recht gehört? ... / Den Handschuh sucht sie – / *Er sieht bald den Handschuh, bald die Prinzessin an*' (1:644). When confirmation finally comes, Homburg is described as '*verwirrt. Ist das der Eure?*' Clearly, this is the first time he gains conscious awareness of Natalie as the unknown third person. '*Der Prinz von Homburg steht einen Augenblick, wie vom Blitz getroffen da; dann wendet er sich mit triumphierenden Schritten wieder in den Kreis der Offiziere zurück*' (1:646). Also he makes no attempt to cover up his findings: 'Was! Sahst du [Hohenzollern] nichts?'

26 Ellis, 48

27 Cf. ibid

28 Ellis discusses Hohenzollern and Golz together in this episode and by so doing tends to underestimate the former's despicable behaviour: 'The quietest avoidance of the issue, the failure to accept responsibility or give real support to the Prince, is shown in the parallelism of the two figures and in the stage direction which shows them both moving away from the Prince' (48).

29 Samuel, 172

30 Ellis, 49–50

31 Ibid, 50

32 Ibid

33 Ibid

34 Ellis further proposes, 'Hohenzollern's report is consistent with the view that the Elector was angered by the Prince's proposal of marriage to Natalie as soon as the Elector was thought dead, i.e. the indecent haste could have upset him. Or, the Elector's anger may have been aroused by the Prince's attempt to replace him as Natalie's protector' (50–1). However, these conjectures which may well be true still suggest that uncomplimentary personal motives, not altruistic considerations, are responsible for the Elector's insistence upon the death sentence.

35 Samuel, 172. Thum shares my view on this issue: 'Hohenzollern's insinuation of "base" motives on the part of the Elector has been much criticized. Nevertheless, it would seem from the evidence that he presents that his conjectures are more than justified' (8).

36 Silz, 505

37 Ellis, 88

38 This is the only time in the whole play when Homburg makes a decision completely on his own, if one excludes the engagement to Natalie; but even this step was indirectly encouraged by Hohenzollern's garden performance.

39 Significantly, many of the pro-Elector productions of the nineteenth and early twentieth centuries presented the sovereign fully dressed throughout this scene.

40 Ellis, 51–2

41 Thum sees a change in heart occurring in Hohenzollern from the battle scene onward, a view which I feel the text does not support. Our divergent views become especially noteworthy in Thum's interpretation of the Count's alleged defence of Homburg: 'Hohenzollern defends his friend courageously in act 5, and he does so with the certainty that he will incur the wrath of the Elector. This altruistic act surely atones for his malicious behavior and his disloyalty to his friend in the first scene of the play' (5).

42 Ellis, 92. 'But [the Elector] has an angry reaction to Hohenzollern, in spite of the fact that the latter is more careful and even more deferential than Kott-witz.' Ellis is correct in imputing anger to the Elector, but incorrect in attributing more care and deference vis-à-vis the Elector from Hohenzollern than from Kottwitz.

43 Samuel, 181

44 See Silz, 514, note 37: 'Hohenzollern, arguing with the bias of a friend, over-simplifies the case, and the Elector is quite right in rejecting the extreme formulation (1622–1627) which would make him the *sole* [Silz's emphasis] culprit.' Although I generally agree with this analysis, I feel that Silz, along with all other critics, has failed to see that the biased defence is really an excuse for a veiled attack upon the Elector.

45 Heinz Politzer writes in reference to this episode, '[Die Eingangsszene] ist sozusagen der Kreuzweg, an dem sich das Los des Helden entscheidet; jedenfalls erscheint dem Herrscher jetzt der *Scherz* nicht nur als *harmlos*, sondern auch sehr *zweideutig* [Politzer's emphasis]': 'Kleists Trauerspiel vom Traum: *Prinz Friedrich von Homburg*,' *Euphorion* 64 (1970): 205. Silz sees it in a more general light: 'The strongest force in Hohenzollern's argument is its revelation – more implicitly than explicitly – of the infinite intricacy of life. It brings home to the Elector not merely his own complicity in the case, but, beyond that, the questionable nature of the world in which we live' (514). Charles M. Barrack's view most closely approximates my own position: 'The fact that the Elector transfers the blame to Hohenzollern is irrelevant. The Elector has admitted, by implication, that the Prince was not totally responsible for his transgression. This is pointed out even more sharply by the Elector's use of the term "Versehen" [sic]. Prior to Hohenzollern's lengthy argument, the Elector refers to the Prince's disobedience at Fehrbellin as "Frevel"': 'Prince Friedrich: Hero or Victim?' *The Germanic Review* 56 (1981): 15. Interestingly enough, Barrack and I reached the same conclusion independently in the same year and in the same journal.

46 Ellis, 52

47 'In the last act, [the Elector] recognizes the importance of that scene [in the garden] by going back to it, and this is an indication that he has been swayed by what Hohenzollern has said,' Ellis, 97.

48 HOHENZOLLERN 'Ruf ihn bei Namen auf, so fällt er nieder' (1:632).

49 In all fairness to Hohenzollern, another difference should be noted. Before, Homburg was in a somnambulistic state which the Count knew how to handle from previous experience. Now, Homburg's faint occurs while he is in a more conscious state of mind. Bearing in mind Hohenzollern's previous cal-

lousness, I sincerely doubt, however, that this line of reasoning motivates his response.

50 Ellis, 72

51 'And it is doubtful whether [Homburg] welcomes the outcome, robbing him of the glory he thought he was to achieve': Ellis, 96. Furthermore, Ellis has outlined the predominant shades of darkness and obscurity, even in reference to the sun, which govern the drama's general atmosphere (78–81). The only positive light streams forth from Homburg's isolated inner world, but it must be seen against the background of death.

52 'At all stages a ruler must weigh the respect of his subjects against their affection. Any ruler wants both, but since they cannot readily be reconciled, it is safer to command respect when it comes to the choice of either' (M 89).

53 In this context Machiavelli observes, 'Affection is a tie like duty which, such is the worthlessness of men, is easily broken by self interest' (M 89).

54 'No ruler should ever believe in taking sides that he is on the right one; in fact, it is best to treat all commitments as dangerous' (M 109).

55 'Moreover, a lesson may be drawn from it [the rise of parliament in France], which is that a ruler must always let others administer distasteful and corrective medicine, but distribute the sweets himself' (M 96).

56 The magnitude of this implied authority Fontane demonstrated ironically towards the end of the century when Briest objects to the subservient form of address of a Käthchen-Effi to a Strahl-Innstetten in an amateur adaptation of Kleist's *Käthchen von Heilbronn*: 'Ich will nicht, dass ein Briest oder doch wenigstens eine Polterabendfigur, in der jeder das Widerspiel unserer Effi erkennen muss – ich will nicht, dass eine Briest mittelbar oder unmittelbar in einem fort von "Hoher Herr" spricht. Da müsste denn doch Instetten wenigstens ein verkappter Hohenzoller sein, es gibt ja dergleichen': Theodor Fontane, *Sämtliche Werke*, ed. Walter Keitel (Munich: Carl Hanser 1963), 4:26. A mere name, but *the* name in the Prussian context, has the power to confer instant respectability and prestige.

57 Thum posits a similar rivalry when he speaks of Hohenzollern's 'malicious voyeurism ... which permits him to ridicule his more successful "competitor" for the highest position in the state, and at the same time to injure the despot, whom he simultaneously admires as his leader [I find no evidence of this] and resents as his superior' (3).

CHAPTER FIVE

1 Richard Samuel, 'Heinrich von Kleists *Robert Guiskard* und seine Wieder-

belebung 1807/8,' *Kleist-Jahrbuch 1981/82*, ed. Hans Joachim Kreutzer (Berlin: Erich Schmidt 1983), 326

2 Ibid, 323

3 Cf. 'Sie alle, die nacheinander auftreten, bezeugen ihre Abhängigkeit von Guiskard, so dass dieser selbst als Mittelpunkt der ganzen Welt des Dramas erscheint': Friedrich Koch, *Heinrich von Kleist. Bewusstsein und Wirklichkeit* (Stuttgart: Metzler 1958), 93.

4 Siegfried Streller, *Das dramatische Werk Heinrich von Kleists* (Berlin: Rütten und Loening 1966), 54

5 Ulrich Vohland, *Bürgerliche Emanzipation in Heinrich von Kleists Dramen und theoretischen Schriften* (Bern/Frankfurt a.M.: Lang 1976), 283

6 Iris Denneler, 'Legitimation und Charisma. Zu *Robert Guiskard,'* in *Kleists Dramen. Neue Interpretationen*, ed. Walter Hinderer (Stuttgart: Reclam 1981), 78

7 'Der Greis ... verheimlicht die Information des Normannen ... und später sein Wissen ... um Guiskards Pesterkrankung': Denneler, 89–90, n27.

8 Streller's more negative assessment of the people in *Robert Guiskard* strikes me as more accurate than the view proposed by Vohland who maintains, 'Das "Volk" ist im *Guiskard* keineswegs mit dem als "Pöbel" bezeichneten Volk in Kleists erstem Drama identisch' (269).

9 Denneler, 85

10 Some critics, especially before the Second World War, made the mistake of taking Abälard at his word, thus failing to recognize the deceptive game he is playing. Friedrich Braig, for example, comments: 'Zudem weiss er [Abälard], dass mit dem Tode Guiskards an ihn die Pflicht herantritt, die Führung an sich zu reissen nicht bloss um des Erbrechtes, sondern um des Volkes und seiner Rettung willen': *Heinrich von Kleist* (Munich: J.H. Beck'sche Verlagsbuchhandlung 1925), 138. Recently, however, Abälard's opportunism has been acknowledged by several commentators, among them Samuel who notes: 'es ist offensichtlich, dass er in [Abälard] nicht ein strahlendes Gegenbild zu dem störrischen, aufreizenden und dazu schwachen jüngeren Robert schaffen wollte, sondern einen kühlen, egoistischen Realisten, ja Intriganten' (341).

11 Cf. 'Durch den zu erwartenden Tod Guiskards kommen bislang verdeckte Machtkämpfe um die Nachfolgeschaft zum Ausdruck ... Die scheinbar homogene Gruppe des Adels bricht auseinander': Denneler, 78.

12 Abälard is referred to as '[der wahre Erbe] aller Eigenschaften, die den Ruhm und die Grösse des Guiskard begründen' by Lawrence Ryan ('Kleists Entdeckung im Gebiete der Kunst: *Robert Guiskard* und die Folgen,' in *Kleists Aktualität*, ed. Walter Müller-Seidel [Darmstadt: Wissenschaftliche Buchgesellschaft 1981], 93), as 'das Ebenbild Guiskards' by Braig (150) and as '[Guis-

kards] verjüngtes Abbild' by Heinrich Meyer-Benfey (*Das Drama Heinrich von Kleists* [Göttingen: Otto Hapke 1911], 223). Only Samuel insists, but somewhat unconvincingly: 'Abälard ist nicht das Abbild Guiskards, geboren zum Herrschen und Führen' (346).

13 In commenting upon the significance of Abälard's seemingly contradictory statement, Friedrich Gundolf has noted quite perceptively '[die] lauernd vorsichtige und zugleich wagemutige Tücke Abälards, dessen zweideutiger Charakter in dem Akzent und der Aussage seiner zwei Verse gegenwärtig gebärdet ist.' *Heinrich von Kleist* (Berlin: Bondi 1932), 57.

14 Hence I disagree with note 44 to Hans Joachim Kreutzer's *Die dichterische Entwicklung Heinrich von Kleists* (Berlin: Erich Schmidt 1968) which reads: 'Auch die Worte 411 ff bedeuten wohl keine Drohung' (212). If one assumes, and one must, that Robert has fully informed his father of his nephew's machinations, and if one bears in mind that Guiskard has agreed to accept the Greek traitors' conditions, thus depriving Abälard of a share of the eastern empire as Helena's betrothed, it strikes me as inappropriate to assume: 'Guiskard ist Abälard vermutlich wohlgesonnen' (212).

15 Although Samuel ultimately recognizes Abälard for what he truly is, i.e., 'einen kühlen, egoistischen Realisten, ja Intriganten' (341), he fails to realize that the apparent contradiction between his actions and his words is resolved by his Machiavellian drive for power and political survival.

16 Cf. 'Das Charisma Guiskards tritt an die Stelle erbrechtlicher Legitimation und gesetzlicher Rechtfertigung seiner Handlungen; politische Autorität wird mit religiöser Begründung kombiniert': Denneler, 82.

17 Cf. In a similar vein, Streller comments: 'Aber nun ergibt sich der Widerspruch: der gleiche Guiskard, der auf Grund seiner Tüchtigkeit das Erbrecht beiseite geschoben hat, beansprucht es für seinen Sohn, obwohl dieser weniger tüchtig ist als der von ihm verdrängte Abälard' (52).

18 Cf. '[Caesar Borgia's] future prospects depended on the succession to the Papacy, and he had to face the possibility of a hostile Pope attempting to deprive him of all his father, Alexander VI, had gained for him' (M 52).

19 Streller, 52

20 Vohland, 266

21 Ibid

22 Ryan, 85

23 In this instance, Samuel would appear to be the only critic not to underestimate the role of cunning in Guiskard's politics: 'Der Pakt ermöglicht es Guiskard, sein hohes Ziel auf billige Weise zu erreichen – wie es seinem Beinamen entspricht, ebenso wie der historischen Überlieferung, das Heroische aber von ihm abstreift' (347).

24 '[States] are not difficult to overrun with the support of a disgruntled or
   ambitious noble or two. Such men, by reason of their position, which I have
   described, can open the gates to an invader and make the conquest possible'
   (M 40).

25 Although the circumstances and the sympathies of the author are quite different, I am still reminded of an episode in Brecht's *Leben des Galilei* where
   Ludovico, the representative of the landed aristocracy, informs Galileo:
   'Wenn [die Bauern] aufs Gut kommen, sich über eine Kleinigkeit zu be-
   schweren, ist die Mutter gezwungen, vor ihren Augen einen Hund auspeit-
   schen zu lassen, das allein kann sie an Zucht und Ordnung und Höflichkeit
   erinnern': *Gesammelte Werke* in 20 volumes, vol. 3 (Frankfurt a.M.: Suhrkamp
   1968), 1309.

26 Cf. 'Diese Redeweise suggeriert Vertraulichkeit und Jovialität. Guiskards
   sprachlicher Niveauverlust muss jedoch auf seine hierarchische Position be-
   zogen werden. Nur die "obere" Stellung erlaubt es ihm, sein sprachliches
   Verhalten dem Volk anzupassen': Denneler, 81–2.

27 Samuel, 348

28 Hans Heinz Holz has provided an excellent, detailed analysis of this speech:
   'Wer so spricht, ist nicht unbefangen. Der ruhige, gemessene Rhythmus der
   Sprache hat sich verändert, hektisch werden die Worte hervorgestossen,
   laufen in rhetorische Fragen aus ... Eine forcierte Munterkeit, die jedoch
   merkwürdig kurzatmig ist, charakterisiert diesen Ausbruch': *Macht und Ohnmacht der Sprache* (Frankfurt a.M.: Athenäum 1962), 48. Generally, Holz makes
   a good case for maintaining that *Robert Guiskard* illustrates 'die Erkenntnis,
   dass die Sprache mächtig ist, die Wahrheit zu verbergen' (45).

29 Much has been written on this topic, most notably by Katarina Mommsen,
   Kleists Kampf mit Goethe (Heidelberg: Lothar Stiehm 1974). Although the struggle for fame informs Kleist's correspondence and his dramas from the beginning to the end (the 'Kranz' motif in *Prinz Friedrich von Homburg*), it is
   particularly noticeable during the period Kleist spent struggling with the
   Guiskard material. From the Aarinsel bei Thun, he wrote to Wilhelmine on 20
   May 1802: 'Kurz, kann ich nicht mit Ruhm im Vaterlande erscheinen,
   geschieht es nie' (2:726) and from St Omer he sent a letter to his sister dated
   26 October 1803 in which he stated, 'Ich habe in Paris mein Werk [*Robert
   Guiskard*], soweit es fertig war, durchlesen, verworfen, und verbrannt und
   nun ist es aus. Der Himmel versagt mir den Ruhm, das grösste der Güter der
   Erde; ich werfe ihm, wie ein eigensinniges Kind, alle übrigen hin' (2:737).

30 Josef Kunz, 'Das Phänomen der tragischen Blindheit im Werke Kleists,'
   Germanisch-Romanische Monatshefte, N.F. 13 (1963): 180

31 Meyer-Benfey, 224

32 I have already dealt with Vohland's contention that Guiskard took upon himself the conquest of Constantinople 'nicht für sich, sondern für Helena und Abälard' and that the plague is 'die Ursache seiner rechtswidrigen und unmoralischen Entscheidung,' 268.

33 Streller, 55

34 Samuel, 347

35 Hermann also has a strong sense of mission but realizes that it can only be accomplished by the will of the gods. He resolutely makes his decision to follow through to the end but with the saving awareness that he could lose if the gods so decreed. When Luitgar suggests sending two additional messengers to Marbod, Hermann remonstrates: 'Wer wollte die gewaltgen Götter / Also versuchen?! Meinst du, es liesse / Das grosse Werk sich ohne sie vollziehn? / ... / Du gehst allein; und triffst du mit der Botschaft / Zu spät bei Marbod, oder gar nicht, ein: / Seis! Mein Geschick ists, das ich tragen werde' (1:562). As Josef Kunz has noted, however, 'Robert Guiskard, schon von der tödlichen Krankheit befallen, lebt im ungebrochenen Vertrauen auf seinen Erfolg und sein Glück' (181).

36 Vohland recognizes the beneficial consequence in terms of Guiskard's relationship to his army, but fails to acknowledge the possibility of calculated intent: 'Sein [the people's] Vertrauen in Guiskard, der sich um die Pestkranken sorgt und keine Gefahr für sein Volk scheut, ist ungetrübt' (270).

37 Cf. 'Doch von Augenblick zu Augenblick wird nun spürbar, dass Guiskards Kräfte sich erschöpfen. Zunächst drängt er selbst auf Abschluss der Verhandlung, solange er sein Gesicht noch wahren kann: "sei kurz und bündig! Geschäfte rufen mich ins Zelt zurück":' Holz, 49.

CHAPTER SIX

1 For example, Richard Samuel in his annotated edition of *Prinz Friedrich von Homburg* (London, Toronto, Wellington, Sydney: Harrap 1962) has indicated the extent to which the character Kottwitz is indebted to Shakespeare's Falstaff: '"Bin ich ein Pfeil, ein Vogel, ein Gedanke ..." cf. *Henry* IV, Part II, Act IV. iii: Falstaff to Lancaster, in reply to the latter's rebuke for having been absent from battle: "Do you think me a swallow, an arrow, or a bullet?"' (165).

2 Hardin Craig, *The Complete Works of Shakespeare* (Chicago, Atlanta, Dallas, Palo Alto, Fair Lawn, NJ: Scott, Foresman & Co. 1961), 945–6. All quotations from Shakespeare's plays have been drawn from this edition.

3 In the very first speech of the play, Richard announces, 'I am determined to prove a villain' (I i, 30). It was in fact usual for the Machiavellian villain of the

Elizabethan theatre to proclaim his evil purpose directly to the audience in a soliloquy. Edmund and Iago also follow this practice.

4 Craig, 301
5 Mme la Baronne de Staël-Holstein, *Considérations sur les principaux événements de la Révolution Française. Oeuvres posthumes* (Geneva: Slatkine Reprints [reprint of Paris edition of 1861] 1967), 196
6 Hyppolyte Taine, 'Le Régime moderne,' in *Les Origines de la France contemporaine*, IX, vol. 1 (Paris: Librairie Hachette 1911), 54
7 Felix Markham, *Napoleon* (Toronto: Mentor 1965), 55
8 Friedrich Nietzsche, 'Zur Genealogie der Moral,' in *Werke in zwei Bänden* (Munich: Carl Hanser 1967), 2:205
9 Interestingly enough, Mme de Staël also saw *Il Principe* as a treatise outlining the necessary means, however deplorable, to expel foreign occupational forces: 'Il me semble plutôt que Machiavel, détestant avant tout le joug des étrangers en Italie, tolérait et encourageait même les moyens, quels qu'ils fussent, dont les princes du pays pouvaient se servir pour être les maîtres, espérant qu'ils seraient assez forts un jour pour repousser les troupes allemandes et françaises ... [S'il] a souillé sa vie par son indulgence pour les crimes des Borgia, c'est peut-être parce qu'il s'abandonnait trop au besoin de tout tenter pour recouvrer l'indépendance de sa patrie' (238).
10 Markham, 20–1
11 Taine, 78
12 Ibid, 26
13 Ibid, 61
14 Cf. 'Mme de Staël et, plus tard, Stendhal, remontent jusqu'où il faut pour le [Napoleon] comprendre, jusqu'aux "petits tyrans italiens du XIVe et du XVe siècle",' ibid, 25.
15 Staël, 238
16 Richard Samuel, 'Goethe – Napoleon – Heinrich von Kleist. Ein Beitrag zu dem Thema: Napoleon und das deutsche Geistesleben,' *Publications of the English Goethe Society* N.S. 14 (1939), 54–5
17 Staël, 231
18 Samuel, 62–3
19 'Ein neues Sinnbild fiel Kleist zu, als er nach der Schlacht bei Jena ausrief: "Wir sind die unterjochten Völker der Römer." Damit drängte sich die Frage auf, ob einer aufstehen werde, der Napoleon gewachsen sei, ein Anti-Napoleon, der, wie einst Arminius, die Deutschen vom Joche der "Römer" befreie': Samuel, 61–2. I shall try to demonstrate that Kleist's 'Anti-Napoleon' acts and speaks very much like Napoleon himself.
20 Cf. Samuel, 56–7.

21 Ibid, 65

22 Staël, 228

23 Siegfried Streller, *Das dramatische Werk Heinrich von Kleists* (Berlin: Rütten & Loening 1966), 51

24 As I noted previously in the chapter on *Robert Guiskard*, Samuel has made a good case for seeing in the fragment, as it has come down to us, the stylistic influences of 1807 rather than of 1802–3. He also concedes, although indirectly, that 'Handlungsverlauf und Gehalt des Stückes' may also reflect political events between the years 1803 and 1807: 'Heinrich von Kleists *Robert Guiskard* und seine Wiederbelebung 1807/8,' *Kleist-Jahrbuch 1981/82*, ed. Hans Joachim Kreutzer (Berlin: Erich Schmidt 1983), 326–7.

25 Iris Denneler, 'Legitimation und Charisma. Zu *Robert Guiskard*,' *Kleists Dramen. Neue Interpretationen*, ed. Walter Hinderer (Stuttgart: Reclam 1981), 86

26 Willi Friedrich Könitzer first noted this parallel in an article: 'Robert Guiskard – Napoleon? Gedanken zu Kleists Trauerspiel-Fragment,' written for the *Berliner Börsenzeitung*, Nr. 329. Beilage 'Kunst, Welt, Wissen,' 17 January 1935.

27 J.M. Thompson, *Napoleon Bonaparte* (New York: Oxford 1952), 142. However, more recently, Felix Markham has written: 'The truth appears to be that Napoleon suggested this form of euthanasia for the victims who could not be transported, but that he dropped the suggestion when his surgeons opposed it. They could not accuse him of callousness, because he had already tried to allay panic by visiting and even touching the plague victims in hospital,' an interpretation giving a more positive slant to the incident (66).

28 Richard Samuel, 'Heinrich von Kleists *Robert Guiskard* und seine Wiederbelebung 1807/8,' 338

29 Pieter Geyl, *Napoleon. For and Against* (London: Jonathan Cape 1964), 94. Geyl is actually paraphrasing the historian Pierre Lanfrey.

30 Thompson, 70

31 Cf. Geyl, 90.

32 Thompson, 94

33 Markham, 140–1

34 Staël, 207

35 Cf. '[Goethe findet] in den Taten Napoleons die Lehre Fichtes bestätigt, das ungeheure Ich ist Gestalt geworden, der faustische Charakter, der über sich hinaus zum Übermenschen strebt, ist verwirklicht': Samuel, 'Goethe – Napoleon – Heinrich von Kleist,' 56.

36 Taine, 35

37 In my view, Rudolf Vierhaus is correct when he speaks of Kleist's political ideal as being a form of government in which 'sich ihm in merkwürdiger Mischung von Militär-Mentalität und ästhetisch-politischen Vorstellungen der Staat im Monarchen darstellte, der seinen politischen Willen dem Volke mitteilt.' 'Heinrich von Kleist und die Krise des preussischen Staates um 1800,': *Kleist-Jahrbuch 1980*, ed. Hans Joachim Kreutzer (Berlin: Erich Schmidt 1982), 32.

38 'The prudent ruler must therefore so order his rule that his subjects will always have need of him and his government, whatever the political climate may be, and this need will ensure their fidelity.' (M 64).

39 Cf. 'Bonaparte, lorsqu'il disposait d'un million d'hommes armés, n'en attachait pas moins d'importance à l'art de guider l'esprit public par les gazettes': Staël, 210.

40 Samuel, 'Goethe – Napoleon – Heinrich von Kleist,' 54

41 Staël, 196

42 Ibid, 208

43 Taine, 94

44 Samuel, 'Kleists *Hermannsschlacht* und der Freiherr vom Stein,' *Heinrich von Kleist*, ed. Walter Müller-Seidel (Darmstadt: Wissenschaftl. Buchgesellschaft 1967), 448

45 Ibid, 449

46 Samuel, 'Goethe – Napoleon – Heinrich von Kleist,' 58

47 Ibid, 64

48 Ibid, 69

49 Ibid, 70

50 Mme de Staël fails to mention Kleist's works in her biggest success, *De l'Allemagne*, first published in 1814 but eagerly awaited during the final years of Kleist's life. See Sembdner, *Heinrich von Kleist*, 2:949–50.

51 Geyl, 136. The chapter Geyl refers to comes from Taine's monumental work *Les Origines de la France contemporaine*, published between the years 1875 and 1893.

52 Staël, 196

53 Taine, 132

54 Staël, 202

55 Taine, 41

56 Ibid, 31. Cf. also 'Tout était chez lui moyen ou but': Staël, 238

57 Incident reported in Taine, 55.

58 Staël, 196

59 Markham, 140

60 Staël, 228

61 Cf. 'He was guided more by calculation than by principle': Geyl, 89.

62 Le comte Chaptal, *Mes Souvenirs sur Napoléon*, quoted by Taine, 90

63 Taine, 91–2

64 Cf. 'Le général Bonaparte, à cette même époque, à la fin de 1797, sonda l'opinion publique relativement aux directeurs; il vit qu'ils n'étaient point aimés, mais qu'un sentiment républicain rendait encore impossible à un général de se mettre à la place des magistrats civils': Staël, 198.

65 Taine, 93

66 Staël, 226. Cf. also 'A tout les moins, il veut être seul maître des réputations pour les faire ou les défaire à son gré': Taine, 97. Molé, one of Napoleon's ministers, once commented, 'He was much less concerned to leave behind him a "race" or dynasty than a name which should have no equal and glory that could not be surpassed,' quoted in Markham, 56. Markham even suggests that 'the theme of heroic thirst for glory' determined Napoleon's preference for Macpherson's *Ossian* (139).

67 Taine quotes one of Napoleon's famous sayings, 'Ma maîtresse, c'est le pouvoir' (94).

68 Staël, 203

69 Taine quotes Merlin de Douai (97).

70 Taine, 130

71 Staël, 238

72 Taine, 78

73 Ibid, 41–2

74 Ibid, 42. Cf. also 'Wenn ich [Nietzsche] meine höchste Formel für *Shakespeare* [Nietzsche's emphasis] suche, so finde ich immer nur die, dass er den Typus Cäsar konzipiert hat. Dergleichen errät man nicht – man ist es oder man ist es nicht. Der grosse Dichter schöpft *nur* [Nietzsche's emphasis] aus seine Realität ... ': 'Ecce Homo,' *Friedrich Nietzsche. Werke in zwei Bänden* (Munich: Hanser 1967), 2:421.

75 *Faust, Goethes Werke* (Hamburg: Wegner 1957), 3:17–18

76 'This then is the message which we have heard of him and declare unto you, that God is light, and in him is no darkness at all': King James Version of the Bible, I John 1:5.

Index